D1616014

FREEDOM FROM THE SELF

Sufism, Meditation and Psychotherapy

FREEDOM FROM THE SELF

Sufism, Meditation and Psychotherapy

Mohammad Shafii, M.D.

Professor of Psychiatry
Child Psychiatric Services
Department of Psychiatry
and Behavioral Sciences
University of Louisville School of Medicine
Louisville, Kentucky

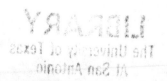

Copyright © 1985 by Human Sciences Press, Inc.
72 Fifth Avenue, New York, New York 10011

Printed in the United States of America
123456789

Library of Congress Cataloging in Publication Data

Shafii, Mohammad.
  Freedom from the self.

  Bibliography: p.
  Includes index.
  1. Sufism—Psychology.   2. Psychoanalysis and
religion.   I. Title.
BP189.65.P78S53   1985   150.19'0882971   84-10878
ISBN 0-89885-231-5

Only when you drink from the river of silence shall you indeed sing.

And when you have reached the mountain top, then you shall begin to climb.

And when the earth shall claim your limbs, then shall you truly dance.

Kahlil Gibran*

* Gibran, K. (1923). *The Prophet,* New York: Alfred A. Knopf, 1963, p. 81.

To Sharon
  a Sufi at heart

CONTENTS

ACKNOWLEDGEMENTS

The author is grateful to the publishers for permission to quote from the following sources:

Assagioli, R. *Psychosynthesis*. New York: Penguin Books, 1981.

Attār, F. (d. 1220). *Muslim Saints and Mystics: Episodes from the Tadhkirat al-Auliya (Memorial of the Saints.)* The Persian Heritage Series. (trans.), A.J. Arberry. Chicago: University of Chicago Press, 1966.

Balint, M. The three areas of the mind. *International Journal of Psychoanalysis,* 1958, *39,* 328–240.

Bibring, E. Psychoanalysis and dynamic psychotherapies. *Journal of the American Psychoanalytic Association,* 1954, *2,* 745–770.

Cage, J. *Silence.* Cambridge, Mass.: MIT Press, 1971 (Published Earlier by Middletown, CT: Wesleyan University Press).

Erikson, E.H. *Childhood and society.* Second Edition. New York: W. W. Norton & Co., 1963.

Erikson, E.H. *Insight and responsibility. Lectures on the ethical implications of psychoanalytic insight.* New York: W. W. Norton & Co., 1964.

Fingarette, H. *The self in transformation: Psychoanalysis, philosophy and the life of the spirit.* New York: Basic Books, 1963.

Frankl, V.E. *Man's search for meaning: An introduction to logotherapy.* Original title: *From Death-Camp to Existentialism.* New York: Washington Square Press, 1963. (Boston, MA: Beacon Press).

Fromm, E. *The art of loving.* New York: Harper & Row, 1956.

Hujwiri, A.H.J. *Kashf al-Mahjub. The oldest Persian treatise on Sufism (The Uncovering of the Veils).* Trans. by R.A. Nicholson. (The Gibb Memorial Trust) London: Luzac and Co., 1967.

Khan, H.I. *The Sufi message of Hazrat Inayat Khan. Volume X.* London: Barrie and Jenkins (Claremont, CA: Hunter House Publishers Inc.), 1964.

Kretschmer, W. Meditative techniques in psychotherapy. Argentina: Buenos Aires. *Psicológica, Revista Argentina de Psicologia Realista,* 1962, Vol. 5, pp. 76–83.

Kris, E. On some vicissitudes of insight in psychoanalysis. *International Journal of Psychoanalysis,* 1956, *37*:445–455.

Luthe, W. Autogenic training: Method, research, and application in medicine. In C. Tart (Ed.), *Altered states of consciousness. A book of readings.* New York: John Wiley & Sons, 1969.

Nacht, S. Silence as an integrative factor. *International Journal of Psychoanalysis,* 1964, *45*:299–303.

Naranjo, C. and Ornstein, R.E. *On the Psychology of Meditation.* New York: Viking Penguin Inc. (England: George Allen & Unwin Ltd.), 1971.

Nasafi, A. (d. 13th century). *Kitab al-Insan al-Kamil (The book of the integrated human being). (Le Livre de l'Homme Parfait).* Ed. M. Molé, Tehran: Département d'Iranologie, de l'Institue Franco-Iranien, 1962 (In Persian).

Rumi, M.J.M. (d. 1273). *Masnavi-Ī-Ma'navi, The Spiritual Couplets.* Translated and abridged by E.H. Whinfield, Republished under *Teachings of Rumi.* London: Octagon Press, 1973.

Rumi, M.J.M. *The Mathnawi of Jalaluddin Rumi. 6 Volumes.* Edited and Translated by R.A. Nicholson (The Gibb Memorial Trust; Spicer and Pegler) London: Luzac and Co., 1968.

Schimmel, A. *Mystical Dimensions of Islam.* Chapel Hill: University of North Carolina Press, 1975.

Scholem, G. *On the Kabbalah and Its Symbolism.* Translated by R. Manheim, New York: Schocken Books, 1965.

Shafii, M. The pir (sufi guide) and the western psychotherapist. *The R.M. Bucke Memorial Society Newsletter,* 1968, *3*, 9–19.

Shafii, M. Adaptive and therapeutic aspects of meditation. *International Journal of Psychoanalytic Psychotherapy,* 1973, *2*, 364–382.

Shafii, M. Silence in the service of ego: Psychoanalytic study of meditation. *International Journal of Psychoanalysis,* 1973, *54*, 431–443.

Shafii, M. & Shafii, S.L. *Pathways of Human Development: Normal Growth and Emotional Disorders in Infancy, Childhood, and Adolescence.* New York: Thieme-Stratton, 1982.

PREFACE

Sufism, Islamic mysticism, is one of the predominant mystical traditions of the East. Within Sufism, over the last 1,000 years, a holistic concept of human development and integration has evolved. Basic personality structure in Sufism has striking similarities to the concept of personality structure in psychoanalysis and ego psychology. In this book human development and integration in Sufism will be compared and contrasted with the concepts of human development and maturity in Western psychologies, particularly psychoanalysis and ego psychology.

The Sufis believe that separation from nature and Reality is the origin of emotional suffering, dualistic thinking, and personality fragmentation. They have evolved insightful psychotherapeutic methods for remedying these problems through the development of an intense psychomystical relationship between the seeker and the Sufi guide (*pir*). Comparing the psychotherapeutic practices of Sufism with Western psychotherapies, particularly dynamic psychotherapy, may assist us in deciphering the fundamental principles of the psychological healing processes transcending the chasms of time and culture.

Meditation is the essential core of most mystical traditions, particularly Sufism. Varieties of meditative techniques in Yoga, Zen Buddhism, Judeo-Christian traditions, Sufism, and clinical therapeutic methods derived from meditation, such as autogenic training, biofeedback, Psychosynthesis, Transcendental Meditation, and Relaxation Response are described. Relevant physiological, psychological, and psychoanalytic studies regarding the effect of meditation on health and disease, along with side effects, contraindications, and the usefulness of meditation for clinicians are explored.

11

The seven stages of human development on the Sufi path of integration are discussed with references to original Sufi stories, anecdotes, poetry, and psychological works. These stages are compared with stages of human development in ego psychology and Erikson's Eight Ages of Man. The Sufis discuss four additional stages of human development unparalleled in Western psychologies. Awareness and understanding of stages of human development in Sufism may help us to explore the uncharted areas of the mind and personality integration beyond our present psychological knowledge.

Every word and sentence of this book was written jointly, in the spirit of love, joy, and communion, with my wife, Sharon Lee Van Daalen Shafii. *Freedom from the Self* was written and rewritten many times in our hearts and minds before finding outward expression on paper. We have evolved together through this labor of love. We hope that this book becomes for others, as it has for us, a stimulus for further development and integration. By reading and rereading the Sufi stories, anecdotes, and poems, the reader may deeply experience the spirit of the materials beyond written form.

We completed the first draft of the book while we were on sabbatical from the University of Louisville School of Medicine in the small, peaceful, mountainous village of St. Jeannet, Cote d'Azure, France, in the fall of 1980. While we were in St. Jeannet, we learned that this 3,000-year-old village was cultivated by the Greeks, settled by the Romans, and spiritualized by the Carmelite Contemplative Order of St. John of the Cross. This setting inspired us beyond our expectation and imagination. The subsequent drafts of the book were written during 1981–1984, while we were back at home, and I was busy with the daily tasks of teaching, clinical service, and administration.

The tireless efforts of Carolyn Gero and Lois Chapman throughout the typing and retyping of this book are deeply appreciated. Jonathan Cowan, Ph.D., made helpful suggestions for improving the organization of the manuscript and for including relevant materials on meditation. Vernon Pearson, B.A., Research Assistant, verified the references. Patricia Hughes assisted in proofreading some of the typed material. We are grateful to Pamela Holden, Business Administrator, who helped us in many ways while we were on sabbatical.

Wayne Oates, ThD, Professor of Pastoral Counseling in the Department of Psychiatry and Behavioral Sciences at the University of Louisville School of Medicine, generously devoted time from his busy schedule to read Chapters 1 and 3 and provided insightful comments.

We hope that *Freedom from the Self* may be helpful to students of human behavior and to anyone sincerely searching for the truth and reality within and around.

Mohammad Shafii, M.D.

St. Jeannet, France

Louisville, Kentucky

Part I

THE ELEMENTS

Chapter 1

THE TRAVELER

Basic Personality Structure in Sufism and Ego Psychology

The Essences are each a separate Glass through which the Sun of Being's Light is passed—Each tinted fragment sparkles in the Sun: A thousand colors, but the Light is One.

Jāmi, a Sufi poet, fifteenth century.[1]

The magic of the past is the science of the present. The mysticism of today is the psychology of tomorrow. The word "mysticism" often brings to mind unfounded beliefs or vague speculations. In actuality, mysticism is the direct experience of nature and Reality (Truth, God). The essential core of mysticism is the communion of human beings,

---

[1] Nasr, S.H. (1975) in R. Beny, *Persia: Bridge of Turquoise*. Boston: New York Graphic Society, p. 70.

nature, and God. It is the experience of the oneness of all within the multiplicity of forms. If we view mystical traditions as experiencing and discovering mysteries within the self and the universe, then we will be able to perceive the unbounded possibilities of mysticism.

In human beings, mystical experiences are expressed in a variety of esoteric traditions, such as Egyptian monotheism, Judaism, Zoroastrianism, Yoga, Buddhism, Christian mysticism, and Sufism (Islamic mysticism). We will be exploring Sufism (*Tasawwuf*), the spiritual and psychological core of human development in Islam and one of the predominant mystical traditions of the East.

In this book we will focus on the holistic concept of human evolution, development, and integration which has evolved in Sufism. During the last 1,000 years, the Sufis have written in detail about basic personality structures which have striking similarities to those in psychoanalysis and ego psychology. This comparison is not only of historical value, but also may help us to discover the significant aspects of personality development and integration beyond the limitations of language, time, and culture.

In exploring psychological concepts in Sufism, we should remember that the Sufis feel that any adherence to a closed system, although comforting, limits human perception and perpetuates the distortion of reality. In essence, Sufism, although it has structure and consistency, is an open system, which attracts, receives, digests, and integrates the prevailing relevant scientific, religious, creative, and artistic ideas of the time.

HUMAN EVOLUTION

Sufis believe that human evolution progresses through the following forms: inorganic matter, organic, vegetative, animal, human, spiritual, nonbeing, and, finally, universal being. The evolution of humanity, then, does not end with our present human form. There is a potential to become a universal being. This progressive, hope-inspiring perspective is a dynamic force in the Sufi's journey toward personality integration and existential communion.

Rumi, a Sufi poet of the thirteenth century, portrayed this progression:

> I died from minerality and changed to the vegetative state.
> I died from the vegetative state and became animal.
>   I died from animality and became human: Why, then, should
> I fear? When have I become less by dying?

At the next stage I shall die from human form, that I may
soar and lift up my head amongst the angels;
Then, will be freed from being an angel: *everything is perishing
except His Face.*
Once more I shall be sacrificed and die . . . I shall become
that which enters not into the imagination.
Then I shall become non-existence: Non-existence saith to
me, . . . *Verily, unto Him shall we return.*

Modified and adapted from Nicholson's
translation, *Mathnawi, Book III*, pp. 218–219.

In Sufism, one becomes experientially aware of past states, early
life experiences, levels of personality development, and connection
with the universe. Seeing oneself within and as a part of the universe
helps in alleviating internal fragmentation, alienation from others,
and separation from nature.

BASIC PERSONALITY STRUCTURES

To understand basic structures of personality in Sufi psychology,
it is necessary to understand the concept of *nafs*. "*Nafs*" is an Arabic
word meaning breath, animal life, soul, spirit, self, individual, sub-
stance, and essence (Steingass, 1892). *Nafs* is related to the word "*neph-
esh*" (soul) in Hebrew. Finding a parallel word in English is difficult.
Frequently, *nafs* is translated into English as "soul" (Morewedge, 1973).
However, the word "soul" has limited theological and metaphysical
associations and does not represent the depth and breadth of the
concept of *nafs* or, more specifically, the psychological meaning of
nafs. The closest meanings in English would be "personality," "self,"
or "levels of personality development." Because of the lack of an
equivalent English word, the original word, *nafs*, will be retained.

Avicenna (d. 1037 A.D.), the Persian physician, philosopher-scien-
tist, and psychologist, approximately 1,000 years ago in *The Book of
Healing*, (*al-Shifā'*), wrote extensively about basic personality structures
and the variety of *nafses*. He relied heavily on Al-Fārābi's (d. 950 A.D.)
writings for understanding Greek philosophy. Avicenna integrated
Sufi ideas with Aristotle's writings on the psychology of the human
personality as found in *De Anima* and developed an integrated and
holistic concept of personality structure (Nasr, 1964).

According to Avicenna and Sufi psychology, all living things, in
addition to their mineral or inorganic state, have *nafs* or several *nafses*,
depending on their level of development in the circle of evolution

(Figure 1, chapter 1). *Nafses* are recognized by their energies and functions. All plants, animals, and human beings have three functions in common: nutrition, growth, and reproduction. These three functions are essential for any form of life. Animals and human beings are differentiated from plants by their ability for voluntary movement and sensory perception. Human beings are differentiated from animals by their intellectual ability.

VEGETATIVE NAFS

The vegetative *nafs (nafs-i-nebāti)* is the most basic *nafs* existing in plants, animals, humans, and all living things. Nutrition, growth, and reproduction, which are essential functions of all forms of life, are manifestations of this *nafs* (Avicenna, p. 41).

ANIMAL NAFS

In addition to the vegetative *nafs*, animals and human beings are endowed with animal *nafs (nafs-i-haiwāni)*. Animal *nafs* consists of two major forces: the driving forces *(quwā-i-muharrika)* and the perceptual forces *(quwā-i-mudrika)* (Avicenna, p. 41). We will begin with a discussion of the driving forces and their comparison to the concept of the id in ego psychology.

DRIVING FORCES

Driving forces *(quwā-i-muharrika)*: The word *quwā* means forces, energies, and powers, and *muharrika* means impulse, stimuli, and that which induces action and movement. Driving forces are composed of two types (Avicenna, p. 42):

1. Sensual force *(qūwat-i-shahwāni)* means sexual or libidinous force. This force stimulates animals and humans to pursue and experience pleasure.

2. Rage force *(qūwat-i-ghazabi)* means the force of rage, anger, and aggression. Fight or flight, along with destructive tendencies, are the manifestations of this force.

The driving forces, a combination of sensual and rage forces, are also referred to as *nafs-i-ammāra*, meaning driven, depraved, or commanding *nafs* (Koran, Sūra 12:53). According to the Sufis, these forces drive animals and human beings to action without pause, inhibition, or thinking. Human beings, like animals, can be impulsively driven by this *nafs* to perform acts which they generally would not do. Indulgence in sexual wishes, immediate need gratification, and loss of control in the form of rage, destruction, homicide, or suicide, are the extreme forms of expression of driven *nafs*. Selfishness, greed, preoccupation with having and possessing are also manifestations of this *nafs* (Shah, 1964, p. 394).

Schimmel (1975), in her scholarly work, *Mystical Dimensions of Islam*, observed that when the Sufis use the word *"nafs"* by itself, they are usually referring to the animal *nafs* (p. 112). *Nafs* is perceived by the Sufis as being a concrete entity. It is not merely a concept or an abstract idea. The animal *nafs* has been compared to a conniving dog, a dangerous snake, a cunning fox, a camel in heat, and often to a wild horse. The Sufis' approach to this "animal within" is not to kill or to destroy it, but to develop the ability of harnessing its energy for further psychospiritual growth. Especially in the early phases of psychomystical development, one needs to be constantly aware of wishes, impulses, and driven tendencies. Being aware of and harnessing the energies of this "animal within" can provide the traveler with the psychological ability for moving further along the Path of Reality (Chapter 6).

DRIVING FORCES IN SUFISM AND ID IN EGO PSYCHOLOGY

A comparative study of Sufism and ego psychology begins with the study of the driving forces of the animal *nafs* in Sufism, which are similar to the concept of the id in the structural theory of psychoanalysis (Figure 1, chapter 1). Freud (1923), after more than 30 years of developing and changing his psychoanalytic concepts, proposed in *The Ego and the Id* a major theoretical construct known as the structural theory. Strachey, the translator of Freud's work from German to English, in the Editor's Introduction wrote:

> *The Ego and the Id* is the last of Freud's major theoretical works. It offers a description of the mind and its workings which is at first sight new and even revolutionary; and indeed all psycho-analytic writings that date from after its publication bear the unmistakable imprint of its effect . . . (p. 4).

PERSONALITY

SUFISM

ACCUSING NAFS
(NAFS-I-LAWWĀMA)
- ABSTINENCE
- AWARENESS OF WISHES, THOUGHTS, AND ACTIONS
- SELF-ACCUSATION--BLAME
- EXPERIENCE OF GUILT AND SHAME
- RELIGIOUS PROHIBITION

HUMAN NAFS
(NAFS-I-INSĀNĪ)
- HEART (DIL) (unconscious)
  - REAWAKENING
- INTELLECT ('AQL) (conscious and unconscious)
  - ABSTRACT-UNIVERSAL INTELLECT ('aql-i-ālima)
  - PRACTICAL INTELLECT ('aql-i-āmila)

ANIMAL NAFS
(NAFS-I-HAIWĀNĪ)
- PERCEPTUAL FORCES (quwā-ı-mudrika)
  - UNCONSCIOUS FORCES (quwā-i-bātina)
    - MEMORIES (tazakkur)
    - ILLUSIONS-INSPIRATIONS (tawahhum)
    - IMAGINATION (takhayyul)
    - ASSOCIATIONS (hiss-i-mushtarak-- pre-conscious)
  - CONSCIOUS AND SENSORY PERCEPTIONS (hawāss-i-zāhiri)
    - CONSCIOUS AWARENESS
    - VISUAL
    - AUDITORY
    - OLFACTORY
    - TASTE
    - TACTILE
- DRIVING FORCES (quwā-ı-muharrika)
  - RAGE FORCE (qūwat-i-ghazabi)
  - SENSUAL FORCE (qūwat-i-shahwāni)

VEGETATIVE NAFS
(NAFS-I-NEBĀTI)
- REPRODUCTION (taulid)
- GROWTH (numuw)
- NUTRITION (taghziya)

MINERAL OR INORGANIC STATE
(JUMADI)

STRUCTURE

EGO PSYCHOLOGY

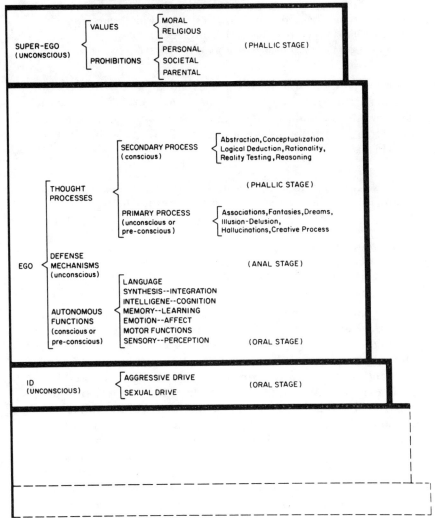

According to the structural theory, the mind is comprised of three parts: id, ego, and superego. "These are called 'structures' because of the relative constancy of their objectives and consistency in modes of operation." (Moore & Fine, 1968, p. 90).

The id is the totally unconscious part of the mind, and it represents the instinctual drives of sex and aggression. The term "id," or as it is called in German,

> ... "*das Es*" ... was derived in the first instance from Georg Groddeck, a physician practicing at Baden-Baden, who had recently become attached to psycho-analysis and with whose wideranging ideas Freud felt much sympathy. . . .the use of the word certainly goes back to Nietzsche. (Freud, 1923, p. 7)

The id represents the passionate, irrational, and driven part of human beings. Freud, by choosing the term "id," meaning "it" in English, specifically underlined the animalistic nature of these forces. According to Freud, the id is comprised of two major instincts or drives. He stated (1923) that there are

> ... two classes of instincts, one of which, the sexual instincts or Eros, is by far the more conspicuous and accessible to study. . . . The second class of instincts was not so easy to point to; in the end we came to recognize sadism as its representative. On the basis of theoretical considerations, supported by biology, we put forward the hypothesis of a death instinct, the task of which is to lead organic life back into the inanimate state; . . . (p. 40).

The concept of the death instinct proved to be controversial, and later was modified and enlarged by Hartmann (1939) and Anna Freud (1965), and is now conceptualized as the aggressive drive.

It is incredible how astute observers of human behavior in both the East and the West, 1,000 years apart, transcended cultural differences and the chasm of time to reach the same conclusions. Sufis, from personal mystical experiences, became aware of the animal part within human beings and developed the idea of the driving forces of the animal *nafs*, consisting of the sensual force and rage force. Freud and other ego psychologists, through their own experiences in personal analysis, careful and meticulous observation of patients in psychotherapy, and naturalistic observation of the behavior of infants and children, recognized the existence of the animal forces within, in the form of the id composed of sexual and aggressive drives.

PERCEPTUAL FORCES

As you recall, in Sufi psychology, animal *nafs* is composed of two major forces: the driving forces and the perceptual forces. Now perceptual forces and their components will be discussed (Figure 1, chapter 1).

Perceptual forces *(quwā-i-mudrika)*: the word *"mudrika"* means understanding, comprehension, and memory. In this situation, it refers to external sensory perceptions, consciousness, and internal perceptions. (Avicenna, pp. 41–51) Perceptual forces are divided into two types:

1. Conscious and sensory perceptions.
2. Unconscious forces.

Conscious and Sensory Perceptions

Conscious and sensory perceptions are called *hawāss-i-zāhiri:hawāss* means senses; *zāhiri* means outward or external. *Hawāss-i-zāhiri* refers to what we call sensory perceptions and conscious awareness. Sensory perceptions include tactile, taste, olfactory, auditory, and visual perceptions.

The Sufis conceptualize conscious awareness as originating from sensory perceptions. Sensory perceptions are closely related to the driving forces of animal *nafs*.

Unconscious Forces

Unconscious forces *(quwā-i-bātina)*: The word *quwā* means forces, and *"bātina"* originating from the word *"batn"* means abdomen, the womb, interior part, and the heart. *Quwā-i-bātina* refers to internal sensations, internal forces, and the unconscious areas of the mind. Imagination, illusions, and memories are representations of these internal forces (Figure 1, chapter 1).

Associations, although perceived as part of the unconscious forces, actually represent the interface between unconscious forces and conscious awareness.

The various components of the unconscious forces will now be discussed.

Associations (hiss-i-mushtarak).   The word *"hiss"* means sense; *"mushtarak"* means shared, common, and paying tribute to two masters (Steingass, 1892).

In Sufi psychology, *hiss-i-mushtarak* refers to the frontiers or the borders between conscious awareness and unconscious forces. Although associations are perceived by the Sufis as part of the unconscious forces, they are still thought of as that part closest to the senses and to the conscious process. Attachment of thoughts and fantasies to sensory perceptions are the manifest expression of associations.

According to Avicenna, all stimuli, after being received by the body, go through the frontiers of associations where past memories and experiences are reawakened and become attached to sensory perceptions (pp. 168–169). The experiences of pleasure and pain are related to this process. Both human beings and animals have associations. Avicenna differentiated between associations and the intellect, which will be discussed later.

Imagination (takhayyul).   The word "*takkayyul*" means imagination, fantasies, daydreams, and visions. Sensory perceptions pass through associations and are stored in the form of fantasies and imaginations in the unconscious. Some perceptions are stored exactly as perceived and some are changed or distorted. The unconscious has the ability to create and express new fantasies and images. Most expressions of imagination are in the form of images and visual perceptions. These images can originate from internal or external experiences. The forces of imagination are more active when the forces of intellect are quiet or silent.

According to Avicenna, imagination has a direct relationship with attention. Attention to external forces and reality inhibits the individual from becoming aware of internal forces. Fantasies and memories fade temporarily. Also, when the individual is stimulated by the sensual force, the expression of the rage force diminishes, and vice versa.

Therefore, when an individual is not involved in action, movement, or perceptions, imagination and fantasy take over. It is interesting to note that the Sufis realized that body movement, sensory perception, and speech inhibited the forces of fantasies and creative imagination. They observed that through quiescence, limitation of body movement, silence, and meditation, it was possible to tap the unbounded forces of fantasies and creative imagination (chapters 3 and 4).

Avicenna divided imagination into two types. In the first type, imagination is used for adaptation to daily life and external reality. In the second type, imagination overtakes wisdom and intellect and expresses itself in the form of irrational fears and massive anxiety.

When this occurs, the power of imagination is reinforced. These internal perceptions and fantasies are then externalized as though real. This happens in individuals who have become psychotic, severely phobic, or who are suffering from major physical illness (pp. 175–176). These phenomena are now referred to as hallucinations.

Illusions and Inspirations (tawahhum).   The word "*tawahhum*" means thinking, suspecting, and supposing. It originates from the word *wahm*, meaning twisting an idea around in one's mind or conceiving a false idea, particularly regarding fearful, distressing, or anxiety-producing experiences. Generally, *wahm* is related to distorted sensory perceptions, similar to the concept of illusion in psychiatry and Western psychologies.

According to Avicenna, illusions are a major force in the life of both animals and human beings. Human beings, through the process of reasoning and intellect, are able to overcome their illusions, but animals are not able to do so. Some people are not able to free themselves from illusions, and they become prisoners of their misperceptions, fantasies, and distortions (pp. 189–192).

In Sufi psychology, illusions are divided into the following types:

1. *Instinctual*—these are inborn behaviors for survival, such as sucking, grasping, and blinking. These behaviors resemble our present understanding of the early inborn reflexes.

2. *Experiential*—these refer to the individual's past experiences, whether pleasurable or painful. Pleasure or pain is associated with the shape, smell, consistency, or other aspects of a particular stimulus. A human being or animal exposed to a stimulus is attracted to or repelled from it based on past experiences.

3. *Associative*—these illusions originate from past instinctual or experiential illusions and, at times, are expressed in new inspirational or creative combinations.

The concept of *wahm* does not have exactly the same meaning as illusion or delusion. Illusion and delusion have a maladaptive and pathological connotation. *Wahm* in Sufi psychology has three levels of meaning: at one level it is instinctual and adaptive for survival; on another level, it can become pathological and troublesome; and, finally, on the highest level, it can be a source of creativity and mystical inspiration.

Memories (tazakkur).   Tazakkur, meaning remembering or keeping on one's memory, originates from the word *"zikr,"* meaning remembrance. According to Avicenna, memory is unique to human beings. Animals have the ability to re-experience sensory perceptions, associations, imaginations, and illusions; however, they do not have the cognitive ability to remember or recall past experiences or events. Avicenna recognized that the ability of cognitive recall is directly related to the ability to use language, which is a human function.

Avicenna differentiated between memory and learning. Memory is when a situation which has already been preserved in the mind is recalled through internal or external forces. Learning is remembering past experiences and applying them to new situations, thereby making the unknown known (p. 192).

According to the Sufis, memory, or the ability to recall and remember past experiences, is a double-edged sword: on one hand, it helps to preserve knowledge and develop rationalistic and intellectual reasoning; but, on the other hand, it hinders further personality integration because one can become preoccupied with self-aggrandizement. There is a danger in seeing ourselves as being totally different from and unique among all creatures of nature and in perceiving ourselves as the masters of the universe. Overpreoccupation with rationalistic thinking and intellectual reasoning induces further feelings of separation resulting in delusions and alienation from other human beings, nature, and God.

PERCEPTUAL FORCES IN SUFISM AND EGO IN EGO PSYCHOLOGY

The word *"ego"* means "I," or more commonly the self. *Ego*, in psychoanalytic theory, refers to the reasoning and adaptive part of the personality. Freud (1923) wrote:

> The ego represents what may be called reason and common sense, in contrast to the id, which contains the passions. . . .Thus in its relation to the id it is like a man on horseback, who has to hold in check the superior strength of the horse; with this difference, that the rider tries to do so with his own strength while the ego uses borrowed forces (p. 25).

Freud (1923, 1926, 1937), Anna Freud (1936, 1965), Hartmann (1939, 1964), Erikson (1950), and Kohut (1971, 1977, 1978) have contributed significantly to the development of the field of ego psychology. Ego psychology is a general psychology of human development and adaptation within the psychoanalytic framework.

Originally, in classical psychoanalytic theory, internal conflicts between the impulses and wishes of the id and parental and societal prohibitions against these wishes were conceptualized as the origin of personality development and of psychopathological disorders. Traumas and conflicts were experienced on a conscious level, then went through the preconscious level, and were subsequently repressed and stored in the unconscious. This form of conceptualization of the human mind and the division of the mind into the Conscious System (CS), Pre-Conscious System (PCS), and Unconscious System (UCS), which was prevalent until Freud's publication of *The Ego and the Id* (1923), is known as the topographical theory of psychoanalysis.

Although Freud's discovery of the unconscious, with its significant impact on the human mind in health and disease, was a major milestone in understanding human beings, the topographical theory was not sufficient in explaining human beings' tendencies toward forgetfulness, repression, and, particularly, healthy adaptation to external reality.

Freud's proposal of the structural theory and the development of the concepts of id, ego, and superego helped in creating the field of ego psychology. Ego psychology takes into consideration human ability for adaptation to external and internal reality, not only during pathological stress, but also during healthy and growth-producing experiences. Ego psychology integrates advances in other scientific fields, particularly in the behavioral sciences—for instance, findings in the field of developmental psychology, cognitive psychology, learning theory, behaviorism, ethology, biology, and psychophysiology.

Ego Functions

We need to remember that "ego" is an abstract concept. It is not an entity by itself. It is defined by its functions. Most commonly, ego functions are divided in the following manner (Figure 1, chapter 1):

1. Autonomous Functions
2. Defense Mechanisms
3. Thought Processes

Autonomous Ego Functions.   Hartmann (1939) proposed that some of the ego functions are conflict-free. He wrote:

Not every adaptation to the environment, or every learning and maturation process, is a conflict. I refer to the development *outside of conflict* of perception, intention, object comprehension, thinking, language, recall-phenomena, productivity, to the well-known phases of motor development, grasping, crawling, walking, and to the maturation and learning processes implicit in all these and many others (p. 8).

Autonomous ego functions are usually conscious or preconscious. Generally, the following functions are perceived as autonomous ego functions: sensory-motor functions, expression of basic emotions, perception, affect, memory, learning, intelligence, cognitive ability, synthetic-integrative functions, and language.

The Sufis' concept of the perceptual forces of the animal *nafs*, with its components of conscious-sensory perceptions and unconscious forces, parallels the psychoanalytic concepts of ego in the structural theory and Conscious and Preconscious systems in the topographical theory. The Conscious System, which is also referred to as consciousness, is "A state of awareness of *perceptions* coming from the outside world and from within the body and mind" (Moore & Fine, 1968, p. 28). The Conscious System is a very small part of the mind.

The Preconscious System in psychoanalysis refers to ". . . memories, ideas, and images, and their verbal symbols as well as motor habits, which are for the most part capable of achieving *consciousness* by the act of focusing *attention*." (Moore & Fine, 1968, p. 74)

The concept of associations in Sufi psychology has similarities to the concept of preconscious in psychoanalysis. Unconscious memories, fantasies, and perceptions are reawakened by daily sensory or experiential events. They are attached to thoughts or body sensations in the preconscious state and finally come to the level of conscious awareness.

Conscious and sensory perceptions in Sufism are comparable to the concepts of Conscious and Preconscious Systems in the topographical theory of psychoanalysis. However, conscious and sensory perceptions go beyond the concept of Conscious and Preconscious Systems in that they also include sensory perceptions. It was much later in psychoanalysis (1923), with the development of the structural theory, that the sensory perceptions of vision, hearing, smelling, tasting, and touching were included as functions of the ego and later referred to as autonomous ego functions.

The Sufi's concept of conscious and sensory perceptions integrates the concept of conscious awareness and sensory perception. In psychoanalytic and psychodynamic theories it is difficult to reconcile the topographical theory with the structural theory. Some psycho-analysts have advocated discarding the concepts of conscious, precon-scious, and unconscious, and adhering to the structural theory of id, ego, and superego. But, in actuality, the concepts of conscious, precon-scious, and unconscious have practical and clinical application in the practice of psychoanalysis and psychotherapy. From the beginning, Sufis have integrated conscious awareness with other sensory mo-dalities and refer to all cumulatively as conscious and sensory percep-tions.

Defense Mechanism.   Anna Freud (1936) in *The Ego and the Mechanisms of Defense* perceived that in the early stages of human development, mental defenses emerge from the ego as an outcome of the struggle between wishes and impulses of the id and the limita-tions and constrictions of outside reality.

These defenses are for the most part unconscious and help in human adaptation in health and disease. Defense mechanisms are classified in the following way (Meissner et al., 1975, pp. 535–536):

1. Narcissistic Defenses

   a. Projection—distortion of external reality by at-tributing one's own internal feelings to others.

   b. Denial—perceiving but refusing to recognize or negating external reality.

2. Immature Defenses

   a. Introjection-Identification—internalization of liked or disliked characteristics or qualities of others.

   b. Regression—return to an earlier stage of develop-ment in order to avoid anxiety or distress.

   c. Acting Out—direct behavioral expression of un-conscious wishes or impulses without conscious aware-ness.

3. Neurotic Defenses

   a. Repression—forgetting unwanted memories, ex-periences, and fantasies. This is one of the major de-fense mechanisms. Overdependence on repression contributes to the development of neurotic disorders and other forms of psychopathology.

   b. Rationalization—finding justification for unac-ceptable behaviors, attitudes, and beliefs.

c.   Displacement—unconscious shifting of feelings, behaviors, and instinctual desires from one person or object to another.

d.   Intellectualization—using thought processes and excessive thinking to control emotions and impulses rather than experiencing them.

e.   Reaction Formation—expression of unaccepted feelings and emotions in an opposite manner.

f.   Isolation—separation or splitting of affect and emotion from the content of thoughts or fantasies.

4.   Mature Defenses

a.   Altruism—experiencing internal gratification by serving others.

b.   Anticipation—assessment of reality and planning for the future.

c.   Asceticism—renouncing base pleasures and experiencing gratification from renunciation.

d.   Humor—expression of feelings and emotions openly without discomfort and not at the expense of others.

e.   Sublimation—expression of internal wishes and impulses from a socially and morally unacceptable aim to a socially and humanistically valuable purpose.

f.   Suppression—conscious or preconscious attempt to delay or postpone a conscious conflictual behavior or impulse.

Although the Sufis did not use the term "defense mechanism" to describe the functions of animal *nafs* in human beings, they had keen awareness of the psychological mechanisms—such as forgetfulness, blaming others, distortion of reality, tendency toward indulgence in wishes and impulses, return to earlier stages of development, altruism, asceticism, humor, conscious control of unhealthy wishes and desires—and emphasis on harnessing the driving forces of animal *nafs* in the service of humanity, creative expressions, and further personality integration. In chapters 2 and 6, the Sufis' description and suggestion for freeing the self from unhealthy and troublesome habits (narcissistic and neurotic defense mechanisms) for further personality integration will be discussed.

Unconscious Forces in Sufism
and the Unconscious in Psychoanalysis

As you recall, the unconscious forces of the perceptual forces of animal *nafs* in Sufi psychology play a significant role in human development. Associations, imagination, illusions and inspirations, and memories are some of the components of the unconscious forces. On a higher level, intellect and heart (affective, emotional, and spiritual experiences) of human *nafs* are other components of unconscious forces.

The concept of the unconscious and its major component, primary process thought in psychoanalysis, will now be reviewed and compared with unconscious forces in Sufism. (Figure 1, chapter 1)

The Unconscious in Psychoanalysis

In psychoanalysis and ego psychology, that part of the mind of which one is unaware is called the unconscious. According to psychoanalytic and psychodynamic theories, mental contents, wishes, and drives "...which are unacceptable, threatening or abhorrent to the moral, ethical and intellectual standards of the individual" are repressed in the unconscious (Moore & Fine, 1968, p. 94). These repressed fantasies and wishes continuously strive for expression, resulting in intrapsychic conflicts and feelings of anxiety or guilt. When the defense mechanism of repression fails, neurotic and psychopathological symptoms are manifested in the individual.

The contents of the unconscious are irrational and regulated by the forces of the id—sexual and aggressive drives. According to psychoanalytic theory, memories, events, sensory and perceptual experiences, thoughts and fantasies, after being perceived consciously, go through the process of repression and are stored in the unconscious. This is particularly true for painful events and traumatic experiences.

Perceptual experiences and thought processes are stored in the unconscious in the form of primary process thoughts and memories. Primary process thoughts are expressed in the form of free associations, fantasies, dreams, daydreams, illusions, delusions, hallucinations, and creative processes.

Primary process in psychoanalysis refers to "...a primitive, irrational type of wishful thought, dominated by the emotions and close

to the *instinctual drives*; ..." (Moore & Fine, p. 76) Symbolic representations, particularly visual symbols, are manifestations of the primary
process. These representations are frequently preverbal, sensory-
visual, and have the quality of timelessness and spacelessness. The
primary process does not follow Aristotelian logic, causality, or deductive reasoning. It is inclusive and holistic rather than deductive. A
symbol in primary process has multiple representations and meanings
Dreaming, daydreaming, fantasies, spontaneous creative expressions,
and mystical visual or auditory experiences are manifestations of the
primary process. The primary process in the true sense is the language
of the unconscious. In severe forms of psychopathological disorders,
and in alcohol and drug toxicity and brain insult, the primary process
may be manifest in the form of hallucinations, delusions, and illusions.

As discussed earlier, unconscious materials pass through the preconscious state in the form of free associations, fantasies, and daydreams before becoming conscious. The Preconscious System is like
a border between two countries; everything which passes from the
land of the unconscious to the land of the conscious has to go through
the Preconscious System and vice versa.

The development of the concept of the unconscious and the
dynamic forces of libido or sexual instinct were the significant contributions of psychoanalysis in helping to understand the human mind
in health and disease.

Freud, at the beginning of this century in the year 1900, with the
publication of his epoch-making book, *The Interpretation of Dreams,*
carefully described the role of the unconscious in the development
of dreams and the role of psychic traumas in the formation of dreams.
Also, he conceptualized that overwhelming psychic traumas and unconscious conflicts contribute to the expression of neurotic symptoms
as a compromise between forbidden sexual wishes and societal, parental, and familial taboos against these wishes.

Psychoanalysis as a psychotherapeutic method emphasizes the
process of free association as a way of bringing to awareness unconscious fantasies, wishes, and traumatic experiences. The underlying
premise of this therapeutic process is that the patient will verbalize
any thoughts, feelings, ideas, or sensations that come to mind without
censoring them. The psychoanalyst, through the process of active
silence and occasional exploratory questions, helps the patient to bring
up fantasies, wishes, and past memories from the depth of the unconscious to consciousness. Then, the patient, with the help of the analyst,
re-examines these fantasies, wishes, and distorted memories, with the
hope of perceiving them in the light of reality (chapter 2).

In psychoanalysis the basic premise is that the dark and evil forces of the unconscious constantly torment the individual, and these forces need to come under the control of the conscious, reality-oriented, and rationalistic forces of the mind—the Conscious System and the ego.

The concept of associations in Sufi psychology resembles the Pre-Conscious System in psychoanalysis and ego psychology. Imagination, with emphasis on visual representation and illusion-inspiration, are clearly similar to the concept of primary process. Sufis emphasize that, through the experiences of silence in meditation and transcending the boundaries of thought processes and language, one can gradually experience the deepest level of the unconscious forces of animal *nafs* within (chapters 3 and 4).

The Sufis feel that it is an illusion to see human beings as different and separate from nature and the universe. Distortion of values and preoccupation with having and possessing rather than with living and being is also an illusion. Hoarding, possessing, dividing, fragmenting, and destroying are related to these illusionary perceptions. As long as we are blinded by illusions, we can only experience a part, but not the whole, of reality.

One of the Sufi's major tasks is freeing the self from illusions. Here, psychoanalysis, dynamic psychotherapy, and Sufism are again on a common path. In psychotherapy, through the process of free associations and the re-experiencing of past traumas, whether real or fantasized, one is able gradually to free the self from past illusions and distortions. The events of the past, the experience of the present, and the possibilities of the future can then be perceived in the light of reality. Sufis follow the same path for basically the same purpose. Sufis approach the problem through meditation and by emphasizing internal experiences and deeds instead of words (chapters 3, 4).

Sufis, through the process of meditation and the suspension of rational thinking, along with becoming acutely aware of inner sensations, developed a technique for tapping the unbounded forces of the unconscious. The fascinating part of Sufi psychology is that the unconscious in Sufism is not a psychological abstract, but has concrete reality. It originates from the gut, viscera, and the heart. It has a physiological basis. Vegetative and autonomic functions of the nervous system are a part of the unconscious. The concept of the unconscious in psychoanalysis has been plagued by the limitations of the topographical theory. Psychoanalytic theory has not paid enough attention to the role of visceral, autonomic, and vegetative aspects of the central nervous system as a building block for the development of unconscious fantasies, perceptions, and thought processes.

Another difference between Sufi psychology and psychoanalysis is that the Sufis believe that animals are also endowed with pre-conscious and unconscious perception (Figure 1, chapter 1). The Sufis elaborated even further on the concept of the unconscious in that they perceived it as a force uniting human beings with animals, plants, and minerals. Sufis, at the same time, also view the unconscious as an integrative force which unites human beings with the Universal Reality, Cosmic Consciousness, or God.

UNCONSCIOUS FORCES IN SUFISM AND THE COLLECTIVE UNCONSCIOUS

Jung, who had been the most promising of Freud's disciples, and heir apparent, expanded the concept of the sexual drive of the id or libido theory (1909-1910). He, like most of the Eastern thinkers, Sufis, and Yogis, believed that libido not only represented the sexual desires in human beings, but also represented the unifying and unitary force in nature which transcended sexuality. He referred to libido as "love" or "life energy," and felt that it underlay all natural phenomena. Freud was afraid that this idea would dilute the scientific and rationalistic aspects of psychoanalysis and would decrease his significant contribution concerning the role of sexual instinct in the development of personality.

Jung journeyed to the East to explore the psychomystical traditions of the orient, particularly India. This exposure helped Jung formulate the idea of "collective unconscious." The concept of collective unconscious transcends Freud's concept of the unconscious. According to Jung (1940), the collective unconscious is the cumulative psychic life of our ancestors.

> This psychic life is the mind of our ancient ancestors. . . .As the body is a sort of museum of its phylogenetic history, so is the mind. There is no reason for believing that the psyche, with its peculiar structure, is the only thing in the world that has no history beyond its individual manifestation. . . .It is only individual ego-consciousness that has forever a new beginning and an early end. But the unconscious psyche is not only immensely old, it is also able to grow unceasingly into an equally remote future. (pp. 24–25).

The concept of unconscious forces in Sufism encompasses the unconscious in psychoanalysis, but also includes Jung's concept of collective unconscious. At the same time, it transcends human experience—present, past, or future. Unconscious forces in Sufism encompass animal, vegetative, and inorganic states of our being along with the human, spiritual, and universal states.

Sufis believe that the conscious is like a cup and that the unconscious is like an ocean. How can the whole ocean be put into a cup? Each individual is like a cup, and all of us and nature collectively are the ocean, unconscious Reality, or God. The individual, by losing the limitation of the cup and freeing the self, can be reunited with the ocean of being. Then, human beings can become one with all aspects of life and lose the anxieties of separation, loneliness, and isolation. The Sufis believe that when a drop of water returns to the ocean, although it outwardly loses the identity of its dropness, it gains the permanency of the everlasting ocean (chapter 5).

The Unconscious Before Freud

The discovery of the unconscious did not begin with Freud or psychoanalysis, although Freud and the psychoanalysts after him have used it effectively for therapeutic purposes and for creating an elaborate theoretical system.

Lancelot L. Whyte (1960), in his scholarly book, *The Unconscious Before Freud,* credits Shakespeare, Leibniz, Goethe, Schopenhauer, Von Hartmann, and Nietzsche with the discovery of the unconscious in the West. He stated:

> The discovery of the unconscious by self-conscious man occupied some two centuries roughly from 1700 to 1900 . . . *the idea of unconscious mental processes was, in many of its aspects, conceivable around 1700, topical around 1800, and became effective around 1900,* thanks to the imaginative efforts of a large number of individuals of varied interests in many lands (p. 57).

According to Whyte, even ". . . Descartes could not avoid——that the facts do not support the assumption of the autonomy of consciousness" (p. 57). A number of forces were moving in the direction of developing and conceptualizing the concept of the unconscious in the West. First of all, from the eleventh century onward, two developments in the West showed great interest in personal religious experiences and the experiences of the individual. These culminated with the work of Goethe and Schelling, with the romantic and transcendental ideas of human beings, and with the *Naturphilosophie* (pantheistic monism) movement in Germany from the 1790s to the 1830s. The *Naturphilosophie* movement, which was a pervasive one at that time in the intellectual circles of Western Europe, owed a great deal to Eastern thoughts and traditions (Whyte, p. 58). Around this time, with the colonial expansion of the West to the Middle East and Asia, the East was being rediscovered as happened also during the Crusades in the eleventh and twelfth centuries. A large number of books about travels to the East, especially Persia, Egypt, India, and China, were published at that time and became popular reading.

At the same time, along with Napoleon's conquest of Egypt, a number of Persian and Arabic classical Sufi poetries and books were translated into German, French, and English. One of them was a partial translation of Hafiz's book of poetry entitled *Dīvān-i-Hāfiz*. Hāfiz was a Sufi Persian poet who lived in the fourteenth century.

Goethe came across a German translation of this book, and was so moved and inspired by the work of Hāfiz, that he isolated himself from the public for a period of time, meditated on each verse, and consequently wrote his famous book, *West-Eastern Divan*, in 1819. He dedicated this book to Hāfiz of Shiraz. The hero and heroine of his romantic book of poems have Persian names, and frequently the events occur in a Persian landscape as Goethe conceived it. It is thought that exposure to Sufi thoughts and ideas rekindled the creative urges in Goethe and contributed to the completion of the second part of his masterpiece, *Faust*, in the late 1820s.

We know also that Freud was an avid reader of Goethe. According to Ernest Jones (1953), Freud, as a young medical student, was also interested in mystical and speculative aspects of *Naturphilosophie* (Vol. 1, p. 43). Also, we know that Freud won a major literary award because of his scholarly interest in and contribution to Goethe's studies. Could it be that the discovery of the unconscious by Freud had its roots in Jewish mystical traditions and in German romantic and mystical movements of the eighteenth and early nineteenth centuries, specifically Goethe's work and, through Goethe, exposure to Sufi thoughts and ideas?

Unconscious forces in Sufism have similarities to the concept of the unconscious in psychoanalysis. They are both composed of past associations, fantasies, imaginations, illusions, inspirations, and memories. The unconscious forces are part of the animal *nafs* and receive energy from sensual and rage forces. Interestingly, according to the Sufis, animals as well as human beings are endowed with unconscious forces. Sufis believe that animals also have the ability to dream or daydream, just as human beings, although animals cannot verbalize it. It is only within the last 20 years that dreaming in animals has been documented by electroencephalographic studies and the observation of rapid eye movement while sleeping.

The Sufi idea of the unconscious is more inclusive than Freud's concept of the unconscious. The Sufis conceptualize the unconscious as being composed of not only fantasies, dreams, illusions, and earlier forms of thought processes, but also as the organic and psychospiritual link between human beings, nature, and the Universal Reality *(Haqq)*.

Human Nafs

In the eleventh century, Avicenna (pp. 209–216) elaborated on specific characteristics of human beings as differentiated from animals. Human beings:

1. Are social animals;
2. Need to change some products of nature to survive; for example, they use animal skins or plant fibers for clothing to protect against the elements;
3. Are tool makers;
4. Are able to observe natural phenomena and use this information for survival; for instance, they use knowledge of seasonal changes for farming;
5. Are able to use symbols and signals for verbal and nonverbal communication;
6. Have a capacity for laughing and crying;
7. Experience shame;
8. Are able to differentiate between good and bad, beauty and ugliness, and right and wrong;
9. Are capable of having a belief system, a faith;
10. Have intellectual and reasoning ability, particularly the ability to perceive the part and generalize the whole.

According to Avicenna and the Sufis, the major components of human *nafs (nafs-i-insānī)* are intellect and heart. (Figure 1, chapter 1)

INTELLECT ('AQL)

In Persian and Arabic the word "'*aql*" means confining, tying up a camel's foot, standing erect on a high rock, and finding out. '*Aql* specifically refers to intellect, reason, discrimination, and the mind. It is interesting to note that by the choice of the word "'*aql*" three

major functions of intellect—inhibition, cognition, and reasoning—
are concomitantly described:

1. '*Aql*, although literally meaning tying an animal's foot,
    here refers to the inhibiting forces of the mind for
    harnessing the animal instincts and desires within.

2. Another meaning of '*aql* is standing erect. One of the
    major differences between human beings and pri-
    mates is the ability to stand erect, leaving the hands
    for tool making and tool using. As we know, ancestors
    of *Homo sapiens* are referred to as *Homo erectus*. Could
    it be that the Sufis unknowingly or knowingly chose
    the word "'*aql*" to refer to this human quality?

3. The most common meaning of '*aql* is reasoning and
    intellect.

Types of Intellect

According to Avicenna (pp. 213–216), intellectual ability, reasoning, and the discovery of meaning in objects or actions is a unique
quality of human beings. Avicenna believed that there were two types
of intellect:

1. Practical Intellect (*'aql-i-āmila*), or the performing in-
    tellect. This type of intellect is concerned with the
    practical aspects of daily life. The following functions
    are included: discrimination, analysis, attention to de-
    tail, differentiation, and deductive reasoning. Practi-
    cal intellect helps the individual in assessing daily re-
    ality and in struggling for survival.

2. Abstract and Universal Intellect (*'aql-i-ālima*). This
    type of intellect refers to the theoretical and abstract
    ability of the mind. The following functions are in-
    cluded: the ability to perceive wholeness, inductive
    reasoning, psychological and philosophical acumen,
    religious aspirations, and aesthetic values.

On a higher level, the creative expression of the human mind in
the areas of industry, art, architecture, scientific discoveries, and particularly spiritual and mystical expressions are manifestations of
abstract intellect (chapter 3).

For Avicenna, Universal Intellect had independent reality, with its own existence separate from the individual's body and mind. Most human beings have the potential to be inspired by the Universal Intellect which transcends concrete realities and dualities of daily life. Universal Intellect is all-encompassing, inclusive, holistic, and seeks existential communion.

The concepts of practical and abstract intellect parallel secondary process thoughts which are the highest level of ego functions in ego psychology. Secondary process thoughts evolve from sensory-motor intelligence, autonomous ego functions, defense mechanisms, and primary process thoughts.

Reality testing, reasoning, rationality, and logical deductions of secondary process thought are similar to the practical intellect in Sufi psychology. Conceptualization and abstraction, the highest level of secondary process thought according to the developmental psychology of Jean Piaget and ego psychology, resemble the concept of abstract intellect in Sufism. Ego psychology does not discuss the concept of Universal Intellect.

HEART (DIL)

Frequently, Sufis refer to the highest level of the unconscious as *dil*. The Persian word *dil*, which in Arabic is *qalb*, means heart, mind, and soul. As used by the Sufis, it means the core of the unconscious *(bātin)*. It is that part of the unconscious which links human beings with the Universal Reality.

The Sufis feel that all human intellectual development is a steppingstone toward experience and knowledge. This knowledge is not intellectual, rationalistic, or cognitive. It transcends all of these. It is the knowledge of the heart, or *dil*, which frees the mind and the body from dualities. The Sufis believe that it is important for a seeker on the path of truth or knowledge to become aware of all levels of *nafses* within. At the same time, the goal is to transcend temporal self and temporal knowledge.

Imam Mohammad-i-Ghazzali, referred to in the West as "Al Ghizal," lived approximately 800 years ago. He reconciled religious dogma, philosophical concepts, and Sufi ideas in a synthetic and creative way. He himself, after spending many years as a theologian, scholar, and philosopher, became painfully aware that all of his knowledge was an outward form of knowledge. He realized that real knowledge was found through personal psychomystical experiences which transcend the limitations of words and books.

The following story is attributed to Ghazzali:

> One day Ghazzali was journeying through the desert from
> one city in the province of Khorasan to another. As was the custom
> of the time, he was traveling with a caravan. All of his books,
> manuscripts, and scholarly works on philosophy and theology
> were loaded on a donkey. Suddenly the caravan was attacked by
> a group of bandits. The bandits took everything. They were going
> to take his donkey with its load. Ghazzali became agitated and
> panic-stricken. He went to the head of the bandits and asked him
> whether he could read or write. The leader, who was a young
> man, saw that the elderly scholar was in deep distress. In puzzle-
> ment, he answered, "No, I can neither read nor write." Ghazzali
> began to beg, "Take all of my belongings, everything I have,
> except these books and my notes and manuscripts. I have invested
> all of my life to gather these things. These are the source of all
> my knowledge. They are of no use to you." The young bandit
> paused a moment and then said, "Old man, you claim that you
> are a scholar and a man of knowledge. What kind of knowledge
> is it that an illiterate bandit can steal from you?"

This encounter shook Ghazzali to the roots of his being and was
a catalyst for his reawakening—the first stage on the Sufi path of
integration (chapter 6). He decided to give up all outward learning
and began his journey on the Path. After years of meditation and
traveling on the Sufi path, Ghazzali again began to write, now integrating philosophical and theological schools of thought with Sufi
meditative experiences.

Ghazzali began his book, *Alchemy of Happiness,* written in the
twelfth century, with the following famous saying, "He who knows
his *nafs,* knows his God."

According to Ghazzali (1973):

> There is nothing closer to you than yourself; if you don't
> know yourself, how will you know others? You might say, "I know
> myself," but you are mistaken! . . . The only thing you know about
> yourself is your physical appearance. The only thing you know
> about your *bātin* [unconscious] is that when you are hungry you
> eat, when you are angry you fight and when you are consumed
> with passion you make love. All animals are equal with you in this
> regard. You have to seek the truth within yourself . . . What are
> you? Where have you come from and where are you going? What
> is your role in this world? Why have you been created? Where
> does your happiness lie? If you would like to know yourself, you

should know that you are created by two things. One is your body and your outward appearance *(zahir)* which you can see with your eyes. The other is your unconscious forces *(bātin, dil)*. This is the part you cannot see but you can know it with your insight. The truth of your existence is in your bātin. Everything else is a servant to your *bātin* or *dil* (pp. 9–10).

When describing *dil*, Ghazzali uses the following metaphor:

> . . .the body is like a country. The artisans are like the hands, feet and various parts of the body. Passion is like a tax collector. Anger or rage is like the sheriff. The *dil* [heart] is the king. Intellect is like the *vazir*. Passion, like a tax collector using any means, tries to extract everything. Rage and anger are severe, harsh and punishing like a sheriff and want to destroy or kill. The king not only needs to control passion and rage but also the intellect and must keep a balance between all of these forces. If the intellect becomes enslaved by passion and anger, the country will be in ruin and the king will be destroyed. (pp. 14–15).

One way an individual can manage all of these contrasting forces is by observing one's deeds, behavior, thoughts, and feelings. Ghazzali elaborated further:

> If you follow the pig of passion you will become shameless, greedy, hypocritical, divisive, jealous and vengeful. If you conquer your passion and keep it under the control of intellect and reason, you will become satisfied, quiet, peaceful, caring and in control of yourself. You will become generous and free of greed.
>
> If you follow the dog of rage, you will become very proud, fearless, unscrupulous, deceitful, self-indulgent and berate others. If you keep this dog is check, you will become patient, tolerant, steadfast, forgiving, brave, secure, and generous.
>
> Satan within you constantly instigates this pig and dog. If you follow Satan's path you will become deceitful and treacherous. If you keep these impulses under control and join the army of reason and intellect, you will become intelligent, knowledgeable, psychologically minded and caring for others. These are the ingredients for leadership. Seeds of happiness will germinate within you . . . .
>
> The heart is like a shining mirror. Troublesome deeds are like smoke and will cover the mirror. Then you will be unable to see your true self. You will be veiled from the vision of Universal Reality or God. (p. 19).

The heart is the core of the unconscious. It is the integrative force which harnesses the animal *nafs* from within and guides the energies of the body and mind toward the path of knowledge beyond the boundaries of intellect and outward sciences. The heart is a catalyst between emotion, affect and thought processes, religious values, and, above all, human beings' constant drive toward and search for existential communion. The heart is the river which brings the restless soul to the vast Ocean of Reality *(haqq)*.

Universal Intellect is similar to Ghazzali's and the Sufis' concept of heart. Avicenna conceptualized the existence of the Universal Intellect from a medical, psychological, and philosophical point of view. He tried to reconcile Aristotelian philosophy with Islamic theology and particularly with Sufism. Heart *(dil)* in Sufism transcends intellect, particularly the practical and rationalistic intellect which is bound by Aristotelian logic and reasoning. The concepts of heart in Sufism and Universal Intellect of Avicenna both transcend individual being and have a universal, transconscious quality. All the manifest phenomena of existence begin and end with heart and Universal Intellect. Heart and Universal Intellect are the expression of the core of the unconscious, *bātin*, and the creative energy in life.

The accusing *nafs* in Sufism and superego in ego psychology, along with the higher levels of personality development, will be discussed in chapter 6 (Figure 1, chapter 1; Figure 1, chapter 6). In the following chapter, the role of the Sufi *pir*, or guide, will be explored and compared with the role of the Western psychotherapist.

Chapter 2

THE GUIDE

Sufi Pir and Western Psychotherapist [1]

Do not take a step
on the Path of Love without a Guide,
I tried it
one hundred times and failed.

Hāfiz, Sufi Poet, fourteenth century

The development of psychotherapies in the West during this century has given a new perspective for helping the emotionally troubled person. Psychoanalysis and cultural anthropology have provided useful tools for studying other cultures, their ways of alleviating emotional suffering, and their methods of furthering personality development and integration.

---

[1] A considerably shorter and earlier version of this chapter was published under the title, "The *Pir* (Sufi Guide) and the Western Psychotherapist," *The R.M. Bucke Memorial Society Newsletter*, 1968, *3*, 9-19.

The West is gradually recognizing that the East has used effective psychotherapeutic techniques in dealing with human suffering for thousands of years (Watts, 1953; Maslow, 1959; Kelman, 1960; Suzuki et al., 1960; Frank, 1963; Arasteh, 1965a; Laing, 1965; Shafii, 1968, 1973; Tart, 1969, 1975; Naranjo & Ornstein, 1971; Bloomfield et al., 1975; Benson, 1975; Carrington, 1978). Comparative study of Western psychotherapeutic techniques with Eastern "psychomystical" practices can further our knowledge of human development, health, and integration. In this chapter, the Sufis' concept of emotional and spiritual suffering and their methods of alleviating these sufferings and achieving human integration will be discussed and compared with the concepts of psychopathology and treatment methods in psychoanalysis and dynamic psychotherapy.

SEPARATION: SICKNESS OF THE MIND

According to the Sufis, human beings are separated from their origin in nature and from Reality, Truth, God *(haqq)*. They believe that emotional suffering or "sickness" originates from this separation *(firāq)*.

Rumi (d. 1273), in the introduction to the first story of the *Mathnawi*, expressed the human dilemma of separation from nature through the symbolic story of the reed (bamboo flute):

> 'Listen to the reed how it tells a tale,
> complaining of separations,
> 'Saying, "Ever since I was parted from the reed-bed,
> my lament has caused man and woman to moan.
> 'It is only to a bosom torn by severance that I can
> unfold the pain of love-desire.
> 'Everyone who is left far from his source wishes back
> the time when he was united with it . . ." (Rice, 1964, p. 68).

The intensity of the sickness of separation, including a possible remedy for it, is exemplified in Rumi's first story of the *Mathnawi:*

> A King fell in love with a slave maiden. He bought the maiden, but before enjoying her company, she became sick, lost weight, looked pale and each day became weaker. The King consulted many physicians, and numerous remedies were prescribed to no avail. As time passed, the slave maiden came close to death. The King was in agony and despair. In the depths of hopelessness

during a dream the King heard a voice saying that a spiritual physician would arrive the next day to relieve the girl's misery.

The next day, a Sufi *pir* appeared in the court. The King knew at once that he was the physician revealed in the dream. The physician examined the maiden carefully and realized that her sickness was "of the heart and the mind," a sickness of separation and love.

The maiden would not reveal to the physician whom she loved. The physician through an ingenious method tried to uncover the identity of her beloved. While taking her pulse he mentioned the names of all the provinces. The name of one of the provinces caused "her pulse to jump." Then he mentioned the names of the cities of that province. When he mentioned Samarqand the maiden's pulse jumped again. Then he asked for someone who was quite familiar with the city of Samarqand and the people living there. After mentioning quarters, streets, and finally a particular household, it was discovered that the maiden was deeply in love with a certain goldsmith.

The physician felt the remedy for the girl's sickness was temporary reunion with her lover. They brought the goldsmith and the two enjoyed each other's union. Gradually the goldsmith was given "a poisonous draught." He became weak, lost his strength, charm, and finally the favor of the maiden. Later the maiden and the King were reunited (Rumi, 1925, Vol. 1, pp. 3–17).

In this story, the King symbolically represents the self of the seeker who is in search of a spiritual physician to uncover the reason for anxieties and sorrows and for guidance on the path of security and integration. Recognition of separation and fragmentation as the origins of all sickness of the mind and heart, and overcoming this separation through the fire of love and the intense relationship with the spiritual physician, are the first steps on the way to recovery, communion, and integration.

The maiden and the goldsmith symbolize the male and female aspects of nature which are hidden in all of us, and also reflect manifest phenomena of life, such as physical appearance and animal desires. The goldsmith symbolizes the temporal self and the animal *nafs*. Temporal love—which originates from animal desires—can be transformed through loss of self by the help of a spiritual physician into the permanent love of existential communion (chapters 5 and 7).

The King also represents the searching soul who is seeking relief and comfort from the anxieties of separation. The King, with all his power and gold, was not able to find comfort. Reunion and integration occurred with the help of a Sufi guide. Rumi, himself, insightfully concluded the story by saying that, in actuality, the King, the maiden, and the goldsmith are metaphors for various parts of the self at odds with each other. The integration of all these fragmented parts can occur through love and with the help of a *pir*.

HUMAN ORIGIN IN SUFISM

Based on the Koran (Sūra 15:29; 38:72), the Sufis believe that

> God kneaded Adam's clay forty days before . . . giving . . . him life and spirit by breathing into him with His own breath. (Schimmel, 1975, p. 188).

This idea of human origin is very similar to that found in the Old Testament (Genesis 2:7):

> And the Lord God formed man of the dust of the ground, and breathed into his nostrils the breath of life; and man became a living soul.

Sufis feel that God's life-giving breath bestows on human beings the potential for existential communion, the oneness of all with All. In human beings, maturity and freedom may be achieved by completing the circle of evolution and returning to the origin, which is Universal Reality (God, *haqq*). Rumi wrote:

> 'I am a bird of God's garden, I do not belong to this dusty world.
> 'For a day or two they have locked me up in the cage of my body.
> 'I did not come here of myself, how should I return of myself?
> 'He who brought me must take me back again to my own country.'
> (Rice, 1964, p. 67).

Nasafi, in *The Book of the Integrated Human Being (Kitāb al-Insān al-Kāmil)*, wrote more than 700 years ago:

> . . .everything in the world of existence has an end and a goal. The end is maturity and the goal is freedom. For example fruit grows on the tree until it is ripe and then falls. The ripened fruit represents maturity and the fallen fruit freedom.
> The final goal is returning to one's origin. Everything which reaches its origin has reached its goal. A farmer sows grain in the ground and tends it. It begins to grow, eventually seeds, and again becomes grain. It has returned to its original form. The circle is

complete. Completing the circle of existence is freedom. (1962, pp. 132–133).

In human beings, according to the Sufis, maturity and freedom occur in the same way—by returning to one's origin.

FORGETFULNESS AND IGNORANCE

Sufis feel that we human beings have a tendency to forget our origin in nature in order to avoid the sadness and anxieties of separation. This forgetfulness (ghaflat) expresses itself in the form of forgetting, neglecting, heedlessness, and ignorance.

However, forgetfulness does not alleviate the anxieties of separation, but actually intensifies them. In the state of forgetfulness, the individual behaves like a wounded beast imprisoned in a cage. The beast does not know the source of its pain, the remedy for it, or the way to freedom. The beast hits itself against the cage, attacks the doctor and jailers alike, and eventually exhausts itself.

Forgetfulness results in hijāb, meaning veiling, concealing, a partition, a curtain, and, specifically, ignorance. In Sufism, ignorance refers to the individual's psychospiritual blindness, lack of insight, preoccupation with pride, and self-conceit. Hujwiri, more than 900 years ago, pointedly entitled his book on Sufism The Uncovering of the Veils (Kashf Al-Mahjūb). He explored and described the ways of overcoming forgetfulness and ignorance on the Sufi Path. According to him, the only way one can overcome forgetfulness and ignorance is through awareness and knowledge of Reality. "Knowledge is the life of the heart, which delivers it from the death of ignorance . . ." (1967, pp. 16–17) Abu Yazid of Bistam said: "I strove in the spiritual combat for thirty years, and I found nothing harder to me than knowledge and its pursuit" (1967, p. 18). Hujwiri, in discussing ignorance, wrote:

> Man, enamoured of his gross environment, remains sunk in ignorance and apathy, making no attempt to cast off the veil that has fallen upon him. Blind to the beauty of Oneness, he turns away from God to seek the vanities of this world and allows his appetites to domineer over his reason, notwithstanding that the animal soul . . . is the greatest of all veils between God and man. (p. 9).

Indulgence in animal desires (nafs) and enslavement in habits are the core of ignorance and veiling. Al-Amuli, a Sufi pir said: "Acquiescence in natural habits prevents a man from attaining to the exalted degrees of spirituality, . . ." (1967, p. 149).

The Sufis were acutely concerned about remaining ignorant. Ignorance, they felt, was worse than being condemned forever in the fires of hell. No punishment was worse than ignorance. The following meditation of Sar'i Al-Saqat'i, the Sufi *pir* of the ninth century, expressed his fear of being veiled from Reality:

> O God, whatever punishment Thou mayst inflict upon me, do not punish me with the humiliation of being veiled from Thee, because, if I am not veiled from Thee, my torment and affliction will be lightened by the remembrance and contemplation of Thee; but if I am veiled from Thee, even Thy bounty will be deadly to me. There is no punishment in Hell more painful and hard to bear than that of being veiled. (1967, p. 111).

The following saying is attributed to al-Tirmidhí: "You wish to know God while your lower soul subsists in you; but your lower soul does not know itself, how should it know another?" (1967, p. 200). Freedom from ignorance is through freedom from the self.

> Thou thyself art the greatest of all veils between thee and God: when thou hast become absent from thyself, the evils implicit in thy being are annihilated in thee, and thy state undergoes a fundamental change: . . . thine eye is closed to thyself and to all that is other than God, and thy human attributes are consumed by the flame of proximity to God. . . . (p. 249).

SEPARATION SICKNESS IN SUFISM AND SEPARATION ANXIETY IN EGO PSYCHOLOGY

In classical psychoanalysis, emotional suffering and neurotic disorders were conceptualized as symptomatic expressions of repressed intrapsychic traumas and conflicts between id impulses and superego prohibitions. Fear of parental punishment and societal prohibitions, in the form of castration anxiety in the phallic-oedipal stage of psychosexual development, were the roots of emotional suffering and psychopathology. This theoretical position has been modified extensively during the last few decades with the advancements in ego psychology and with the contributions of child psychiatry, cognitive psychology, and studies of animal behavior (ethology).

At the present time, attachment behaviors in animals and human beings are perceived as essential for the survival of the human species. John Bowlby (1958), inspired by the works of ethologists, suggested that attachment behaviors in human beings (sucking, clinging, following, crying, and smiling) are instinctual. In the infant six to twelve months of age, these behaviors are integrated in the form of an innate instinctual attachment toward mother beyond the need for satiation or sexual and aggressive drives of the id (Shafii & Shafii, 1982, p. 15).

In an infant six months and older, attachment behavior to mother expresses itself dramatically in the form of separation anxiety:

> When the infant cannot see or hear mother, he becomes quiet, subdued, and apprehensive. Then, suddenly, the infant cries loudly and shows moderate to severe signs of physical and psychological distress, such as agitation, increase in heart beat and respiration, sweating, pupil dilation, and at times panic reaction. This reaction to separation from mother is called separation anxiety. It subsides with mother's return.
>
> Throughout life, separation anxiety is reactivated in different forms and intensity whenever a loss is experienced, whether it be the loss of a loved one, of self-esteem, or of a cherished possession (Shafii & Shafii p. 23).

Disturbances in human attachment, disorders of mothering, and the experience of a loss of a loved one in early childhood contribute significantly to the development of chronic anxiety, sadness, depression, and, in severe cases, to narcissistic disturbances of personality, such as self-indulgence, self-aggrandizement, preoccupation with the self, and selfishness (Bowlby, 1973). In some cases, antisocial behavior, drug and alcohol addiction, or psychotic disturbances are the outcome.

It appears that the Sufis, more than 1,000 years ago, became aware of the anxieties of separation and their possible pathological influence on the self, not only within the context of the mother-child relationship, but also separation sickness from the animal, vegetative, and mineral parts of the self, other human beings, and, above all, Universal Reality.

Erich Fromm (1956) in *The Art of Loving* lucidly discussed man's separation from nature as the origin of anxieties.

> . . . man . . . has emerged from the animal kingdom, from instinctive adaptation, . . . he has transcended nature—although he never leaves it; he is a part of it—and yet once torn away from nature, he cannot return to it; once thrown out of paradise—the

state of original oneness with nature . . . Man can only go forward
by developing his reason, by finding a new harmony, a human
one, instead of the prehuman harmony which is irretrievably lost
(p. 6).

According to Fromm, the development of reason brings with it
a sense of awareness; awareness of the moment, the past, the future,
the self and others. Awareness contributes to seeing the self "as a
separate entity." Separateness brings with it the possibility of choice
and freedom. But at the same time, separateness makes one aware of
being alone. This aloneness generates the feeling of

> . . . helplessness before the forces of nature and of society, all this
> makes . . . [a human being's] separate, disunited existence an un-
> bearable prison. He would become insane could he not liberate
> himself from this prison and reach out, unite himself in some
> form or other with men, with the world outside (p.7).

Erich Fromm's formulation concerning human beings' separateness from nature is similar to the Sufis' ideas of separation. As you
recall, Sufis perceive separation as sickness, and the anxieties of separation as the essence of fragmentation of personality and the cause
of disturbances of the mind and spirit. As Fromm wrote: "The experience of separateness arouses anxiety; it is, indeed, the source of all
anxiety" (p. 7). Some psychoanalysts and ego psychologists have
reached the same conclusion as the Sufis that separation is the origin
of all anxieties.

FORGETFULNESS AND IGNORANCE IN SUFISM
AND REPRESSION AND DENIAL IN EGO PSYCHOLOGY

The concept of "forgetfulness" in Sufism is similar to the defense
mechanisms of repression and denial in psychoanalysis and dynamic
psychotherapy (chapter 1). Repression is a psychological defense
mechanism which ". . . consists of the expelling and withholding from
conscious awareness of an idea or feeling," which is usually painful
and related to anxiety or guilt (Moore & Fine, 1968, p. 30). Although
some element of repression is necessary for daily adaptation, extensive
repression contributes to the development of inhibition, neurotic tendencies, lack of curiosity, mediocrity, and ignorance.

One of the major goals of exploratory psychotherapy and psychoanalysis is helping the individual modify the defensive posture of

repression through free associations in order to become aware of the origin of earlier traumatic experiences and anxieties which have been repressed and forgotten. Sufis, Western dynamic psychotherapists, and psychoanalysts feel that extensive forgetfulness or repression may contribute to feelings of fragmentation, psychic suffering, and arrest in development.

Forgetfulness in Sufism also has similarities to the defense mechanism of denial. Denial is "A defense mechanism of a primitive or early variety in which the *ego* avoids becoming aware of some painful aspect of *reality*." (Moore & Fine, p. 31) The extensive use of denial may contribute to the development of severe psychopathology in the form of psychosis, borderline psychosis, and disorders of personality and character. Denial may result in ignorance, dishonesty, and psychological insensitivity.

Ignorance and veiling in Sufism also have similarities to the concept of "psychological blindspots" in psychoanalysis. Psychological blindspots refer to the individual's psychological unawareness of tendencies and shortcomings. In Sufism, being unaware and ignorant of oneself is worse than being veiled from Reality. Martin Lings (1971) quoted a Sufi *pir* of the 20th century, Shaykh Al-'Alawi:

> The veiled are ranged in hierarchy: the veiled from his Lord, and the veiled from himself. And the veiled from himself is more heavily veiled than the veiled from his Lord (p. 205).

The Sufis' concept of ignorance goes beyond the present concepts of repression, denial, and psychological blindspots in psychoanalysis. For instance, Nasafi, in the thirteenth century, regarding forgetfulness and ignorance, wrote:

> [Most people] fall to the animal level of existence and never reach the human level because they are preoccupied in this world with the passions of consuming, sexual desires and preoccupation with their offspring. From the beginning of life to the end of life all of their efforts are for these. They do not know anything else but these three things . . . A few when they are freed from these fetishes become enslaved by three bigger fetishes. They pass these three veils but become entangled by three larger veils. The three larger veils are preoccupation with physical appearance, possessions, and position (pp. 228–229).

According to Nasafi, there are seven veils on the Path of Reality: worship of the self, passion of consumption, indulgence in sexual desires, preoccupation with offspring, preoccupation with appearance, preoccupation with possession, and love of position. These seven veils consume a person's life and contribute to the continuation of ignorance and forgetfulness (p. 230).

OVERCOMING THE SICKNESS OF SEPARATION

Internal conflicts, such as the struggle between moral values and impulsive wishes, intellect and emotion, certainty and insecurity, and the conscious and unconscious, which are manifestations of the sickness of separation, can only be overcome through union of all internal and external forces. Rumi expressed this conflict resolution poetically:

> I have resolved conflict within myself,
> I feel only as an identity;
> I seek unity, I speak unity;
> I know oneness and I see oneness.
>
> (Arasteh, 1965a, p. 7).

Sufis believe that union is achieved by the intensive emotional involvement of the seeker with the Sufi *pir*, or "spiritual physician." The seeker totally devotes and surrenders the self to the *pir*. Intense love, *ishq*, is the essence of this relationship and its integrative energy.

Again, the Sufis and some psychoanalysts, such as Erich Fromm (1956), are in agreement:

> Man—of all ages and cultures—is confronted with the solution of one and the same question: the question of how to overcome separateness, how to achieve union, how to transcend one's own individual life and find at-onement. The question is the same for primitive man living in caves, for nomadic man taking care of his flocks, for the peasant in Egypt, the Phoenician trader, the Roman soldier, the medieval monk, the Japanese samurai, the modern clerk and factory hand. The question is the same, for it springs from the same ground: the human situation, the conditions of human existence. The answer varies. The question can be answered by animal worship, by human sacrifice or military conquest, by indulgence in luxury, by ascetic renunciation, by obsessional work, by artistic creation, by the love of God, and by the love of Man. (p. 8).

Fromm felt that there are a number of ways in which human beings try to overcome separateness and to experience union:

1. "Orgiastic" states, created through trancelike experiences or by the use of drugs or alcohol;

2. "Conformity" in civilized societies, whether democratic or totalitarian;

3. "Creative Activity," in which the individual unites the self with the material and created object;

4. "Love"—the interpersonal union and fusion of one person with another, or mystical union of man with God.

INTENSE LOVE (ISHQ): THE INTEGRATIVE ENERGY

"*Ishq*" is an Arabic word meaning intense love, passionate attachment, and dying for love. It does not have an English equivalent. The closest meaning of *ishq* in English would be intense love and devotion. The word "love," however, does not represent the totality, intensity, dynamism, and irrationality of *ishq*.

The word "*ishq*" originates from "*ashiqa*." *Ashiqa* is the name of a type of vine which attaches itself to a tree. This vine grows on the tree, taking nourishment and sustenance from it. Eventually, the tree dies and loses itself to the vine (Valiuddin, 1972, p. 1). The loss of self in the Beloved through intense love *(ishq)* is the essential core of Sufism. Rumi portrayed this loss:

> One went to the door of the Beloved and knocked.
> A voice asked, "Who is there?"
> He answered, "It is I."
> The voice said, "There is not room for Me and Thee."
> The door was shut.
> After a year of solitude and deprivation
>   he returned and knocked.
> A voice from within asked, "Who is there?"
> The man said, "It is Thee."
> The door was opened for him.
>
> (Idries Shah, 1964, p. 317).

Sufis feel that intense love is dormant in all beings. When it is activated in human beings through psychological reawakening, it starts to grow. The fertile ground of intense love is the heart and the unconscious (chapter 1). Gradually, animal instincts, such as anger and passion, are transformed through the alchemy of intense love to an integrative energy for existential communion.

INTENSE LOVE, DEATH, AND REBIRTH

The Sufi's experience of *ishq* (intense love) cannot be fully understood unless one becomes familiar with the concepts of *mihr* and *mahabbat*. "*Mihr*" is a Persian word encompassing a broad spectrum of related meanings—sun, light, matter, mother, love, and death. "*Mahabbat*" is an Arabic word meaning affection, and originates from the word "*hubb*," meaning seed.

The Sufis believe that the rays of the Sun of Reality (God, *haqq*) manifest in the world of existence in the forms of love and light *(mihr)* and find concrete representation in human beings in the form of affection *(mahabbat)*. Affection which exists in all of us is the dormant seed of *ishq* (intense love).

In Sufi thinking, the seed welcomes the pain and suffering of cold winter and the torment of spring. Finally, the seed loses its identity (dies) and becomes a new plant which flowers and bears seeds. By loss of the temporal self, the seed continues its permanent existence (chapter 5). Sufis call this process *mahabbat*. They feel strongly that the seed of growth and integration is dormant in each person in the form of intense love. Through psychological reawakening, and by the help and affection of a Sufi *pir*, the dormant seed of intense love germinates and unleashes the energy for final integration and existential communion. A human being, then, loses temporal individuality and becomes one with the existential cycle of life—transcending the self to become human (chapters 5, 6 and 7).

ATTRIBUTES OF THE SUFI GUIDE (PIR)

Pir is a Persian word meaning aged, old, or elder. In Sufism, *pir* means spiritual guide or physician of the soul. The *pir* plays a significant role in the psychospiritual development of the disciple, seeker, or *murid*. In Sufi literature, many words are used synonymously with *pir*:

> *kāmil*—perfect, complete, full. In Sufism this refers to the one who is complete with all qualities of humanity.
> *murād*—wished, willed, desired. In Sufism this refers to the one who leads the seekers on the path of truth toward freedom from the self *(fanā)*.
> *murshid*—a guide to the right way, a spiritual advisor, and a guide on the path of integration.
> *shaykh*—a venerable old man, a chief, a superior of the dervishes.

tabib ruhani—physician of the soul.
qutb—pole, axis, or pivot. In Sufism this refers to the one who is
the head of the Sufi order. (Nurbakhsh, 1953, pp. 3–4).

A description follows of some of the attributes of a *pir* such as
maturity, patience, trust in God, freedom from illusion, freedom from
the self, and being of the world while free of the world.

MATURITY (PUKHTA)

A Persian phrase beautifully describes the concept of *pir*. The *pir*
is called *mard-i-pukhta-va-johān-didah*—*mard* meaning man; *pukhta*
meaning cooked, ripe, mature; *johān-didah* meaning seeing or having
seen the world and knowing mankind. A *pir*, then, is a seasoned and
mature human being, who has travelled extensively both in the world
and on the Path of Reality.

PATIENCE (SABR)

A *pir* spends years as a seeker while progressing through the
various stages of human development on the Sufi path. Reaching the
stage of patience, the fifth stage of human development in Sufism, is
essential for becoming a *pir* (chapter 7).

Ibn ‘Arabī (d. 1240), the Sufi saint of Andalusia, described an
interaction with his Sufi *pir*:

> One day, while we were walking together by the sea, he [my
> *pir*] asked me a question concerning God's saying, "I require no
> provision from them, nor do I need them to feed Me." [Koran,
> Sūra 101:57] I did not answer him, but left him. Four years later
> I met him and told him that I had the answer to his question. He
> said, 'Let me have your answer, for after four years the time is
> ripe for it.' I then gave him my answer and marvelled that he had
> remembered the verse. (1971, p. 119).

The question asked by the Sufi *pir* transcended the intellectual
and manifest meaning of the Koranic verse. Although Ibn ‘Arabī
from a very young age had a reputation for understanding and inter-
preting verses from the Koran, he perceived his *pir's* question on a
deeper experiential and spiritual level. Ibn ‘Arabī realized that he was
not ready to comprehend or appreciate the meaning of the verse with

his whole being. He knew that an immediate or impulsive response would be merely an intellectual exercise. He left his *pir* without saying a word, and patiently meditated upon the verse for 4 years. Through patience and continuous internal experience of the verse, Ibn 'Arabī became enlightened.

The experience of patience is essential for both the *pir* and the seeker. The Sufis frequently use the metaphor of ripened fruit to illustrate the need for patience and readiness. When fruit is not ripe, it tastes bitter and may cause indigestion. When fruit ripens, it gives joy to others and through the seed has the potential for rebirth.

A Sufi attains the stage of patience after experiencing the stages of repentance, abstinence, renunciation, and poverty (chapter 6 and 7). Although readiness to become a *pir* cannot be measured in terms of time, generally it takes at least 12 years under the guidance of a *pir*.

TOTAL AWARENESS OF THE DISCIPLE

It is essential for the *pir* to be emptied of self-preoccupation in order to be in tune with the disciple's physical, psychological, and spiritual states. The *pir* becomes a mirror, not only for reflecting the Beloved Reality and the Beauty of Nature, but also for intuitively perceiving the disciple's inward state and outward condition. Through psychospiritual communion beyond words, thoughts, time, space, and temporal reality, the *pir* helps the disciple become aware of the unconscious and Universal Reality.

The following story about Jonaid and his *pir*, Sari-Al-Saqati, vividly demonstrates this process:

> As is well known, Junayd refused to discourse to his disciples so long as Sari [his *pir*] was alive, until one night he dreamed that the Apostle [Prophet Muhammed] said to him: "O Junayd, speak to the people, for God hath made thy words the means of saving a multitude of mankind." When he awoke the thought occurred to him that his rank was superior to that of Sari, since the Apostle had commanded him to preach. At daybreak Sari sent a disciple to Junayd with the following message: "You would not discourse to your disciples when they urged you to do so, and you rejected the intercession of the Shaykhs of Baghdád and my personal entreaty. Now that the Apostle has commanded you, obey his orders." Junayd said: "That fancy went out of my head. I perceived that Sari was acquainted with my outward and inward thoughts in all circumstances, and that his rank was higher than mine, since

he was acquainted with my secret thoughts, whereas I was ignorant
of his state. I went to him and begged his pardon, and asked him
how he knew that I had dreamed of the Apostle. He answered:
'I dreamed of God, who told me that he had sent the Apostle to
bid you preach.'" This anecdote contains a clear indication that
spiritual directors are in every case acquainted with the inward
experiences of their disciples. (Hujwiri, pp. 128–129).

This story exemplifies two things. One is the special relationship
between the *pir* and the disciple. They are in tune with each other
verbally and nonverbally. Frequently, communication and revelations
occur in both of them simultaneously while they are meditating or
during dreams. Instead of using words to communicate, the *pir* and
the seeker are in psychological communion beyond the limitations of
time and space. Secondly, one does not become a Sufi *pir* by desire
or choice. Wishing or desiring to become a *pir* is, itself, a sign of
self-aggrandizement and a veil on the Path of Reality. A true Sufi *pir*
does not claim to be a *pir*.

The Sufis use another psychological process called *khátir* (passing
thought) for becoming more receptive to others. Passing thought resembles the first thought which comes to mind in free association in
psychoanalysis and psychotherapy. Hujwiri described a passing
thought *(khātir)* as the occurrence in the mind of an initial thought
which is quickly replaced by a succeeding thought. The Sufis give
special attention to the initial thought because they believe that it
comes directly from God:

> . . . the thought occurred to Khayr Nassáj that Junayd was waiting
> at his door, but he [decided] to repel it. The same thought returned
> twice and thrice, whereupon he went out and discovered Junayd,
> who said to him: "If you had followed the first thought it would
> not have been necessary for me to stand here all this time." (Huj-
> wiri, p. 387).

FREEDOM FROM ILLUSIONS

Attributes of the *pir* have been exalted in Sufi poetry. Depending
upon the era, the cultural situation, and the seeker's own needs,
metaphysical powers, such as mental telepathy, clairvoyance, and even
miracles, have been ascribed to the *pirs*. But, in most Sufi writing,
emphasis is on the *pir* as an integrated or universal human being
rather than as a person with magical or omnipotent powers.

The following story is attributed to Rabe'a, a Sufi of the eighth century, A.D.; this story describes her encounter with Hasan of Basra, another Sufi:

> . . . he [Hasan] saw Rabe'a when she was near a lake. Throwing his prayer rug on the surface of the water, he called,
> "Rabe'a, come! Let us pray . . . here!"
> "Hasan," Rabe'a replied, "when you are showing off your spiritual goods in this worldly market, it should be things that your fellow-men are incapable of displaying."
> And she flung her prayer rug into the air, and flew up on it.
> "Come up here, Hasan, where people can see us!" she cried.
> Hasan, who had not attained that station, said nothing. Rabe'a sought to console him.
> "Hasan," she said, "what you did fishes also do, and what I did flies also do. The real business is outside both these tricks. One must apply one's self to the real business." (Attār, Arberry's translation, 1966, p. 45).

FREEDOM FROM THE SELF (FANĀ)

Although not every *pir* can reach freedom from the self *(fanā)*, it is essential that every *pir* constantly work on freeing the self from self-conceit, selfishness, greed, thirst for power, and prejudice (chapter 5). The *pir* is ready to give up and sacrifice everything for humanity. He or she lives by serving others willingly, enthusiastically, and humbly.

BEING OF THE WORLD

A Sufi *pir* is of the world, but, at the same time, free from the world. A Sufi is expected to have a job and be useful in the community. He or she is encouraged to be married. Marriage and the responsibility of parenthood are helpful in dealing with daily reality and are essential for the development of maturity.

The biographies of the Sufi *pirs* reveal that most of them excelled in a profession or a skill. For example, Attār, a Sufi *pir* and author of many books on Sufism in the twelfth century, A.D., was an apothecary. While tending his shop, he would use spare moments to write

Sufi poetry or biographies of other Sufis. No job, however, was below a *pir's* dignity. Some of the greatest Sufi *pirs* have had jobs, for instance as porters, water carriers, and janitors. Even though some of these *pirs* were highly respected by the rulers of the time and were sought after for advice, they were not influenced by the rulers' wealth, power, or glory.

FREE FROM THE WORLD

The *pir* treated rulers and beggers alike. Frequently, the *pir* directly questioned and confronted the worldly preoccupation of the ruler. The following story is an example of such an encounter between Ebrahim Ibn Adham, the King of Balkh, and a Sufi *pir*.

> Suddenly a man with an awful mien entered the chamber, so terrible to look upon that none of the royal retinue and servants dared ask him his name; the tongues of all clove to their throats. He advanced solemnly till he stood before the throne.
> "What do you want?" demanded Ebrahim.
> "I have just alighted at this caravanserai," referring to the king's palace as a motel, said the man.
> "This is not a caravanserai: this is my palace. You are mad," shouted Ebrahim.
> "Who owned this palace before you?" asked the man.
> "My father," Ebrahim replied.
> "And before him?"
> "My grandfather."
> "And before him?"
> "So-and-so."
> "And before him?"
> "The father of So-and-so."
> "Where have they all departed?" asked the man.
> "They have gone. They are dead," Ebrahim replied.
> "Then is this not a caravanserai which one man enters and another leaves?" With these words the stranger vanished. (Attar, pp. 63–64.)

This encounter, among others, blazed the flame of reawakening and repentance in Ebrahim. Soon after, he renounced the Kingdom of Balkh and pursued abstinence and renunciation on the Sufi Path of Reality.

Hujwiri summarized the attributes of the *pir*:

> ... he must be a man of rectitude ... who has traversed all
> the hills and dales of the Path, and tasted the rapture of "states"
> and perceived the nature of actions, and experienced the severity
> of the Divine majesty and the clemency of the Divine beauty.
> Furthermore, he must examine the state of his disciples and judge
> what point they will ultimately reach: whether they will retire
> [regression], or stand still [fixation], or attain [maturity and inte-
> gration]. If he knows that some day they will abandon this Path,
> he must forbid them to enter upon it; if they will come to a stand,
> he must enjoin them to practice devotion; if they will reach the
> goal, he must give them spiritual nourishment. The Sufi Shaykhs
> are physicians of men's souls. (p. 55)

NEED FOR A PIR

The Sufis believe that maturity cannot be achieved alone.
They feel that there is a great need for guidance and discipline.
The Path is unknown, the night is dark and the road is full of
danger. Danger of preoccupation with selfishness, false visions,
misinterpretation of mystical states, arrest in development, fixation in a particular state, appeal to various drugs to create false
mystical experiences and not infrequently overwhelming anxiety
and insanity. (Shafii, 1968, p. 11)

Transcending the temporal self cannot be accomplished by the
self alone.

> O seeker
> without the shadow of a *pir*
> the clamor of the beast (self)
> will torment you.
>
> (Rumi, *Mathnawi*, Book 1, p. 181)

Emotional readiness is necessary to benefit from the psychological
and spiritual guidance of the *pir*. The metaphor of making wine is
frequently used to describe this readiness. The grapes are picked
when ripe. Then they are crushed by the wine-maker and allowed to
sit for some time to ferment. The final quality of the wine depends
more on the grape than on the ability of the wine-maker. In this
metaphor, the grape is the seeker, the wine-maker is the *pir*, the

crushing is the process of freeing the self, and the quiescence is meditation.

The danger of preoccupation with the self and self-conceit is ever present on the Path. Abu Yazid vividly portrays this pitfall:

> "For twelve years," said Abu Yazid, "I was the blacksmith of my soul. I thrust my soul into the furnace of discipline and made it red hot in the flames of arduous endeavour, then I placed it upon the anvil of reproach and hammered it with the hammer of self-blame, till I had fashioned out of my soul, a mirror. For five years I was my own mirror, and I polished that mirror with every manner of godly service and obedience. After that I gazed upon my own reflection for a year, and I saw about my waist an infidel girdle of delusion and coquetry and self-regard, because I relied upon my own acts of obedience and approved of my own conduct."
> (Attār, Arberry's translation, p. 113)

Abu Yazid's story exemplifies the seeker's tendency toward self-regard and pride even while on the Path. There is a danger of taking pride in abstinence, renunciation, and meditation, and these practices then become obstacles rather than means of further integration.

THE SEARCH FOR A PIR

After a seeker becomes aware of the need for further integration, the search for a *pir* begins. The search may take a short time or many years. A true search is not a whim of the moment. It is a serious endeavor originating from the seeker's heartfelt need. If the search is undertaken out of self-conceit, pride or material or societal gain, it becomes an obstacle on the Path and will further fragment the seeker's soul. The more sincere and devoted the seeker is in this search, the closer the goal.

Rumi, in Book 3 of *Mathnawi*, wrote of the search for a *pir*:

> Search, no matter what situation you are in.
> O thirsty one, search for water constantly.
> Finally, the time will come when you will reach the spring.
>
> (Ghani, 1951, pp. 219)

The need and search for a guide is not unique to Sufism. The guru in yoga, the Zen master in Zen Buddhism, and the spiritual director in Christianity are all guides on the Path. Also, the need for a spiritual teacher is mentioned in the Cabala, the Jewish mystical tradition. According to the Cabala, to understand the *Book Yetsirah*, even God's chosen Prophet, Abraham, needed a teacher:

> He [Abraham] sat alone and meditated (*me'ayyen*) on it, but could understand nothing until a heavenly voice went forth and said to him: "Are you trying to set yourself up as my equal? I am One and have created the *Book Yetsirah* and studied it: but you by yourself cannot understand it. Therefore take a companion, and meditate on it together, and you will understand it." Thereupon Abraham went to his teacher Shem, son of Noah, and sat with him for three years and they meditated on it until they knew how to create a world. And to this day there is no one who can understand it alone. (Scholem, 1965, p. 176)

Rumi, in Book I of *Mathnawi* symbolically illustrated the need for a guide:

> There was a certain merchant who kept a parrot in a cage. Being about to travel to Hindustan on business, he asked the parrot if he had any message to send to his kinsmen in that country, and the parrot desired him to tell them that he was kept confined in cage. The merchant promised to deliver this message, and on reaching Hindustan, duly delivered it to the first flock of parrots he saw. On hearing it one of them at once fell down dead. The merchant was annoyed with his own parrot for having sent such a fatal message, and on his return home sharply rebuked his parrot for doing so. But the parrot no sooner heard the merchant's tale than he too fell down dead in his cage. The merchant, after lamenting his death, took his corpse out of the cage and threw it away; but, to his surprise, the corpse immediately recovered life, and flew away, explaining that the Hindustani parrot had only feigned death to suggest this way of escaping confinement in a cage. (Whinfield's translation, 1973, p. 28)

The parrot represents the seeker; the cage, the animal *nafs* and the temporal self; and the Hindustani parrot, the *pir* or Sufi guide. The merchant's parrot was suffering from "sickness of separation." The only way it could be freed from the cage was by identifying with the Hindustani parrot. Through the process of *fanā*, "dying" or freeing the self from the temporal self, the parrot gained freedom. The story also teaches that one must always keep searching for a *pir*. As long as one is searching and remains receptive, a *pir* will be found.

PIR AND SEEKER RELATIONSHIP

The relationship between the *pir* and the seeker is intense. The process of *fanā* (annihilation of the self, loss of the self, or freedom from the self) cannot be achieved without intensive identification with the *pir* (chapter 5).

Initially the *pir* interviews the seeker privately. The nature and the content of the interview are not disclosed and are considered "secrets of love." Often, the *pir* asks the seeker about motivation, internal pain and suffering, visions, dreams, past experiences, and misdeeds. The seeker at this time experiences feelings of excitement, turbulence, and ecstasy. With humbleness and honesty, the seeker gives mind and heart to the *pir*.

Generally, the *pir* does not accept a seeker immediately. He or she advises patience, self-observation, repentance, and purification. The seeker is put through many tests to assess sincerity of commitment, intensity of devotion, and strength of personality for tolerating the trials and tribulations of the Path. In the past it was common for a seeker to be tested for three years before initiation. Hujwiri wrote:

> The Súfí Shaykhs observe the following rule. When a novice joins them, with the purpose of renouncing the world, they subject him to spiritual discipline for the space of three years. If he fulfills the requirements of this discipline, well and good; otherwise, they declare that he cannot be admitted to the Path. . . . The first year is devoted to service of the people, the second year to service of God, and the third year to watching over his own heart. (p. 54)

The following story exemplified the seekers' need to undergo trials before becoming ready for initiation on the Path. 'Abu Bakr al-Shebli (d. 846 A.D.) was the son of a court official. At a relatively young age, he was appointed Governor of Demavend (an important region close to present day Tehran, Iran). Shortly afterwards, he was reawakened, renounced the governorship, and became a seeker on the Path. He sought Jonaid as a *pir*, and said to him:

> "You are recommended as an expert on pearls [enlighten-ment and wisdom], . . . Either give me one, or sell one to me."
> "If I sell you one, you will not have the price of it, and if I give you one, having so easily come by it you will not realize its value," Jonaid replied. "Do like me; plunge head first into this Sea, and if you wait patiently you will obtain your pearl."

"Now what shall I do?" asked Shebli.

"Go and sell sulphur for a year," said Jonaid.

Shebli did so. When the year was up, Jonaid gave him new instructions.

"This work brings notoriety and commerce. Go and beg for a year, so that you be not busied with aught else."

For a whole year Shebli wandered throughout Baghdad. No one gave him anything. He returned and reported to Jonaid.

"Now realize your own worth, for you count for nothing in the eyes of your fellows," said Jonaid. "Fasten not your heart on them, neither have any regard of them. For some days you were a chamberlain and for some days you acted as governor. Now repair to your former province and seek quittance [recompense] of the inhabitants there."

Shebli returned to Demavend and went from house to house, till only one victim of oppression remained. That man he could not trace.

"With him in mind," Shebli recalled, "I distributed a hundred thousand dirhams, but still my heart did not find rest."

Four years went by in this way. Then he returned to Jonaid.

"Some fragment of pomp and pride still lingers in you," said Jonaid. "Beg for another year."

"Every day I went begging," Shebli recalled. "I brought him all I got, and he would give it to the poor. At night he kept me hungry. When a year had gone by, he said to me, 'Now I admit to you my companionship, but on one condition, that you shall be the servant of my companions.' So for a year I served the companions. Then Jonaid said to me, 'Abu Bakr, what is your view of yourself now?' 'I regard myself as the least of God's creatures,' I replied. 'Now,' remarked Jonaid, 'your faith is whole.' "
(Attar, Arberry's translation, pp. 278–279)

From a psychodynamic perspective, Jonaid perceived extensive arrogance, self-conceit, and narcissistic tendencies in Shebli. Jonaid, with the psychological acumen of an experienced clinician and psychotherapist, communicated with Shebli within the metaphor of the pearl, confronting Shebli directly. Shebli became more receptive and asked for guidance. Jonaid was not satisfied with Shebli's quick acquiescence, and prescribed bitter medicine to free him from his plight of arrogance and narcissism. It took many years for Shebli to free himself from these troublesome characterological traits. Shebli then, with fervor and intense love, plunged into the ocean of existential communion. He eventually came to be one of the greatest Sufi *pirs*.

The following story was written by Jāmī in *Nafahāt al-uns*, about Majduddin Baghdādi, a Sufi *pir* of the twelfth century:

> When he entered the service of a Sheikh, he was made to serve "at the place of ablution," i.e, to clean the latrines. His mother, a well-to-do lady physician, asked the master to exempt the tender boy from this work, and sent him twelve Turkish slaves to do the cleaning. But he replied: "You are a physician—if your son had an inflammation of the gall bladder, should I give the medicine to a Turkish slave instead of giving it to him?" (Schimmel, 1975, p. 101)

In the true sense, the *pir* is perceived as a physician of the soul, who has personally suffered the sickness of separation, and has gone through intensive and arduous therapeutic and psychomystical trials. Obedience and total trust in the *pir* are very important steps for the novice (Nurbakhsh, 1978; Royster, 1979).

However, as Hujwiri emphasized more than 900 years ago, the physician has to be worthy of this trust. Throughout the ages, there have been many excellent *pirs*, but also some corrupt ones. These few corrupt *pirs* exploited the trust of their disciples for personal, political, and financial gains. The downfall of Sufi orders in Turkey, Persia, and other Islamic countries may be attributed to corrupt practices of some of the Sufi *pirs*. This is similar to unethical physicians today who exploit their patients, or, through ignorance, prescribe unnecessary medications or procedures. However, the abuse or exploitation by a few physicians does not mean that the field of medicine or the healing arts should be abandoned.

Hazrat Inayat Khan (1964), the founder of the Sufi Order of the West, wrote:

> Then there arises the question of how to find the real guru. Very often people are in doubt, they do not know whether the guru they see is a true or a false guru. Frequently a person comes into contact with a false guru in this world where there is so much falsehood. But at the same time a real seeker, one who is not false to himself, will always meet with the truth, with the real, because it is his own real faith, his own sincerity in earnest seeking that will become his torch. The real teacher is within, the lover of reality is one's own sincere self, and if one is really seeking truth, sooner or later one will certainly find a true teacher. And supposing one came into contact with a false teacher, what then? Then the real One will turn the false teacher also into a real teacher, because Reality is greater than falsehood. (Vol. X, p. 65)

INITIATION

Initiation to the Sufi Path frequently occurs through symbolic and highly emotional ceremonies. At this time, the *pir* instructs the seeker with *zikr*, one of the names of God. The disciple learns to inhale and exhale *zikr* silently. This is referred to as "secret *zikr*." The practice of *zikr* is similar to the practice of *mantra* in Yoga. It is the first step of the meditative experience (chapter 3). The seeker may at times feel elated and at other times sorrowful. Feelings pour out from within. Tears may flow quietly and profusely.

As a seeker, one knows that the *pir* is aware of one's internal states at all times. So one feels there is no need to communicate one's feelings verbally except when the *pir* asks. At this phase, emphasis is upon the internalization of the *pir* and his attributes (chapter 5). At times this internal process is so intensive that the seeker does not think about anything but the *pir*. A well-known example is the relationship between Rumi and his *pir*, Shams-e-Tabrizi:

> "When he stimulated my thought from the depth of my psychic sea, the phantom of light arose. Shams was the light of the eye, the clarity of reason, the brightness of the soul and the enlightenment of the heart. Shams was a universal man who took away my reason and religion. He was the form of every happiness." (Arasteh, 1965b, p. 39)

The seeker is expected to come regularly, usually twice a week, on Sunday and Thursday evenings, to the place of Sufi gathering (*khaneqa*). In the gathering, the seeker serves his brothers and sisters in any capacity, such as cleaning, serving tea, and helping the needy. Serving others helps to decrease selfishness and "I-ness." The Sufis read mystical poetry from Rumi's *Mathnawi* and other Sufi books and are involved in group *zikr*. They chant one of the names of God or a poem together until an intensive emotional experience occurs. Many cry in joy and ecstasy. Some will be blessed by a "vision."

The seeker is expected to keep silence and reveals visions or dreams only to the *pir*. The *pir* at this stage is essential in helping the seeker develop further on the Path of Integration. It is not uncommon for a seeker to express psychomystical experiences in symbolic poetry, but often silence is advised. Silence is considered a sign of growth and maturity.

The *pir* listens attentively to the seeker's visions, dreams, and mystical states (*hālāt*). He may ask the seeker a few questions, and make occasional suggestions, clarifications, or interpretations. This process helps the seeker become aware of animal *nafs* and the tendencies for avoiding and resisting. The *pir* must constantly help the seeker chip away at self-conceit, illusions, and false expectations.

HĀLĀT: MYSTICAL STATES

The seeker's intensive affective and emotional experiences on the Sufi Path are called *hālāt*. "*Hālāt*" is the plural of the word "*hāl*," which means condition, state, and feeling. Hujwiri stated: "*Hāl* . . . is something that descends from God into a man's heart, without his being able to repel it when it comes, or to attract it when it goes, . . ." (p. 181). In this statement, the involuntary and spontaneous aspects of *hāl* are emphasized. Jonaid of Baghdad wrote that mystical states (*hālāt*) ". . . are like flashes of lightning: their permanence is merely a suggestion of the lower soul (*nafs*)" (Hujwiri, p. 182).

Sarraj (d. 988 A.D.) described ten mystical states in detail: observation, nearness, love, fear, hope, longing, intimacy, tranquility, vision, and certainty (pp. 54–72). These states are progressive. The Sufis in each stage of personality development re-experience these mystical states spontaneously (chapter 6 and 7). Affective and emotional experiences are like intense fires which melt away impurities and help in polishing the mirror of the heart.

During mystical states, tears, feelings of sensory vibration, hair-raising goose bumps, and changes in respiration are experienced. There is a temporary suspension of thought processes, as though the individual becomes totally filled with visceral or vegetative sensations. These mystical experiences help the Sufi further along the Path of Truth toward a deeper experience of Reality.

PSYCHOPHYSIOLOGY OF MYSTICAL STATES

Intensive emotional experience and expression of mystical states in Sufi meditation is a puzzling phenomenon. In Zen and Yoga, there is less emphasis on affective and emotional experiences than in Sufism. In mystical states, a massive dis-inhibition and catharsis of emotion occurs. These deep emotional expressions frequently are without accompanying memories, fantasies, or thought processes. They are pure feelings, as though flowing from the depths of one's being. The experience of mystical states is overwhelming and all-encompassing. The seeker experiences joy, sorrow, hope, and fear with all atoms of his or her being. Can we explain these intensive emotional, affective, or psychomystical states from a psychophysiological point of view?

While one is meditating, breathing gradually becomes shallower and frequency decreases by almost one-half. There is no evidence of increased carbon dioxide in the blood. This quiet, shallow breathing is not followed by rapid, deep breathing or hyperventilation. Physiologically, there is increased stimulation of the parasympathetic system which manifests itself by decreased breathing and decreased muscle tonicity (chapter 3).

Gellhorn (1967) applied the term "ergotropic" to the sympathetic nervous system and "trophotropic" to the parasympathetic nervous system (p. 5). Gellhorn and Kiely (1972), in their paper entitled *Mystical States of Consciousness: Neurophysiological and Clinical Aspects*, stated: "The physiological change which accompanies the mental state of meditation is a shift in the trophotropic-ergotropic balance to the trophotropic side" (p. 400).

Through what mechanism does the vagus nerve, or parasympathetic system, become stimulated during meditation? The Sufis believe, as you recall, that a human being is enslaved by rationalistic thinking and deductive reasoning. This results in fragmentation and loss of touch with visceral consciousness. We know that the brain cortex has an inhibitory function over the "lower part" of the brain, such as the hypothalamus, reticular system, mid-brain, medullar oblongata, spinal cord, and the sympathetic and parasympathetic systems. Could it be that, through preoccupation with rationalistic thinking and thought processes, the autonomic and vegetative nervous systems are being overinhibited? Sufis feel that by inhaling and exhaling *zikr* and the practice of meditation, the individual gradually becomes free from rationalistic thinking and dualism. Perhaps, in this manner Sufi *pirs* help seekers come in touch with their visceral system and the animal and vegetative parts of the inner self.

I hypothesize that through the Sufi meditative experience the inhibitory grip of the brain cortex is temporarily released, and the hypothalamus and sympathetic and parasympathetic systems are allowed to function automatically—free from the interference of the cortex. When the hypothalamus and the vagus nerve are free, the affective states (*hālāt*) of hope, fear, love, etc., are experienced without cognitive interference. Tears come freely without any reason. The seeker feels overwhelming joy without explanation. The proprioceptive sensation of vibration and hair-raising goose bumps are experienced with or without cognitive awareness (chapters 3, 6, and 7).

PSYCHOANALYSIS AND DYNAMIC PSYCHOTHERAPY

The term "psychotherapy" is ubiquitous and therefore difficult to define. Everything is called "psychotherapy," or has "psychotherapeutic" benefit. According to Hilda Bruch (1974):

> Psychotherapy itself is in such a state of flux, and the concept has been broadened to such an extent, that nearly every professional interaction between two people, or groups of people, is referred to as "therapy." (p. viii)

Jerome Frank (1963), in *Persuasion and Healing*, examined psychotherapy from a cultural and historical perspective, and provided the following definition:

> Attempts to enhance a person's feeling of well-being are usually labeled treatment, and every society trains some of its members to apply this form of influence. Treatment always involves a personal relationshp between healer and sufferer. Certain types of therapy rely primarily on the healer's ability to mobilize healing forces in the sufferer by psychological means. These forms of treatment may be generically termed psychotherapy. (p. 1)

There are now more than 100 forms of psychotherapy: some examples include psychoanalysis, dynamic psychotherapy, gestalt therapy, reality therapy, behavioral therapy, family therapy, group therapy, psychosynthesis, client-centered therapy, transpersonal psychotherapies, and biofeedback.

ESSENTIAL CORE OF PSYCHOANALYSIS AND DYNAMIC PSYCHOTHERAPY

Psychoanalysis and varieties of dynamic psychotherapies believe in the existence of the unconscious. The concepts of id, ego, and superego describe the structural components of the personality (chapter 1). In human beings, sexual and aggressive impulses of the id are in conflict with parental and societal inhibitions of the superego, resulting in the ego's experience of anxiety and guilt. These painful and unacceptable feelings and conflicts are repressed in the unconscious. At times they break through the barriers of repression and manifest themselves in the form of emotional suffering, with the psychopathological symptoms of neurosis, psychosis, psychophysiological disorders, or disorders of character.

The therapeutic premise of psychoanalysis and dynamic psychotherapy is that by establishing a trusting and meaningful relationship between the patient and the therapist, the unconscious conflicts will be uncovered through the process of free association and verbalization. It is hoped that thereby the patient gradually gains insight and awareness followed by symptom reduction, improvement, and growth.

Edward Bibring (1954), in his classic paper *Psychoanalysis and Dynamic Psychotherapies* described five basic principles and techniques employed in psychoanalysis and dynamic psychotherapy.

> 1. *Suggestion* is a common denominator in all therapeutic techniques, whether surgical, medical, or psychological. According to Bibring, "The psychiatric meaning of the term suggestion refers to the induction of ideas, impulses, emotions, and actions, . . . by the therapist . . . in the patient . . ." (p. 747)
>
> 2. *Abreaction* is the expression of memories and emotions openly and without inhibition. This is also referred to as catharsis. Psychoanalysis and dynamic psychotherapies have their beginnings and roots in suggestive and abreactive therapeutic methods.
>
> 3. *Manipulation*—according to Bibring (1954):
>
> " . . . covers a wide field of therapeutic measures. Crude forms of manipulation such as advice, guidance, and similar ways of running a patient's life . . . do not represent proper curative principles. Manipulation, in the sense used here, can be defined as the employment of various emotional systems existing in the patient for the purpose of achieving therapeutic change . . . " (p. 750)
>
> 4. *Clarification,* according to Bibring, is when "The therapist aids the client or patient to clarify his feelings, including the nature of his fears, object relationships, attitudes, the different choice of actions, etc." (p. 754) Self-understanding, which constitutes " . . . the basic principles of . . . *insight therapy* . . . is based on " . . . clarification and interpretation." (p. 754)
>
> 5. *Interpretation*—". . . in the sense as used here refers exclusively to unconscious material . . ." (p. 757) Through interpretation the therapist explores hidden and unconscious meanings of the patient's attitudes, behavior, and free associations. The psychotherapist makes a connection between the patient's manifest behavior with the unconscious experiences and feelings of the recent past. This is called dynamic interpretation.

Bibring felt that there is also a "genetic" interpretation which is only in the domain of psychoanalysis. The psychoanalyst not only makes a connection between manifest behavior of the patient to the relatively recent past, but also to early infantile and childhood experiences—the genesis of all behavior.

In summary, in psychoanalysis and dynamic psychotherapy, exploration of unconscious conflicts and infantile traumatic experiences and fantasies occurs through the expression of the patient's verbal and nonverbal behavior in the therapeutic situation. Emphasis is on free associations, in the form of spoken words. Working through the defensive postures of transference and resistance is the essence of psychoanalytic therapy.

SUFISM, PSYCHOANALYSIS AND DYNAMIC PSYCHOTHERAPY

Basic personality structure and the stages of human development in Sufism, ego psychology, and psychoanalysis are discussed in chapters 1, 6, and 7. The therapeutic process and methods in Sufism will now be compared with dynamic psychotherapy. The term "psychotherapy" is used to refer to therapeutic processes both in psychoanalysis and dynamic psychotherapy.

Origin of Suffering

Separation Anxiety   In psychotherapy, one of the premises is that the patient needs to experience anxiety before benefitting from therapy. Psychotherapy focuses on symptom alleviation and underlying personality changes for improved adjustment to daily life. In Sufism, the seeker's suffering and awareness of this suffering are also essential.

Sufis and psychotherapists differ on the origin of suffering and anxieties. Classical psychoanalysts emphasize neurotic conflicts originating from the phallic-oedipal phase (ages three to seven years) of psychosexual development as being the origin of patients' anxieties and suffering (chapters 1 and 6).

In the last few decades, with the contributions of child psychiatry, child analysis, and developmental psychology, we have become aware that attachment behavior and the mother-child relationship throughout pregnancy and the first 2 to 3 years of life play an important role in the formation of personality and in the development of psychopathology. Attachment behavior and its manifestation in the form of separation anxiety now seem to have much more impact on the development of the self than the oedipal conflict.

The Sufis perceive "separation" as the basis of anxieties and disorders of the mind. They not only include separation of the child from mother, but also separation of human beings from each other, from nature, and from Universal Reality. Sufis feel that the greater the separation, the more the feelings of fragmentation and distress.

In recent years, psychoanalysts such as Kohut (1971, 1977, 1978) and Kernberg (1975), have recognized that frequent separations of the child from mother or uneven mothering (overvaluation or undervaluation of the child) have significant impact on the development of self-esteem, perception of the self, and the development of a variety of psychopathologies which come under the heading of narcissistic personality disorders. These disorders differ from neurotic disturbances. Clinical data demonstrate that the occurrence of these disorders is increasing. The concept of narcissism will now be discussed.

Narcissism   The term narcissism is used in psychoanalysis and dynamic psychotherapy to describe an individual's love and attachment to the self. The word narcissism originates from Narcissus. In Greek mythology, Narcissus was a beautiful young man who fell in love with his own image reflected in the water. Because of this self-love, he pined away and changed into the narcissus flower. (Shafii & Shafii, 1982, p. 71).

PRIMARY NARCISSISM: In the psychoanalytic concept of human development, the first 2–4 months of life are referred to as the stage of primary narcissism.

> In primary narcissism everything and everyone exists to satisfy the needs of the self. Self-love and lack of feeling for others are the essence of primary narcissism. (p. 71).

SECONDARY NARCISSISM: With the development of the recognition smile at approximately age four months, the infant begins to develop feelings for

> . . . a love object (mother) outside of the self. This is the beginning of secondary narcissism. Secondary narcissism means that the infant begins to recognize that there is a *reciprocity* in his relationship to mother (someone outside the self) in order to fulfill the needs of the self. In secondary narcissism, there is a *quid pro quo* relationship: I do this to get that.

By age 36 months . . . the child begins to consider other people's feelings, needs, and reactions independently from the needs of the self.

The narcissistic concern about the self waxes and wanes throughout childhood and adolescence. Fear of bodily injury in the phallic-oedipal stage, concern about puberty in early adolescence, and extreme preoccupation with appearance in middle adolescence are some of the manifestations of primary narcissism. Creative productivity in children and adults represents symbolic projections of the self into the environment, which is sublimated expression of secondary narcissism.

Self-esteem and ego ideal are the healthy representations of narcissism. Unrealistic omnipotent fantasies are overcompensations for feelings of helplessness, impotence, and narcissistic injury. By late adolescence and early young adulthood, the mature individual develops a healthy balance between the love of the self and the love of others.

Overconcern for others, at the expense of the self, or over-preoccupation with the self, at the expense of others, can result in the development of serious psychopathology, such as depression, narcissistic personality disorders, drug and alcohol abuse, borderline psychosis, and psychosis. (pp. 71–72).

The Sufis have been acutely aware of the human tendency toward self-gratification, self-conceit, and overestimation and underestimation of the self. They do not use the terms neurosis or narcissistic personality disorder, but at the core of their conception of the disorders of the mind is the individual's relationship with the self, others, nature, and God. Sufis feel that separation from nature and God and dualistic thinking are the roots of selfishness, self-conceit, and fragmentation. Constant attacking and chipping away at narcissistic tendencies is the essence of the therapeutic methods in Sufism.

Assessment

The Sufi *pir* interviews the seeker and observes not only verbal expressions, but also actions and attitudes. In the interview, there is less emphasis on early childhood development, although past experiences, especially guilt-ridden experiences and frightening and hurtful behavior towards others, are explored. The Sufi *pir* is particularly interested in assessing the seeker's tendencies toward pride and self-conceit, insincerity, lack of commitment, and emotional instability. The process of assessment may take a short time or years. In classical Sufism, as discussed earlier, it usually took approximately 3 years.

The Sufi *pir* looks for two major things. The first is the extent and nature of the seeker's psychic suffering. Is the seeker looking for a quick relief to avoid pain? Or is the person seeking knowledge and Reality? If the seeker is looking for a quick relief from pain, Sufism is not the answer. On the other hand, if seekers are sincerely seeking Truth and are unhappy and distraught by their present condition, then they are welcomed to the Path. The assessment of the intensity of suffering is primarily nonverbal, observational, and intuitive, rather than dependent on verbalization.

Pointed, and at times apparently irrational, illogical, or even rude and insulting comments are made by the *pir* in the initial interview to put the seeker off guard or jolt him or her. In this manner, the *pir* assesses the individual's response to unfamiliar, paradoxical, or irrational experiences. Flexibility, receptiveness, and thirst for knowledge are important qualities for a seeker. Argumentativeness, rigidity, and particularly rationalistic tendencies are signs of potential limitations.

The Sufis feel strongly about the necessity of being able to tolerate irrational and paradoxical situations. They feel that it is necessary to give up "apparent rationality" and become "deranged and irrational" before experiencing real knowledge. In the *pir's* initial assessment of the seeker, there is less emphasis on healing, treatment, and alleviation of symptoms, and more emphasis on experiencing knowledge and Universal Reality. In this area, Sufis differ from psychotherapists.

Treatment

In psychotherapy, the priority is treatment. The premise is that by gaining insight through self-examination of past traumatic experiences, troublesome symptoms will be alleviated and improvement will occur. The Sufis feel that psychic suffering and pain are essential throughout life. The goals of the Sufis are the vision of Reality, Union with the Beloved, and integration of personality. This requires pain, suffering, and sacrifice. Alleviation of symptoms and the development of health and well-being are not the goals but the side effects.

Let us say, for instance, that a seeker suffers from sleeplessness. If the sleeplessness is felt to be related to psychological or spiritual causes, the *pir* may say, "This sleeplessness is a sign of your psychic suffering. Use the hours of wakefulness to meditate, read Sufi poetry, and, if you feel like crying, let the tears flow. This turmoil will help you become like steel in the fires of agony and despair." The Sufis do not avoid grief, depression, temporary irrationality or the experience of intense feelings. They see all of these experiences as ingredients for purification. However, if a seeker becomes too anxious, distraught, or fragmented, the sensitive and experienced *pir* will advise decreasing the intensity and frequency of meditation, and prescribe concrete and specific tasks in the form of serving others in order to modify the intensity of what we now would refer to as "regression" (chapter 3).

There is a limitation in the therapeutic effects of psychotherapy or psychoanalysis. A number of studies show that it does not matter what type of therapy one applies, whether psychoanalysis, exploratory psychotherapy, behavior therapy, or faith-healing; the outcome is about the same. Approximately two-thirds of the patients experience relief and alleviation of symptoms. In psychoanalysis and insight-oriented psychotherapy, there is now less emphasis on "treatment" and more emphasis on acquiring knowledge and insight about the self and one's relationship with others.

Here again, Sufism and psychotherapy meet. The only difference is that the Sufis' purpose from the beginning is not "treatment." The Sufis feel that knowledge of the self is only the first stage of experiencing True Knowledge or Universal Reality.

Nasafi, in *The Book of the Integrated Human Being,* wrote:

> Know that the requirements of the Path are six. First is giving up—possession and position and the love of them. It is also giving up sins [impulsive behaviors] and troublesome character traits. Second is making peace with all the creatures of the world; hurting no one with deeds or words, and withholding help and kindness from no one. Recognize that everyone is poor, needy and "seeking" like yourself. The third is developing the ability to be alone and not dependent on others. The fourth is practicing silence—experiencing silence in meditation and other situations. The fifth is the ability to experience and tolerate hunger and thirst by fasting and by decreasing one's preoccupation with food and eating. The sixth is wakefulness—sleeping less and developing the ability for self-observation. It is reawakening from the sleep of heedlessness and ignorance.
>
> The fundamentals of the Path are also six. The first is finding a guide, *pir.* Without a guide one cannot achieve the goal. The second is devotion and love toward the *pir.* The seeker's devotion and love for the *pir* is like having a horse to ride on the Path. The stronger the devotion and affection, the stronger the horse . . . the third is obeying the guide and following him. The seeker has to give up the blind following of parental beliefs and follow the guide in words and deeds. The *pir* is like a physician and the seeker like a patient. When the patient does not follow the physi-

cian's order or does the opposite, he will never gain health and
will become sicker. If the patient wants to treat himself by reading
books on medicine he will never recover. The presence of a physician and a cooperative patient are essential for alleviation of disease and its causes. The fourth is giving up one's previous beliefs
and will. Attachment to earlier beliefs is a block on the Path.
Following the order of the *pir* brings the seeker closer to the *pir*.
The fifth is giving up protest and denial of the *pir's* advice. . . . the
sixth is stability and persistence. An unstable person does not
accomplish anything in this world or the next. Oh dervish, anyone
who attains a goal, whether it be wordly or eternal, it is the result
of stability and perseverance . . . (pp. 95–96).

Intense Love in Sufism and Transference in Psychotherapy

Intense love *(ishq)* is the integrative energy in Sufism. Imam Ja'far
as-Sādiq (d. 765 A.D.), one of the greatest teachers of Sufism, stated
that intense love is ". . . a divine fire that devours man completely"
(Schimmel, 1975, p. 41). Sufis from that time on searched for this
"divine fire," which they felt was the source of light.

The intense relationship between the seeker and the *pir* rekindles
the divine fire and unleashes extensive and, at times, overwhelming
emotional experiences in the seeker. The relationship between the *pir*
and the seeker can be compared to the relationship between parent
and child, beloved and lover, candle and moth, rose and nightingale,
and physician of the soul and the patient. Schimmel wrote:

> The novice who has entered the master's group becomes "like
> the son of the sheikh"; he is considered part of him according to
> the tradition, "the son is part of the father." The sheikh helps
> him to give birth to a true "heart" and nourishes him with spiritual
> milk like a mother, . . . (p. 103).

The relationship between the disciple and the Sufi *pir* has
similarities with the transference relationship in psychoanalysis and
psychotherapy, but at the same time transcends it.

Meaning of Transference   One of Freud's major contributions was
the identification of the transference phenomenon and its significance
to the psychotherapeutic process. Transference literally means trans-
ferring unconscious feelings, emotions, and expectations from meaningful persons of the past to meaningful persons of the present. When
one is in physical or emotional distress, these feelings and expectations

are intensified. Sensitivity of the therapist to the various aspects of transference and its effective use can significantly help a patient or troubled person.

Greenson (1967) wrote:

> The development of the technique of psychoanalysis has been determined essentially by the evolution of our knowledge about the nature of transference. The greatest advances in psychoanalytic technique were derived from Freud's (1905) major discoveries about the twofold power of transference; it is an instrument of irreplaceable value, and it is the source of the greatest dangers. Transference reactions offer the analyst an invaluable opportunity to explore the inaccessible past and the unconscious (Freud, 1912, p. 108). Transference also stirs up resistances that become the most serious obstacle to our work ... (p. 151).

Transference, by its nature, is an intense, ambivalent relationship. At times, the patient has intense, positive, affectionate love, and even sexual fantasies toward the therapist. This is referred to as positive transference. At other times, unrealistic anger, hostility, and aggressive and destructive feelings prevail. This is referred to as negative transference.

The goal of psychotherapy is to experience past repressed feelings in the privacy, security, and receptivity of the therapeutic situation. By re-experiencing these feelings, with the help of the therapist, the patient gradually gains insight into the origins of the feelings, and, it is hoped, frees the self from destructive, troublesome, and divisive influences. Some of the energies which had been invested in intrapsychic conflicts become neutralized or freed for healthier adaptation.

The relationship between the seeker and *pir* has a strong transference component, especially in the early phases of psychospiritual development. The most important and significant person in the seeker's life is the *pir*. The seeker projects and displaces inner thoughts, ideas, feelings, wishes, and hopes onto the *pir*. The *pir* is frequently idealized as a benevolent father or mother who is, at all times, aware of the physical, emotional, and spiritual state of the disciple. Occasionally, magical thoughts and omnipotent fantasies are projected onto the *pir*.

Generally, negative, angry, and hostile feelings toward the *pir* are not directly expressed, as is encouraged in psychotherapy. However, in many situations, such hostile and aggressive feelings may find a way of expression through dreams and visual or auditory experiences in meditation. The seeker shares dreams, visions, and thoughts openly with the *pir*. The *pir* then makes comments and interpretations to help the seeker modify anxiety, guilt, and sexual or aggressive impulses of the animal *nafs*. The major emphasis is on confronting and modifying the narcissistic aspects of the self. In Sufism, "working through" varieties of narcissistic postures and tendencies frequently occurs by the process of displacement. Sufi stories, metaphors, symbolic poetry, anecdotes, and brief sayings of past *pirs* are used extensively for clarification, confrontation, and interpretation (Deikman, 1977).

Beyond Transference   In Sufism, the seeker, through intense love and total trust, is expected to give up will and desires and totally follow the will of the *pir*. This is called *iradah*. The word *iradah* literally means "will," but in Sufism it refers specifically to enthusiastically, willingly, and unconditionally giving up one's will to the will of the *pir* and the will of God. This complete giving up of one's will without doubt or ambivalence helps the seeker on the Path of liberation and freedom from the self. The Sufis feel strongly that one cannot be freed from the conditioned self and animal *nafs* until one freely gives up one's will and totally trusts the *pir* as a guide on the Path of Reality. *Iradah* transcends the concept of transference in psychotherapy. Transference is based on infantile wishes and desires of the id, and *iradah* is based upon the highest level of human love for psychospiritual integration and existential communion (Nurbakhsh, 1978).

Avoidance in Sufism and Resistance in Psychotherapy

Sufi *pirs* are aware of the seeker's tendency for avoiding regular meditative practices, for giving in to impulses, and for avoiding pain and frustration on the Path. Total trust or "surrender" to the *pir* helps the seeker in overcoming these avoidances. Rumi, in Book I of *Mathnawi*, portrays the seeker's tendency toward avoidance:

> It was the custom of the men of Qazwin to have various devices tattooed upon their bodies. A certain coward went to the artist to have such a device tattooed on his back, and desired that it might be the figure of a lion. But when he felt the pricks of the needles he roared with pain, and said to the artist, "What part of the lion are you now painting?" The artist replied, "I am doing the tail." The patient cried, "Never mind the tail; go on with another part." The artist accordingly began in another part, but the patient again cried out and told him to try somewhere else. Wherever the artist applied his needles, the patient raised similar objections, till at last the artist dashed all his needles and pigments on the ground, and refused to proceed any further (Whinfield's translation, pp. 44–45).

The artist said, "Who has ever seen a lion without a head, tail, stomach, or back?"

Here, Rumi emphasized the physical and emotional pain which a seeker needs to go through to become a fully integrated being. Sufis do not use the term "resistance" to express the seeker's conscious and unconscious hesitations for further development. They generally use the terms "avoidance," "fear," or "cowardice" to describe what we call "resistance."

In the initial phase of the meditative experience, fantasies and visions occur frequently. At this time, the Sufi *pir* is helpful in assisting the seeker to overcome preoccupations with self-satisfying and self-deluding visions. These visual experiences may become a source of avoidance and resistance on the Path.

> A disciple formed the notion that he had attained a degree of perfection.
>
> "It is better for me to be alone," he thought.
>
> So he withdrew into a corner and sat there for a space. It so fell out that every night he was brought a camel and told, "We will convey you to Paradise." He would sit on the camel and ride until he arrived at a pleasant and cheerful spot thronged with handsome folk and abounding in choice dishes and running water. There he would remain till dawn; then he would fall asleep, and awake to find himself in his cell. He now became proud and very conceited.
>
> "Every night I am taken to Paradise," he would boast.
>
> His words came to Jonaid's ears. He at once arose and proceeded to his cell, where he found him putting on the greatest airs. He asked him what had happened, and he told the whole story to the shaikh.
>
> "Tonight when you are taken there," Jonaid told him, "say thrice, 'There is no strength nor power save with God, the Sublime, the Almighty.' "
>
> That night the disciple was transported as usual. He disbelieved in his heart what the shaikh had told him; nevertheless, when he reached that place he uttered as an experiment, "There is no strength nor power." The company all screamed and fled, and he found himself on a dunghill with bones lying before him. Realizing his error, he repented and repaired to Jonaid's circle. He had learned that for a disciple to dwell alone is mortal poison. (Attār, Arberry's translation, pp. 208–209).

This story clearly illustrates that the seeker, when withdrawn to the self in quiescence and meditation, may experience illusions and hallucinations. This disciple was preoccupied with narcissistic delusions and self-gratifying hallucinations. He perceived these illusions as true mystical experiences. He avoided the rigors of meditation, discipline, and sleeplessness for the pleasures of sleep and illusionary experiences. Also, he became more conceited and felt no need to contact his *pir*. He had the illusion that he had attained the highest level of spiritual development.

Jonaid was acutely aware of the regressive power of meditation and isolation. In this situation, Jonaid recognized that because these visions were so gratifying (ego syntonic) it would be of no use to confront the seeker directly. He decided to redirect the seeker's emotional investment from these illusions.

The verse from the Koran, "There is no strength nor power save with God, . . ." is commonly uttered by the Sufis and other Moslems when they want to determine whether or not they are experiencing something real or illusionary. It is believed that by repeating this verse three times and relying totally on the power of God, illusionary experiences will disappear. Jonaid tactfully, on a nonverbal level, communicated to the seeker the illusionary nature of his experiences by suggesting the utterance of the Koranic verse three times. By this process, Jonaid reawakened the observing part of the seeker's ego without increasing his narcissistic defensive postures and thereby helped him overcome these illusionary experiences.

The seeker "repented" and gave up his delusions. From a psychoanalytic point of view, the seeker was acting out transference resistances and, with Jonaid's help, was able to "work through" these resistances by the process of repentance. As we shall see, repentance, or reawakening, although it is the first stage of human development in Sufism, is at the same time a dynamic process which continues throughout the Sufi's life (chapter 6).

The Self in Sufism and Psychic Trauma in Psychotherapy

Interpretation, whether dynamic or genetic, plays an important role in psychoanalytic therapies. The essence of interpretation is connecting the patient's present behaviors, feelings, and associations in the psychotherapeutic situation with the memories or perceptions of traumatic childhood experiences.

Sufi *pirs* do less interpretation. When they do interpret, it is related to the narcissistic self of the seeker. From a psychoanalytic point of view, the Sufi *pir* focuses more directly on the self and the primary and secondary narcissistic tendencies of the seeker. The *pir* does not permit the seeker to indulge in self-pity because of "earlier traumatic experiences."

Interpretation in Sufism frequently transcends the dynamic and genetic interpretation of psychoanalysis and psychotherapy. It is existential interpretation, facilitating constant examination of the seeker's relationship with the self, others, nature, the cosmos, and Universal Reality (chapter 5).

Therapeutic Methods in Sufism

The Sufis' methods for helping a seeker on the Path toward integration are numerous. Some of them include:

1. *Silent meditation*—at least daily (usually before dawn), and preferably two to three times a day following prayers (chapters 3 and 4);

2. *Regular attendance* at Sufi gatherings;

3. *Regular interviews* with the Sufi *pir*, which are referred to as "experiencing the presence" *(huzūr)* of the *pir*. This presence can be for either a short or long time— as short as a glance, or as long as a day or two. Generally, it is 15 minutes to an hour long, and occurs at least twice weekly in the place of Sufi gathering. Meeting with the *pir* may be more frequent, at times daily, depending upon the *pir's* assessment of the seeker's psychospiritual state;

4. *Group Meditation*—regular contact with other Sufis at least twice weekly is essential. The Sufis sit in a circle on the floor, cross-legged, with knees lightly touching, forming a "chain." They meditate silently for a period of time, usually 30 to 90 minutes;

5. *Chanting*—this is also called *zikr-i-jali*, which means glorious outward meditation. Here, under the guidance of the *pir*, the Sufis rhythmically chant a *zikr*, which is often a short verse from the Koran in praise of God. This group chanting can be a very powerful experience. At times, the whole group functions as one entity, like " a ship in a tumultuous sea of unity." Some of the Sufis temporarily lose consciousness and, for many, silent tears flow. After reaching a crescendo

under the direction of the *pir*, the rhythm becomes slower and finally quiescence prevails. Most of the Sufis experience spiritual uplifting, profound joy, and elation after these sessions;

6. *Use of poetry*—reading mystical poetry or expressing one's psychomystical experiences in the metaphor of poetry is a common phenomenon. Sublimation of urges also finds an expression through Sufi poetry. Frequently, the Sufi poems are sung in melodic tones. This helps the Sufi experience beyond words the feelings and spiritual states of other Sufis.

7. *Use of Music and Dance*—although the use of music in the orthodox Islamic religion is forbidden, the Sufis have discovered that it may help significantly in meditative practices. To them, music transcends words and logic. Music goes to the heart of nature, connecting the seeker to the invisible rhythms of existence. Rumi, the founder of the whirling dervishes, used music extensively in Sufi group meditative practices, *Semā'* (chapter 5). Sufis are aware of the powerful and significant effects of the rhythmical movement of music and dance on catharsis of emotion, creation of a feeling of well-being, and the enhancement of internal peace and tranquility;

8. *Seclusion*—the Sufi *pir* advises some of the seekers, particularly those who have passed the initial phase and still have overwhelming narcissistic tendencies, to isolate themselves from others for a period of forty days *(chilla)*. Also, periods of seclusion may help a Sufi or Sufi *pir* to refocus all energies and attention on Reality.

Chilla

According to Hujwiri:

... the forty days' fast *(chilla)* of the saints are derived from the fast of Moses [Koran, Sura VII, Verse 138]. When the saints desire to hear the word of God spiritually, they remain fasting for forty days. (p. 324).

In the Sufi gathering place, a few small rooms are designated for *chilla*. *Chilla* is usually practiced under strict observation of the Sufi *pir*. During this time, the seeker fasts all day, breaking the fast after sunset with a glass of water and a piece of bread or mouthful of food. The seeker sleeps little, and spends most of the time in silent meditation or chanting. This active withdrawal is a powerful experience and not recommended for everyone. If a seeker is not ready or strong enough to tolerate this long period of isolation, he may become "deranged."

From a psychodynamic point of view, this active sensory isolation and withdrawal from daily life, sleep, and food usually results in profound regression. Inhibition and secondary process thinking decrease with an increased flow of unconscious fantasies and primary process thinking. The Sufi *pir* is the only contact the seeker has with the outside world. The Sufis feel that, in some cases, the only way a seeker may break the crust of avoidance and self-conceit is by *chilla*. The seeker shares visions, thoughts, and feelings with the *pir*. The watchful eyes of the *pir* closely observe the psychological, physical, and spiritual states *(hālāt)* of the seeker. If the seeker appears not able to cope with *chilla*, the *pir* shortens or terminates the experience.

The seeker emerges from *chilla* full of vigor, insight, and internal peace. The seeker has experienced intensive fears, anxieties, pain, loneliness, depression, sorrow, hope, joy, hallucinations, delusions, illusions, spiritual visions, stupor, numbness, hunger, and many other states and emotions. If the seeker can withstand facing the naked self, with all its strengths and shortcomings, he or she will be transformed, or at least gain a new perspective.

Chilla, from a psychological point of view, is an intensive sensory isolation. It reminds one of works on sensory deprivation and the technique of anaclitic therapy (Solomon et al., 1961; Azima et al., 1961). In anaclitic therapy, the patient is isolated in a partially dark room. The therapist is the only one to have contact with the patient during this treatment, which may take from a few days to a few weeks. At times, sleep is induced through chemical means to facilitate the process of regression. The premise of this therapeutic approach is that isolation and increased sleep contribute to acute and intense temporary regression. By regular therapeutic contacts with the therapist, and by resurgence of primary process fantasies, the patient is able to modify maladaptive defensive postures and become aware of deep-seated unconscious conflicts. This intensive therapeutic approach is usually reserved for patients who are so "well defended" that the customary psychotherapeutic and analytic methods have not been effective.

INDIVIDUALITY AND COMMUNION IN SUFISM AND PSYCHOTHERAPY

The goal of psychoanalysis and psychotherapy is helping the individual become more independent, have freedom of choice, and adapt more effectively with the environment, resulting in strengthening of the ego and the self. The Sufis' goal is freeing the self from the self. Emphasis is on interdependence rather than independence. It is becoming one with all; experiencing existential communion. In existential communion, one gives up individuality but gains the essence and spirit of all beings.

In the following chapter, meditation—which is the basic therapeutic and integrative method of most mystical traditions, such as Yoga, Zen Buddhism, Christian Contemplative Orders, and Sufism—is discussed from a psychological, physiological, and clinical perspective.

Part II

THE METHOD AND PROCESS

Chapter 3

HEALING SILENCE

Psychophysiological and Clinical Significance of Meditation[1]

Lamps are many but light is one.[2]

Rumi, Sufi poet, thirteenth century.

In the West, especially in the United States, there has been an increasing interest in the psycho-religious practices of the East, such as Yoga, Zen Buddhism, and Sufism. In all of these practices, meditation and

---

[1]Parts of the paper *Adaptive and Therapeutic Aspects of Meditation* by the author, which was published in *International Journal of Psychoanalytic Psychotherapy*, 1973, *2*, 364–382, are integrated in this chapter.

[2]Arasteh, A.R. *Final Integration in Adult Personality. A Measure for Health, Social Change and Leadership.* Leiden: E.J. Brill, 1965, p. 205.

the experience of internal silence are means of adapting to life's stresses and achieving further growth and integration. It is estimated that, in the United States alone, over 10 million people practice meditation.

In this chapter we will define meditation, describe types of meditative techniques, and explore the psychophysiological effects of meditation. The clinical significance of meditation and the therapeutic techniques adapted from meditation for the treatment and prevention of physical and emotional disorders and alcohol and drug abuse will be discussed. The possible benefits of meditation for clinicians are included. Potential adverse effects of meditation are explored.

DEFINITION OF MEDITATION

Generally, meditation is defined as contemplation and reflection, but this does not represent the totality of meditation. I would define meditation as *a psychophysiological state of active passivity and creative quiescence.* A discussion of the specific meaning of "psychophysiological state" and "active passivity and creative quiescence" follows.

Psychophysiological State

Bagchi and Wenger's (1957), Wenger and Bagchi's (1961), and Wenger et al.'s (1961) psychophysiological studies of Yogis in India demonstrated that they were able voluntarily to control autonomic functions, such as heartbeat and respiration. Studies by Wallace (1970) of subjects meditating showed that "The EEG pattern during meditation clearly distinguishes this state from the sleeping state. There are no slow (delta) waves or sleep spindles, but [α]alpha-wave activity predominates" (p. 1753). Wallace also reported that the meditators had an increase in skin resistance and a decrease in oxygen intake, respiration, and heartbeat. Meditation, Wallace postulated, is a unique psychophysiological state that is different from the states of wakefulness, sleep, and dreaming.

In view of these studies, along with others which will be discussed later in this chapter, the phrase "psychophysiological state" becomes an essential and integral part of the definition of meditation.

Active Passivity and Creative Quiescence

"Active passivity and creative quiescence" are interrelated in our definition of meditation. These phrases make specific reference to the paradoxical nature of meditation. When a person is sitting quietly, phenomenologically speaking, he or she is passive. In most meditative processes, with this passivity or quiescence comes an openness to receive internal and preconscious stimuli. Also, I suggest that quiescence and one-pointed attention facilitate further ego synthesis and integration similar to the creative process or the development of insight in the psychoanalytic situation (chapter 4). The use of the term "creative quiescence" emphasizes the internal experience of meditation rather than concrete creative output.

DESCRIPTION OF MEDITATION

Most commonly, the individual who wants to meditate sits cross-legged on the ground with the back straight, the eyes open, half-opened, or most often closed, while breathing deeply but quietly. The frequency and length of meditation varies. Often, it is once or twice a day for 20 to 45 minutes.

Some meditators, while breathing quietly, inhale and exhale a one-syllable word called *zikr* (remembrance) in Sufism, or *mantra* in Yoga. In Zen Buddhism, instead of a *mantra*, the meditator may be given a paradoxical problem called a *koan* to meditate upon. Often, the solutions to these *koans* are not found in rational or logical thought.

Most beginners in meditation are advised to direct attention to one point of the body, such as the forehead, neck, heart, navel, or genital area. Generally, they are instructed by their guide or *pir* to let thoughts and emotions float freely in their mind and, after observing them, return attention to meditation. In Sufi meditation, emphasis is on letting thoughts and fantasies flow rather than on pushing them away or being preoccupied by them. Meditators are encouraged to experience the present and to be in harmony with the moment rather than to dwell on the past or the future.

METHODS OF MEDITATION

The following schematic classification of meditative techniques gives us a beginning understanding of the similarities and differences between meditative practices in various mystical traditions. However, we should keep in mind that any division of meditation into types and subtypes is, by its very nature, a distortion which emphasizes the form rather than the essence.

Goleman (1977) divided meditative methods into two types: concentrative and mindfulness.

1. Concentrative Meditation

The meditator is instructed to fix attention on a single object. The object of meditation may be sounds *(mantras)*, ideas, images, feelings, or physiological functions, such as breathing. ". . . the mind is not only directed toward the object but finally penetrates it; totally absorbed in it, the mind moves to oneness with the object" (p. 7).

Concentrative meditation may be further divided into active or passive. In *active concentrative meditation*, the meditator is instructed to resist wandering thoughts, suppress daydreams and fantasies, and quickly and forcefully return attention to the object of meditation; some examples are *japa* of the Bhakti Yoga tradition, *samadhi* of Tibetan Buddhism, *siddha yoga* of Kundalini Yoga, and the contemplative traditions of Christianity.

In *passive concentrative meditation*, the meditator is attentive to the meditative object, but does not actively suppress thoughts, fantasies, ideas, or sensations. The meditator follows the thoughts, ideas, and fantasies, and then gently brings attention to the object of meditation; for example, *zikr* of Sufi meditation, *mantra* of Transcendental Meditation, and focusing on the sound of the word "one" in the Relaxation Response (Benson, 1975).

2. Mindfulness

In mindfulness, there is no *mantra* nor predetermined object of meditation. In mindfulness, ". . .the meditator methodically faces the bare facts of his experience, seeing each event as though occurring for the first time. He does this by continuous attention to the first phase of perception when his mind is *receptive* rather than reactive" (Goleman, 1977, p. 21). The meditator focuses attention on sensations and thoughts. He or she avoids judgment, reflection, suppression, or pursuit of thoughts and sensations. Thoughts and sensations are dismissed after being noticed. The premise is that the meditator will become aware of the disjointed, random nature of his or her mind, and, it is hoped, further insight will follow.

Mindfulness can also be further divided into active or passive. *Active mindfulness* is a type of meditation which emphasizes active focusing on thoughts and sensations. An example is the "self-remembering" of Gurdjieff. *Passive mindfulness* is a type of meditation which reflects

freedom from concentration and fixation on meditations or even specific sensory perceptions, thoughts, or ideas. At this level, one transcends the need for *zikr, mantra, koan,* or attention to thoughts, ideas,
or sensory perceptions. Passive mindfulness, which is referred to as
"emptiness" in Zen Buddhism, or *fanā* in Sufism, is the highest level
of meditation. The individual is freed from meditation; the beginning
and the end become one (chapter 5). Examples of this type of experience are *shikan-taza* ("just sitting") of Zen Buddhism, *fanā* of Sufism,
and "nontechnique" of "self-knowledge" of Krishnamurti (Goleman,
pp. 93, 103).

Sufi Meditative Techniques

If we apply Goleman's classification of meditation, we will notice
that the Sufis use a variety of meditative techniques in their practices.
For example, silent meditation *(zikr)* begins with the passive concentrative meditation of quietly and silently inhaling and exhaling one of
the names of God. Thoughts, feelings, fantasies, ideas, and sensations
are not actively suppressed. The mediator allows him or herself to
experience feelings and then gently brings attention to the object of
meditation.

As the Sufi becomes more experienced in meditation, each
meditative session begins with passive concentrative meditation, but
gradually moves to a state of mindfulness. The Sufi transcends the
experience of breathing, *zikr,* and goes through the phase of active
mindfulness by focusing on thoughts, sensations, and feelings, eventually reaching the state of passive mindfulness. In this state, the Sufi
is totally free from concentration on *zikr* or specific sensory perceptions, feelings, or thoughts. The Sufi experiences "moments of *fanā*,"
similar to the experience of "emptiness" in Zen Buddhism and *nirvana*
in Yoga (chapter 5).

The Sufi also practice another type of meditation which they
refer to as *zikr-i-jali* or glorious outward meditation (chapter 2). In
this meditation, a short verse from the Koran, a melodic Sufi poem,
the name of one of the attributes of God, or the name of a Sufi *pir*
is rhythmically chanted and actively concentrated upon. Gradually,
this active concentrative meditation may move the meditator toward
passive concentrative meditation, active mindfulness, and, at times,
culminate in passive mindfulness and the experience of moments of
fanā. This type of meditation is similar to the active concentrative
meditation of Tantric Yoga, *japa* of Bhakti Yoga, *samadi* of Tibetan
Buddhism, chanting in Buddhism, and contemplative traditions in
Christianity.

PSYCHOPHYSIOLOGY OF MEDITATION

During the last few decades there have been extensive physiological studies of Yogis, Zen Masters, and, more recently, Westerners who have chosen to practice some form of meditation. We will discuss the effect of meditation on the central nervous system, dehabituation, hemispheric laterality, skin resistance, respiratory system, cardiovascular system, and on the human response to stress and anxiety.

Meditation and the Central Nervous System

Studies of Eastern Meditators   Das and Gastaut (1956) pioneered EEG studies of experienced yoga masters. They documented increased Beta wave (12-30 cycles per second) activities of the brain (hyperarousal), while the muscles showed hypotonicity and significant relaxation. This paradoxical finding was associated with the meditators' feeling of "ecstasy."

The studies we have cited earlier of experienced yogis in India showed that they were able to significantly decrease their respiration rate, pulse, and heartbeat. In fact, it appeared as though they had stopped their heartbeat. However, electrocardiogram (EKG) readings actually showed a decrease of amplitude and rate; the heart was functioning, although inaudibly. The authors concluded that yogis, through a variety of meditative techniques, were able to stimulate the parasympathetic nervous system and thereby decrease respiration rate, pulse, and heartbeat. Subsequently, Fenwick (1960) and others found that during *mantra* meditation the amplitude of EEG alpha waves (8–12 cycles per second) increased significantly.

The Birth of Biofeedback   In the West, before the above studies, it was thought to be impossible to control or influence the body's autonomic functions, such as brain electrical activity, heart rate, pulse, blood pressure, respiratory rate, muscle tonicity, and body temperature. In fact, these functions were classified as involuntary or vaso-vegetative functions because they were thought to be independent of volition or conscious control.

The yogis' abilities to influence and control autonomic functions were perceived for a long time by most scientists and clinicians with skepticism and disbelief, or, at most, as "epiphenomena" (unpredictable and irrelevant phenomena not worthy of investigation).

However, a few scientists developed "feedback methods," based on physiological findings on yogis, for helping animal and human subjects control and change autonomic functions in the laboratory setting. (Miller, 1969; Engel & Hansen, 1966; Shapiro et al., 1969; Benson et al., 1969; Kamiya, 1969; Basmajian, 1967; Green et al., 1969) Based on these investigations, the new scientific field of biofeedback and self-control was born (Kamiya et al., 1971).

Studies on Western Meditators   Wallace (1970), Wallace et al. (1971), Banquet (1973), and Fenwick et al. (1977) studied a number of subjects in the United States who had been involved in the practice of Transcendental Meditation (TM). These studies confirmed earlier studies of Eastern meditators in which the practice of meditation significantly increased the amplitude of EEG alpha waves. The alpha rhythm is thought to represent a state in which the brain cortex is awake but idling. Large numbers of neurons are thought to be firing synchronously producing alpha rhythm; the higher the amplitude, the greater the number of brain cells involved and the more coherent their activity. In addition to meditation, other internal experiences that are associated with high alpha output are often described as serene, pleasant, and devoid of visual imagery.

Recent studies have indicated that Transcendental Meditators can induce high alpha wave output more quickly and more frequently than controls (Williams & West, 1975). Also, the alpha wave output during Transcendental Meditation increases over the first 6 months of training (Glueck & Stroebel, 1975). However, a more recent study of Transcendental Meditators did not find any increase in alpha activity above the normal wakeful state (Stigsby et al., 1981). There are also indications that alpha output may increase during active meditative concentration, such as in Tantric meditation of Ananda Marga (Corby et al., 1978), and during the active mindfulness of Soto and Rinzai of Zen meditation (Kasamatsu & Hirai, 1966). An increase in alpha rhythms continues in many experienced meditators even when they are not meditating.

Another frequent finding is a decrease in the average alpha frequency (number of cycles per second) during TM (Wallace, 1970; Wallace et al., 1971; Banquet, 1973; Fenwick et al., 1977). Stigsby et al., (1981) also noted that this mean alpha frequency was very stable in meditators as compared to controls. This decrease in mean alpha frequency was also found by Kasamatsu and Hirai (1966) in their sample of Zen meditators.

On the other hand, as discussed earlier, Das and Gastaut (1956) found that, during the deep meditative states of yoga masters who experienced *samadhi*, or "ecstasy," there was an increased frequency in Beta waves of more than 12 cycles per second. Banquet (1973) noticed the same phenomenon in experienced Transcendental Meditators in the higher stages of meditation.

In studying experienced Transcendental Meditators, Levine et al. (1977), Haynes et al. (1977), and Westcott (1977) found that meditation may produce increased coherence (synchrony and similarity in phase and frequency) between the EEG recordings of various parts of the brain, particularly the left and right hemispheres. It is thought that coherence and synchrony may extend to nonmeditative time intervals in experienced meditators.

A Study of a Sufi Meditator   Surwillo and Hobson (1978) reported on the interval histogram of EEG half-wave durations of a person who had been practicing Sufi meditation for 18 years. ". . . the histogram obtained during meditation shows a shift in the direction of higher frequencies by comparison with the histograms obtained in the resting conditions" (p. 141). These findings confirm Das, Gastaut, and Banquet's studies of experienced meditators, which demonstrated that an acceleration in the frequency of electrocortical activity occurs during deep meditation.

A Study of Christian Silent Prayer   Increased electrocortical activity also occurred during silent prayer in the EEGs of six adults of the Protestant faith (Church of God) who were extensively involved in ". . . matters of personal devotion, including prayer, Bible reading, and reflective meditation." (Surwillo & Hobson, p. 136) In this study, none of the subjects showed evidence of sleep or drowsiness, as Pagano et al. (1976) previously reported in over one-half of the Transcendental Meditators.

Meditation and Dehabituation   Psychophysiological studies show that after initial exposure to a stimulus, the nonmeditating subject, upon repetition of the same stimulus, has a tendency to restrict or "tune out" its perception. This phenomenon is called *habituation*. Anand et al. (1961), in EEG studies of Yogi practitioners in India, noticed that while the Yogis were meditating, their EEG showed no reaction to external stimuli. But when they were not meditating, their EEG showed a reaction to these same stimuli. Repeated exposure to the same stimuli was perceived as though anew. This means that experienced meditators did not "tune out" the stimuli as the average person does.

Naranjo and Ornstein (1971) reported on the work of the Japanese scientists, Kasamatsu and Hirai, who

> ... studied the habituation of the orienting response to a repeating click in ordinary people and in Zen masters. The subjects in this experiment sat in a soundproof room and listened to a click repeated each fifteen seconds while an EEG was being taken. The normal subjects showed the customary phenomenon of habituation. There was a decrease in the response after the third or fourth click. After habituation, each time the click occurred there was no response in the brain of the subject: the click had been tuned out of awareness. When the Zen masters were exposed to this same repetitive click over a period of five minutes, they did not show the customary habituation but responded to the last click in the same way as they did to the first. They did not seem therefore to make a "model" of the repetitive stimulation and tune it out. (p. 196).

Through the process of meditation, dehabituation or, as Deikman (1966) called it, de-automatization occurs. This dehabituation enhances the meditator's receptivity and openness to internal and external stimuli (Hirai, 1974, p. 36–65). Also, it modifies the tendency to stereotyped, repetitive behavior and restrictive, defensive postures. Specifically, through meditation one learns to free the self from earlier patterns of behavior, and becomes more open and receptive to all forms of learning. These findings open the door to new areas in the theory of learning, namely *learning through unlearning*. The stage of *fanā* in Sufism, *nirvana* in Yoga, or *satori* in Zen, refers among other things to having attained relative freedom from earlier repetitive but constrictive behaviors and having developed "openness to receive" internal and external reality without distortion (Fromm, 1960) (chapter 5).

This process of dehabituation is a paradoxical construct. In meditation, one sits quietly breathing a *zikr* or *mantra*, which is, in itself, a repetitive behavior. One gradually experiences a freedom from earlier and infantile repetitive and compulsive behaviors that are only partially fulfilling and heavily taxing on psychic functioning. From a psychodynamic point of view, breathing a *zikr* or *mantra*, which is conflict-free from earlier repetitive and automatic habits and behaviors, seems to be less taxing on psychic energy. In Sufi meditative experience, one eventually frees the self from the repetitive behavior of breathing the *zikr*.

Meditation and Hemispheric Laterality Roger Sperry (1967) studied the behavior of chronic epileptic patients who had undergone a type of brain surgery for the treatment of uncontrolled epilepsy called commissurotomy, which means cutting the commissure connecting the right and left brain hemispheres. Sperry found that the two brain hemispheres have specialized cognitive functions which, after being surgically separated from each other, are ". . . capable of sustaining an independent autonomous consciousness" (Galin, 1977, p. 397). This capability is referred to as hemispheric laterality or lateral specialization. Recently, it has been discovered that hemispheric laterality also occurs in healthy people who have not had a commissurotomy.

In a right-handed person, verbal language, arithmetical calculations, logical deduction, reasoning, attention to details, classification into good or bad, and dualistic thinking are functions of the left hemisphere. Spatial and musical ability, and nonverbal representations, in the form of visual imagery, proprioceptive and kinesthetic sensations, holistic and integrative thinking, nonlinear associations, and affective and emotional expressions, are attributed to the functions of the right hemisphere. Creative processes, esthetic perceptions, and mystical experiences are also thought to be the functions of the right hemisphere (Sperry, 1967; Galin, 1974, 1977). Galin (1974) suggested that the right hemisphere may be the neurophysiological locus for the unconscious part of the mind and the left hemisphere for the conscious.

It is postulated that in Western cultures, which emphasize controlling emotions and being rational and logical, that the holistic and synthetic functions of the right hemisphere have been suppressed and dominated by rationalistic and analytical functions of the left hemisphere (Galin & Ornstein, 1972). Internal conflicts between thoughts and emotions, rationality and feeling, and analytical deductions and holistic experiences may be associated with the constant internal struggle between the left and right hemispheres, and, possibly, between the mid-brain area (e.g., the limbic, sympathetic, and parasympathetic systems) and the cortex.

Sperry's discovery resulted in a major revolution in our thinking about the functions of the brain's hemispheres and the possibility of finding anatomical and neurophysiological basis for holistic, integrative, synthetic, meditative, and mystical experiences.

The Sufis have discussed extensively two types of intellect (chapter 1). The first is practical intellect, which deals with the functions of discrimination, analysis, differentiation, deductive reasoning, and rationalistic thinking. Practical intellect is similar to the functions of the left hemisphere, which have only recently been discovered. Second is the abstract-universal intellect, which is manifested by holistic thinking, inductive reasoning, creative processes, psychological and philosophical acumen, religious aspirations, aesthetic values, and mystical experiences. Abstract-universal intellect describes what we now refer to as functions of the right hemisphere.

Is it possible to enhance the functions of the right hemisphere? If so, were mystics and Sufis aware of this possibility and, through meditation, did they attempt to tap the unbounded potential of the right hemisphere for developing a totally integrated human being?

Pagano and Frumkin (1977) addressed this same issue in a study of experienced meditators as compared with beginning meditators and with a nonmeditator control group. They found that experienced meditators were significantly superior to inexperienced meditators and nonmeditators regarding enhanced functions of the right hemisphere, as measured by the Seashore Tonal Memory Test. The authors concluded that meditation has a cumulative effect and ". . . facilitates right hemispheric functioning" (p. 407).

Meditation and Increased Coherence   One idea that has provoked considerable recent interest is that meditation may produce increases in the coherence (similarity in frequency and phase) in the two hemispheres both during and outside of meditative practice periods. It has been suggested that increased coherence between corresponding points on opposite hemispheres is beneficial, perhaps by decreasing internal noises and disjointed thoughts and fantasies (Westcott, 1977; Haynes et al., 1977; Levine et al., 1977). During TM, both alpha and theta activity appear to spread coherently to a larger number of locations in the same cerebral hemisphere (Banquet, 1973; Levine et al., 1977) and to the opposite hemisphere (Levine et al., 1977; Westcott, 1977). The magnitude of overall EEG power output for each hemisphere may also become more nearly equal during meditation (Westcott, 1977; Bennett & Trinder, 1977). There is some suggestive evidence that the latter two findings may also hold during relaxed but nonmeditative states in trained meditators. Bennett and Trinder (1977) also found that Transcendental Meditators were more able than controls to produce a nonsymmetrical EEG pattern when differences in activation of cerebral hemispheres would be adaptive in optimizing performance on assigned tasks.

Future Possibilities for Research   Brain electrical studies of meditation have just begun. Already, exciting findings have been reported and repeated in different laboratory settings using a variety of meditative techniques. It is important to recognize that the EEG recording is a crude and relatively nonspecific technique which attempts to document sophisticated and delicate brain electrical activities and functions through a myriad of obstacles, such as blood vessels, membranes, the skull, scalp, and hair. It is like taking a picture of the surface of the ocean from a distance, and assuming that the picture represents the depth, richness, and inner life of the ocean. We need scientist-meditators, special vehicles, and sensitive measuring techniques to bring to the surface the awesome beauty, invisible rhythms, rich heritage, and ever-evolving life of the mind.

Perhaps instruments which can detect the delicate functions of the brain may open new vistas—vistas already alluded to throughout the ages by the Sufis and the mystics. The development of a positron emission tomography (PET) scanner and Nuclear Magnetic Resonance (NMR), which allows us to portray the physiologic and metabolic functions of the brain and the body through sophisticated color-coded computer tomography, may revolutionize research on the effect of meditation on the human mind.

Meditation and Skin Resistance

Generally, when a person is excited, stimulated, or tense, the sympathetic nervous system is activated in the form of the fight or flight response. Dilation of pupils, increases in respiration rate, heartbeat, muscle tonicity, and perspiration, along with an internal feeling of tension and anxiety, occur. Scientists can study the fight or flight response, or sympathetic stimulation, by a variety of physiological measures, including the level of electrical conduction from one point on the skin to another, which is referred to as skin resistance. When the sympathetic nervous system is stimulated, the subject begins to perspire and, as a result, the sweat glands in the palms conduct electricity more freely. The skin resistance measured between electrodes decreases. Conversely, deactivation of the sympathetic nervous system, which usually accompanies a calmer state, produces an increase in skin resistance.

Skin resistance is measured by:

1. Basal Skin Resistance (BSR), which refers to changes in the baseline level of electrical conduction of the skin which takes place over a relatively long time period (i.e., minutes).

2.   Spontaneous Skin Resistance Responses (SSRR), which are also referred to as Galvanic Skin Responses or Phasic Skin Responses. These responses are momentary and spontaneous (i.e., fractions of seconds). They occur in reaction to a sudden, unexpected stimulus, such as a loud tone, or in changes of the subjects's thoughts, feelings, or experiences.

3.   Habituation, as discussed earlier, refers to a physiological process of decrease or lack of response to a given stimulus when the stimulus is repeated a number of times. The stimulus loses its novelty and the response habituates. Habituation is measured by the number of repetitions that it takes for the change in resistance to decrease below a certain level. It is used as a measure of reactivity to stress.

The weight of evidence strongly supports the hypothesis that TM substantially increases BSR during meditation, indicating that it probably deactivates the sympathetic nervous system (Wallace, 1970; Wallace et al., 1971; Janby, 1977; Laurie, 1977, West, 1977; Orme-Johnson, 1973; Morse et al., 1977). However, Schwartz (1974) and Cauthen and Prymak (1977) argue against these findings.

In active concentrative meditation, such as tantric yoga, Elson et al. (1977) found an increase in BSR. On the other hand, Corby et al. (1978) found that there is a decrease in Basal Skin Resistance indicating alertness, openness, and the potential for increased sensitivity.

Regarding Spontaneous Skin Resistance Responses (SSRR), the number of responses decreases during Transcendental Meditation (Orme-Johnson, 1973) and during Zazen, an active mindfulness type of meditation (Akishige, 1968). However, Corby et al., (1978), in Tantric yoga practitioners, showed a significant increase in SSRR before and during meditation as opposed to the control group.

Goleman and Schwartz (1976) found that experienced Transcendental Meditators exposed to a stress film showed less of an SSRR increase. Meditating before the film was also beneficial in decreasing the number of SSRRs in both experienced meditators and novices.

In summary, a number of studies demonstrate that in beginning meditators (particularly TM meditators) skin resistance increases and this represents a decreased stimulation of the sympathetic system and reflects the subjective feeling of relaxation, calmness, and quiescence (Wallace, 1970; West, 1977; Morse et al., 1977). In more experienced meditators, there is a decrease in skin resistance indicating alertness, openness, and the potential for increased sensitivity and sympathetic stimulation (Corby et al., 1978).

Meditating and the Respiratory System

Most types of meditation are associated with a decrease in respiratory rate. Student yogic meditators in India typically showed a 40 to 60 percent decrease in the normal respiration rate of 16–18 breaths per minute. More experienced yogis had baseline rates of about six breaths per minute, which stayed the same during meditation (Wenger & Bagchi, 1961). Kasamatsu and Hirai (1973) reported that experienced Zen meditators' respiratory rate decreased to four breaths per minute for prolonged periods.

In Transcendental Meditation (TM) and Relaxation Response (modified version of TM), the respiration rate decreased 10 to 20 percent (Wallace et al., 1971; Morse et al., 1977; Beary et al., 1974). Marked slowing of respiration has also been reported in Tantric yoga meditation (Corby et al., 1978). In some cases, slowing of the respiration rate has continued outside of the meditative period (Dwivedi et al., 1977; Fee & Girdano, 1978).

In highly experienced Zen meditators, oxygen consumption decreased 20 to 30 percent (Sugi & Akutsu, 1964; Kasamatsu & Hirai, 1973). In TM and Relaxation Response, approximately a 5 percent reduction of oxygen consumption has been reported (Wallace et al., 1971; Benson et al., 1978; Warrenburg et al., 1980).

Meditation and the Cardiovascular System

Bagchi and Wenger's (1957) studies of yogic practitioners found no consistent changes in heart rate except in subjects making a conscious attempt to decrease their heartbeat by a variety of physiological maneuvers, but they noticed an overall trend toward stabilization of the heart rate in meditators over a period of time.

Wallace et al. (1971), Morse et al. (1977), and Corby et al. (1978) found that during the practice of TM, there was a 3–12 beats per minute decrease of heart rate. When TM meditators were shown a "stress-producing film" following meditation, their heart rate did not increase as much as did that of the controls (Goleman & Schwartz, 1976). Wallace (1970) reported that TM practitioners show an average 25 percent decrease in cardiac output. This study has not been duplicated.

There are some indications that in borderline hypertensive patients a 5 to 10 percent decrease in blood pressure may occur after meditation. However, these changes disappear by 6 months follow-up, indicating that they may be due to a placebo effect. Progressive relaxation training, biofeedback, and self-hypnosis had a similar effect on these patients (Fee & Girdano, 1978; Benson et al., 1978; Seer & Raeburn, 1980).

The meditative experience decreases susceptibility to stress in the sympathetic nervous system. However, meditation is not a substitute for effective treatment of hypertensive disorders, but may act as adjunct therapy for encouraging self-healing and stress management. Meditation may be useful for prevention of hypertensive disorders.

STRESS, ANXIETY, CANCER, AND QUIESCENCE

Cannon and de la Paz (1911) and Cannon (1929) found that ". . . adrenalin secretion from the medullary part of the adrenal gland creates emotional arousal and prepares the animal physiologically for 'fight or flight'" (Shafii & Shafii, 1982, p. 104). Hans Selye (1946, 1950) defined the above physiological action as the animal and human response to stress. Stress response is essential for adaptation in health and disease.

> Selye discovered that a stressful reaction contributes to activation of the reticular formation and the limbic system of the central nervous system. This activation stimulates the hypothalamus, which secretes cortiocotrophin-releasing factor (CRF). CRF stimulates the anterior pituitary gland. The anterior pituitary gland releases cortiocotrophin (ACTH). ACTH stimulates the cortex of the adrenal gland, which synthesizes adrenocortical hormones, particularly cortisol. Cortisol comprises 80% of the total corticosteroids in the blood.
>
> Also, stimulation of the hypothalamus increases the level of secretion of catecholamines, particularly adrenalin and noradrenalin from the medulla of the adrenal gland, and the cells of the sympathetic and central nervous system. (Shafii & Shafii, 1982, p. 105)

Adrenalin and noradrenalin are thought of as emergency hormones, which prepare animals and human beings for fight or flight. Injection of these hormones induces reactions of anger and fear. Increases in blood cortisol in human beings is associated with increased symptoms of stress and anxiety manifested by feelings of apprehension, fear, and terror, shortness of breath, increased respirations and pulse rate, and heart palpitations. Anxiety is also manifested by restlessness, nervousness, sweating, trembling, shaking, and, in severe cases, with dizziness, fainting, nausea, vomiting, diarrhea, and the fears of dying, going crazy, or loss of control.

Although mild forms of stress response and anxiety in appropriate situations help individuals anticipate realistic danger and prepare for it accordingly, overwhelming anxiety or chronic anxiety contributes to the development of a variety of emotional disorders, such as anxiety, depressive and psychotic disorders, alcohol and drug abuse, or antisocial behavior. A large number of psychophysiological disorders, such as asthma, essential hypertension, diabetes, gastrointestinal ulcers, rheumatoid arthritis, and allergies are closely related to overreaction to stress, chronic anxiety, and disturbances in the autoimmune system.

Modern industrialized life has added significantly to constant overtaxing of physiological flight and fight responses and chronic stress reactions. For instance, environmental noise, driving on busy streets, keeping tight schedules, exposure to stressful daily news and radio and television programs, and lack of physical exercise tax the mind-body systems. These stressors contribute significantly to the development of chronic stress syndrome and a variety of emotional and physiological disorders. New fields are developing in the health sciences, such as biofeedback, behavioral medicine, and psychoneuroendocrinology, for studying human beings' reactions to stress and for finding methods of prevention and treatment.

Recently it has been suggested that a direct relationship exists between increased stress and evidence of cancer. Riley (1981) reported on a study of the effect of stress on mice which had been injected with cancer-producing viruses or cancer cells. He had noticed that the normal, noisy environment of the laboratory setting was quite stressful for mice and that the level of corticosterone in the blood of these stressed mice was almost three times higher than levels in mice kept in a quiet setting. Increased cortiocosterone in the blood contributed to a significant decrease in the number of leucocytes (white blood cells), particularly lymphocytes, and a decrease in the size of the thymus gland. The leucocytes and thymus gland are the part of the autoimmune system which helps in destroying virus cancers, cancer cells, and cancer tumors in mice. Riley noticed that the cancer tumors in stressed mice grew 3–4 times faster than did the tumors in the mice that were kept in a relatively quiet and protected environment, with limited exposure to noise or handling. All of the stressed mice died of a tumor, but a large number of the control group survived.

For example, in one experiment, Riley injected three groups of female mice with mammary tumor virus (MTV). One group (nonparous—never been pregnant) of mice was kept in a low-stress, quiet environment. The other two groups (parous and nonparous) were kept in ". . . conventional, open-rack facilities and thus exposed to long-term environmental stress . . ." (p. 1107). Riley found that the group which was kept in a quiet environment and partially protected against stress ". . . showed a less than 10 percent tumor incidence at 13 months of age . . .", and in stressed groups, the tumor incidence at the same age was 92 percent for the parous group and 68 percent for the nonparous group (p. 1107).

A Sociopsychological Survey

In a sociopsychological survey of 126 individuals who had been involved in the practice of Transcendental Meditation, we found that 92 percent of the respondents felt more relaxed after meditation. These subjects had been meditating 1–2 times per day for about 20 minutes each time over a period of 1–39 months. About 75 percent of these subjects, who were between the ages of sixteen to sixty-five years, reported improved ability to concentrate, and decreased tension, anxiety, and nervousness (Shafii, 1973).

Meditation and the Plasma Cortisol Level

Jevning et al. (1978) found that in 12 long-term (3–5 years) TM meditators, as compared with 5 controls with no previous experience in meditation, the mean level of plasma cortisol in meditators was 5.7 μg percent (microgram percent) in the moments before meditation, decreasing to 4.3 μg percent during meditation, and increasing to 4.9 μg percent following meditation. The plasma cortisol of the controls in a similar setting was 9.6 μg percent before relaxing, 10.2 μg percent during relaxation, and 8.9 μg percent after relaxing. From this study it is evident that meditation contributed to a decrease in plasma cortisol. One might postulate that lower blood cortisol helps to minimize overreaction to stress and increase the competency of the autoimmune system. If these studies are confirmed, exciting new possibilities open for the effective use of meditation and healing silence in the prevention and treatment of cancer and the management of autoimmune disorders.

Meditation and the Plasma Norepinephrine Level

Hoffman et al. (1982), in a crossover study of the effect of the "relaxation response" on 10 experimental subjects and 9 controls, found that plasma norepinephrine levels ". . . under high-stress conditions (upright posture and isometric stress) . . ." (p. 192) were associated with a significant increase of plasma norepinephrine as opposed to that of the control group. They concluded: "These data suggest that in subjects eliciting the relaxation response more NE [norepinephrine] is required to produce the normal compensatory increases . . ." in heart rate and blood pressure (p. 192). According to them, the relaxation response ". . . may reduce adrenergic end-organ responsivity" (p. 192). These findings confirm earlier findings by Michaels et al. (1979) ". . . suggesting that subjects eliciting the relaxation response may be less responsive to stress (Hoffman et al. 1982, p. 192).

MEDITATION AND TYPES OF ANXIETIES

Schwartz et al. (1978), in a psychobiological study, differentiated two types of anxiety which are relatively independent of each other: (1) Somatic, and (2) Cognitive. Somatic anxiety is expressed by bodily changes, such as blushing, increased heartbeat, sweating, dry mouth, palpitation, and increased breathing. Cognitive anxiety is experienced by ". . . conscious awareness of unpleasant feeling about self or external stimuli . . ." (p. 322).

Schalling et al. (1975) developed an anxiety scale with separate subscales for somatic and psychic (cognitive) anxiety. The somatic subscale includes items related to autonomic disturbances, diffuse types of mental discomfort, panic attack, difficulties in concentration, and distractibility. The psychic (cognitive) subscale includes items related to frequent worrying and ". . . pronounced anticipatory reactions as well as prolonged post-stress reactions . . . and increased muscular tension . . . nervousness and lack of self-confidence in social situations" (p. 611). Davidson and Schwartz (1976) further subdivided somatic anxiety into skeletal and autonomic types, and cognitive anxiety into right or left hemispheric types.

Schwartz et al. (1978) conducted a study of 77 persons, of which 44 were involved in a physical exercise class, and the other 33 practiced meditation (TM) at least once daily. All subjects practiced either physical exercise or meditation for at least 1 month, with a median duration of 6 months. All of these subjects were given a cognitive-somatic trait anxiety inventory within the context of a larger battery of psychological tests.

The authors found ". . . that meditators report less cognitive and more somatic anxiety than exercisers and, conversely, exercisers report less somatic and more cognitive anxiety than meditators" (p. 326). They proposed ". . . that anxiety is not a diffuse, undifferentiated internal state, but rather reflects a set of patterns of specific psychobiological processes . . ." (p. 326).

Perhaps the Sufis, Yogis, and Zen masters were aware of somatic and psychic components of anxiety because not only do they emphasize silent meditation to alleviate intrusive thoughts, disjointed and fragmented feelings, and internal anxiety, but they also emphasize physical exercise, such as walking meditation, hatha yoga, and Sufi dances to alleviate somatic anxiety.

ADAPTIVE REGRESSION AND THE BENEFICIAL EFFECTS OF ZEN MEDITATION

Maupin (1965) examined the effects of Zen meditation on a college student population and discussed the effect of meditation from a psychodynamic perspective. Maupin compared individual differences in response to Zen meditation. He noticed that tolerance for unrealistic experiences (accepting experiences which do not agree with the individual's perception of reality) and capacity for adaptive regression (ability to experience irrational thoughts, primary process thinking, and return to one's earlier developmental stages) are related to the individual's capacity to meditate deeply. In contrast, individuals who have extensive difficulty experiencing adaptive regression or who have a tendency toward rationalistic thinking and focusing on outward reality experiences, have difficulty meditating.

Maupin wrote:

> . . . satori seems to fit into the class of psychologically adaptive regressions described in the psychoanalytic literature. The meditation process may then be conceptualized as a sequence of states of regression, ... For example, the early response pattern includes a kind of relaxed drowsiness in which primary-process derivatives appear. The ability to deal with them in an accepting, undisruptive fashion enables the student to get through to the next stage, past alterations in body feelings, to "mirrorlike" detachment, in which more "regressed" elements may emerge. The

"nonstriving" quality of this state, . . . constitutes a safeguard against maladaptive reactions, . . . (p. 196).

According to Maupin, the benefits of Zen meditation are: an effective method of learning to be quiet and attentive; a means of becoming aware of minute cues, signals, and sensations by combining suspension of action and waking attention; enhanced calmness; increased ability to cope with internal and external tension; significant improvement in sleep; improvement in bodily functions; enhanced feeling of oneness between body and mind and a solid feeling of the self; increased awareness of one's experiences; and an increased energy for constructive work and problem solving (p. 179).

CLINICAL THERAPEUTIC TECHNIQUES ADAPTED FROM MEDITATION

For more than half a century, a number of clinical therapeutic techniques have been directly adapted from meditation, such as autogenic training, Happich's meditation therapy, psychosynthesis, Morita therapy, and Naikan therapy. These methods of therapy will be briefly reviewed.

AUTOGENIC TRAINING

Schultz (1932), a German psychiatrist and neurologist, inspired by self-hypnosis and Eastern meditative techniques, developed a therapeutic method which is referred to as "autogenic training." The essence of autogenic training is self-healing through special psychophysiological and meditative exercises. Schultz divided these exercises into *standard exercises*, which are related to physiological functions, and *meditative exercises*, which are related to the psychological and mental functions.

According to Luthe (1963):

> Psychophysiologically, autogenic training is based on three main principles: (a) reduction of exteroceptive and proprioceptive afferent stimulation [through auto suggestion by progressively inducing heaviness and warmth of the extremities, warmth of the solar plexus, coolness of the forehead and calmness and regulation of the heartbeat and respiration]; (b) mental repetition of psychophysiologically adapted verbal formulas; and (c) mental activity conceived as "passive concentration." (p. 311)

The patient is instructed in meditative exercises after being trained for a period of 6–12 months in standard exercises and is able to experience the above-mentioned autogenic states for up to 40 minutes without any evidence of side effects.

> The meditative series begins with passive concentration on phenomena of visual imagination, as, for example, the spontaneous experience of certain colors. Later, the trainee may focus on seeing all colors at will. When that is achieved, the meditative series continues with visual imagination of objects. This training phase may take several weeks before results are obtained. It is followed by imagining abstract concepts like "happiness" or "justice" in different sensual modalities (musical, chromatic, plastic). Still later, one may meditate on one's own feelings and, in contrast, try to invoke the image of another person. (p. 314).

Schultz and Luthe strongly suggested that autogenic training should be performed under the guidance of an experienced physician or therapist, who personally has had experience in all phases of this training. Significant improvement has been reported in patients suffering from psychological or organic disorders, such as sleep disorders, asthma, anxiety neurosis, and cardiac and hypertensive disorders. Some of the physiological changes observed in the subject's EEG and EKG following autogenic training resemble the changes in meditation.

Happich's Meditation Therapy

Carl Happich (1932, 1939, 1948), a German internist, developed an elaborate meditative technique based on visual imagery for therapeutic and spiritual purposes.

> The technique . . . is meditation of the most systematic kind, and also of the widest human scope. It begins with physiology and ends in religion. Happich developed it out of his literary and practical knowledge of Oriental techniques. He combined their wisdom with the experience of modern depth psychology. (Kretschmer, 1962, p. 220).

Happich believed that the collective unconscious expresses itself through symbols. He emphasized breathing exercises and guided visual imagery. After helping the patient come gradually into tune with the physiological rhythms of the body through exercises, he advised various visual meditative exercises, such as going to a meadow, passing through a forest on the way to a mountain, going to a chapel, and listening to the murmur of water.

According to Happich, the meadow, mountain, and chapel have not only personal associative symbolic significance, but also have "archetypal" significance which, on a deeper meditative level, stimulates feelings, emotions, and internal psychospiritual experiences. For example, the meadow he feels represents the peace and beauty of Mother Nature and also youth and the mother-child relationship; the forest represents darkness, the unknown, fear, and demons; climbing the mountain represents sublimation and psychospiritual transformation; and the chapel represents

> . . . the innermost rooms of his the meditator's psyche where he faces the simple question of how he relates to the possibilities of psychic transformation within man. When the meditator is able to comprehend the symbolic significance of the chapel, he can learn to use it to uncover and face in himself the central problems of human life. (p. 222).

After mastering specific visual meditative experiences, Happich suggested a higher level of meditation, such as meditating on the abstract design of a *Mandala. Mandala* is a Sanskrit word meaning "circle." In Tibetan Buddhism, mandalas of various shapes and forms are used as objects of meditation. Finally, the meditators are asked to meditate upon a word which is similar to the use of *mantra* in Yoga and *zikr* in Sufism.

These meditative exercises were found useful in the psychotherapeutic treatment of patients suffering from anxiety neurosis, varieties of depression, phobias, obsessional neurosis, and feelings of emptiness, loneliness, and isolation. Individuals are advised not to practice these meditations by themselves, but only under the close supervision and guidance of an experienced psychotherapist-meditator.

Kretschmer, more than 20 years ago, with foresight wrote:

> Meditation has a good chance of eventually becoming one of the leading therapeutic techniques. All the newer systems [of psychotherapy] . . . look for a development in this direction. But whether or not this development takes place depends completely on a deep-going reformulation of psychotherapeutic training and the practice of psychotherapy . . . . We can only hope that psychotherapy will continue to develop into a genuine technique which can aid men in their goal of developing their highest psychic potentialities. (p. 228).

Psychosynthesis

Roberto Assagioli (1965), the Italian physician and psychoanalyst, transcended the therapeutic limitations of psychoanalysis and developed the school of psychosynthesis. Assagioli synthesized and integrated the techniques employed in psychoanalysis and dynamic psychotherapy, such as free association, verbalization, and the transference phenomena, with meditative practices, such as guided visual imagery and Sufi symbolic meditations. For example, in regard to the evolution and development of the higher self, which Assagioli referred to as spiritual psychosynthesis, he recommended the special meditative "exercise of the blossoming of the rose." He wrote:

> The flower has been regarded and used as a symbol of the Soul, of the spiritual Self, of Divinity in both the East and West. China adopted the image of the "Golden Flower," while India and Tibet adopted the lotus (in appearance similar to the water-lily), which has its roots in the earth, its stem in the water, and its petals in the air, where they open under the rays of the sun. In Persia and Europe the rose has been extensively used. (p. 213).

In Sufism, the open rose symbolizes the soul, spirit, and Beloved Reality. The nightingale symbolizes the Sufi seeker's constant search for closeness and communion with the Beloved. The thorns of the rose symbolize the hardship and suffering which the seeker experiences on the path of Reality.

Assagioli adopted from the Sufis the practice of visualizing oneself as a closed rosebud that gradually opens, symbolizing the opening of the center of one's consciousness. This meditation is prescribed to the patients and is practiced over and over.

> The results with patients have varied greatly in different cases; but sometimes they have been apparently out of all proportions to the simplicity of the exercise. There has resulted with some patients a true Self-realization, and awakening of hitherto latent inner qualities that certainly speed up the healing process. (p. 215)

Morita Therapy

Carpenter (1977) discussed the contribution of meditation and Buddhism to psychotherapy in Japan. Buddhism, similar to Sufism, suggests that ". . . the cause of human suffering is man's natural inclination toward dualistic thinking, namely partitioning the world into 'I' and 'other' . . ." (p. 395)

The mission of a Zen master, similar to that of a psychotherapist, is helping the individual gain ". . . insight into repetitive, self-defeating patterns of behavior, desensitization of painful thoughts, and the conditioning of the central nervous system" (p. 394).

A number of psychotherapeutic methods have evolved in Japan from Zen Buddhism integrating meditative practices in the therapeutic process. The foremost of these is Morita therapy, which was developed by Shoma Morita in the 1930s (Kora & Sato, 1958).

Morita therapy, similar to Buddhism or Sufism, perceives that

> . . . neurotic suffering is due to egocentricity—attachment to one's image of oneself; as a therapeutic technique that is similar to the Zen Buddhist disciplines and aims to bring about a detachment from one's ego through an intense personal experience leading to insight to one's nature. (Carpenter, 1977, p. 396)

In Morita therapy, the patient is usually hospitalized, and undergoes four stages of treatment.

1. *Total Bedrest (4–7 days)*

   The patient is isolated from others and is only involved in eating and toilet activities. The patient is also isolated from outside stimuli. This stage of treatment is similar to anaclitic therapy (Azima et al., 1961) and to ". . . a Jungian rebirth episode" (Carpenter, 1977, p. 397). The patient's anxieties gradually decrease during this period of isolation. A decrease in neurotic and psychopathological behaviors also occurs. This period of isolation is similar to meditative retreats under the supervision of a guide in Zen Buddhism or the practice of *Chilla* (40 days' retreat) in Sufism (chapter 2).

2. *Light work (3–7 days)*

   During this second stage, the patient stays in his or her room, but is involved in some form of light work or occupational therapy. The patient is expected to keep a daily diary of experiences, but is not allowed to read, watch television, listen to music, or go out of the room, nor to interact with other patients.

3.   *Heavy Work (7 days)*
The patient is required to do heavy work, even though experiencing pain and discomfort and is allowed to read.

4.   *Life Training Period (1–2 weeks)*
The patient now resumes previous daily work part-time, while still living in the hospital. After successful completion of this period, the patient is discharged.

During hospitalization, the patient has frequent contact with the physician who, ". . . much like the Zen Master . . . answers questions and makes observations on the patient's progress." (Carpenter, 1977, p. 397)

Naikan Therapy

Naikan Therapy is a form of intensive short-term meditation-psychotherapy. The patient is isolated from others for a period of 7 days, beginning the day at 5:30 A.M. by doing naikan meditation exercises. The patient continuously meditates throughout the day until 9:00 P.M., the only interruptions being for eating and personal hygiene.

The patient is supervised very closely by the therapist and is visited every 90 minutes. He or she is required to meditate on various prearranged themes and topics related to "(1) rediscovery of personal responsibility for selfish and irrational behavior toward others in the past; and (2) the discovery of grateful feelings toward those individuals who helped the patient in the past" (Carpenter, 1977, p. 398).

Japanese psychotherapists have more actively integrated Zen Buddhist meditative practices in treatment of psychiatric and psychophysiological disorders. They are years ahead of us in integrating healing practices of the past with modern health sciences.

MEDITATION AND DYNAMIC PSYCHOTHERAPY

Meditation and an Outpatient Psychiatric Population

Bloomfield et al. (1975) and Bloomfield and Kory (1978) have written extensively on the psychotherapeutic significance of meditation, particularly Transcendental Meditation. They reported that in more than 100 psychiatric patients who meditated while under psychiatric care, most experienced enhanced well-being, and a decrease of tension and anxiety, symptoms of obsessive-compulsive neurosis, depression, drug abuse, and psychophysiological disorders. These patients recovered more quickly and spent a shorter period in psychotherapy. After termination of the treatment, the patients who continued to meditate were freer from recurrence of emotional disorders. They experienced a feeling of robust health, effectiveness, and productivity. According to Bloomfield, meditation is not only an effective psychotherapeutic method, but also has significant preventive potential.

Meditation and an Inpatient Psychiatric Population

Glueck and Stroebel (1975) compared EEG alpha biofeedback training, autogenic training, and passive *mantra* meditation (TM) in a number of patients who were admitted to a psychiatric hospital. Of the 187 patients who were taught to meditate, 17 percent stopped meditating regularly, although some of them were meditating occasionally (only 6 percent totally stopped meditating).

Ninety-six patients completed an 8-week intensive course in meditation. Of these patients, 54, as compared to a matched control group ". . . showed a greater level of improvement rates . . ." (p. 309). The patients who were taught to meditate experienced more side effects with psychotropic medications and frequently requested that the medications be decreased or discontinued. Patients who had been meditating showed a decrease in the symptoms of anxiety and depression along with an increase in self-reliance and self-healing. The authors concluded that meditation added significantly to the hospital treatment program. Patients who were instructed in alpha EEG biofeedback for generalized relaxation or autogenic training did not show significant improvement as compared to the meditative group.

It is important to keep in mind that meditation may be useful as an adjunct for the treatment of both inpatient and outpatient psychiatric populations, rather than as a substitute for traditional psychotherapeutic or clinical management.

Carrington (1977) stated:

> Taken together, the research studies and clinical observations suggest that while the effects of meditation can be impressive, it is doubtful whether meditation can change personality in any

basic sense. To effect truly deep change meditation may need to become part of a more general change in the way one lives one's life. However, practical meditation [TM] does reduce tension and improve functioning on a number of levels. (p. 275).

According to Carrington, meditation is not a substitute for psychotherapy, but ". . . the possibilities of using meditation along with psychotherapy . . ." are quite encouraging. (p. 279).

Carrington suggested that meditation is contraindicated for seriously disturbed patients who are not currently involved in psychotherapy:

> While it *may* be effective as a sole treatment, in some instances it creates difficulties for emotionally disturbed people because of the unusually intense stress-release that such an individual may undergo. It is therefore desirable for such a person to be under the care of a trained psychotherapist while adjusting to meditation. (p. 279).

MEDITATION AND THE PREVENTION OF ALCOHOL, MARIJUANA, AND DRUG ABUSE

Clinical experience with patients who were able to free themselves from the use of marijuana, mescaline, and LSD made me wonder some time ago whether the effect of meditation was limited to a few specific individuals, or if it had preventive and therapeutic possibilities on a larger scale.

Also, at that time, Benson and Wallace presented their work on the effect of Transcendental Meditation on the decrease of drug abuse, which was then published a year or so later in 1972. Benson and Wallace gave questionnaires to ". . . approximately 1,950 subjects who had been practicing Transcendental Meditation for three months or more and who were attending . . . meditation training courses . . ." (p. 370) and of these, 1,862 responded. The average length of time the subjects had been meditating was 20 months.

Eighty percent of the subjects used marijuana during the 6-month period before meditation. Six months after beginning the practice of meditation, 37 percent continued the use of marijuana, and 21 months following initiation to meditation, only 12 percent continued the use. There was also a significant decrease or discontinuation of LSD, barbiturates, alcohol, and cigarettes.

We repeated this study using a non-biased questionnaire and a matched control group (Shafii et al, 1974). We found that in 126 meditators and 90 controls, 92 percent of the meditators who had practiced meditation for more than 2 years significantly decreased their use of marijuana. Of this group, during the first 3 months following initiation to meditation, 69 percent totally stopped their use of marijuana, as compared to 15 percent of the control group. We noticed that the longer an individual practiced meditation, the greater was the decrease or discontinuance of marijuana use.

We also noticed a significant decrease or discontinuance of the use of alcohol, cigarettes, hallucinogens, narcotics, nonprescribed barbiturates, tranquilizers, and stimulants in meditators as compared to the control group (Shafii et al., 1975).

It is not clear at this time whether meditation can assist in the treatment of individuals with severe chronic alcoholism, narcotic addiction, or drug abuse. But, one can conclude that the practice of meditation can be an effective method for the *prevention* of marijuana, alcohol, cigarette, and drug abuse.

THE CLINICIAN AS A MEDITATOR

A number of authors have written about the need for clinicians having personal experiences in the practice of meditation in order to become more in tune with and sensitive to their patients' communications, and for handling the stresses of clinical practice more effectively. Having personal experience in the practice of meditation is particularly helpful when the clinician is working with patients who are meditating, or, especially, when the clinician wishes to prescribe meditation as a form of treatment (Schultz, 1932, 1958; Luthe, 1963; Maupin, 1965; Lesh, 1970; Tart, 1971; Shafii, 1973; Bloomfield and Kory, 1978).

Carrington (1977), a practicing psychologist and psychotherapist, reported that after she and her psychiatrist spouse began meditating, they found that their professional skills improved, in that they experienced sharpened sensitivity to their patients' moods (pp. 281–284), and effortless awareness of their patients' deeper unconscious struggles and conflicts (p. 281). Occasionally, they found that when they were meditating they experienced mental and symbolic imagery which helped them to develop further insight into a particular patient's problem. Meditation also enhanced their understanding of symbolic representations in patients' dreams. They became more in tune with the patients' primary process material. They noticed an improvement in their ability to cope with the patients' negative reactions and hostility. Above all, they experienced an increase in evenly suspended attention to the patients' conscious, unconscious, verbal, and nonverbal communications (pp. 281–284).

In summary, the following changes may occur in a clinician or therapist who is actively and sincerely involved in the practice of meditation:

1. Increased awareness of physiological functions and invisible rhythms of one's self and the patient;

2. Increased alertness and attentiveness;

3. Decreased fragmentation, disjointedness, and thought intrusion;

4. Increased ability to listen to the patients' and others' verbal and nonverbal communication;

5. Enhanced empathy;

6. Ability to experience momentary oneness with the patient;

7. Experience of serenity, security, competence, and confidence;

8. Awareness of other dimensions in the healing process beyond techniques and procedures;

9. Realization that the relationship between the patient and clinician may have a healing effect beyond present scientific and cognitive understanding;

10. Being in tune with the patient's spiritual dimension and encouraging healing of the body, mind, and spirit concomitantly;

11. Openly receiving irrational, illogical, or unexplainable behavior or phenomena without bias or undue value judgement;

12. Ability to sit in silence with a patient and accept openly the patient's silence as a vehicle for healing rather than having to interpret the silence as resistance, avoidance, or hostility (chapter 4).

ADVERSE EFFECTS OF MEDITATION

In mystical traditions of the East, such as Sufism, Yoga, and Zen Buddhism, meditation is not prescribed indiscriminately. In chapter 2 we discussed, for example, that in classical Sufism, after 3 years of evaluation, testing, and retesting of the seeker's sincerity, commitment, and personality strength, he or she may be initiated to the circle of meditation.

In the West in recent years, with modifications of some of the Eastern meditative methods, meditation has become popularized and, unfortunately, oversold. It has been promised as a panacea for all ills. Anyone who is curious about or interested in practicing meditation can, by merely paying a sum of money, become initiated into a variety of meditative techniques. The supermarket of meditative techniques in the United States is mind-boggling. Moving from one technique to another, from one guru to another, and from one group to another, is quite common. Indiscriminate use of meditation without close and continuous supervision has pitfalls, dangers, and side effects.

Meditation is based on a dyadic relationship between two people, two souls, transcending books, methods, *mantras*, and self-proclaimed gurus. This dyadic relationship is similar to the relationship of a seed to the earth, which needs silence, quiescence, patience, and continuous nurturance. The *pir* or the guide functions as the earth and, at the same time, as the gardener. The seedling needs continuous care and, particularly, pruning to deepen its roots.

When one is meditating or prescribing meditation, one needs to be aware of adverse effects which have been known throughout the ages. A discussion of some of these effects follows:

1. Active Regression

Meditation is a powerful experience which can drastically change or at least initially destabilize the initiate's life, internal experiences, and self-perceptions. From a psychodynamic perspective, active regression occurs. Increased awareness of sensory perceptions and flooding of primary process thinking, in the form of increased dreams, fantasies, and illusions and sleeplessness, may occur. In some cases, extensive catharsis of emotions by the process of disinhibition and alleviation of repression and suppression may ensue. In an individual who already has a very shaky and tenuous relationship with reality and is vulnerable to the forces of pathological regression, the practice of meditation may be like opening Pandora's box. In some cases, acute psychotic regression, overwhelming anxiety, personality fragmentation, and autistic withdrawal may occur.

Sufism, perhaps more than any other mystical tradition, has been aware of the active regressive pull of meditation. The Sufis recognized that even in a relatively healthy and strong personality a period of temporary derangement (*junun*—acute regression) may occur. Sufis also refer to this acute regression as *masti*, which means intoxication and drunkenness. The seeker in actuality becomes intoxicated with the practice of meditation. He or she may behave irrationally, and give up work and daily habits. The seeker may openly express extreme forms of emotion, such as joy, ecstasy, or sadness. At times, the seeker may speak irrationally, experience autistic withdrawal, or refuse to eat, sleep, or attend to personal hygiene. During this stage, the seeker needs close care and supervision by the Sufi *pir* and the group support of the other Sufis.

The Sufi *pir* may directly recommend a decrease of meditation time, and an increased involvement in daily tasks, such as serving others. The *pir* may also advise individual sessions. If the seeker's acute regression is profound, the *pir* may advise a decrease of meditative exercises, suggest physical exercises, and outside reality-oriented work to modulate and modify the extent of regression. Seekers gradually, with the help of an experienced *pir*, overcome this period of acute and temporary regression and become versatile in adapting and adjusting the length and depth of meditation.

Drunkenness (*masti*) is usually a sign of one's unripeness and overintoxication. If it continues for some time, it is perceived as a sign of immaturity, self-centeredness, and a tendency toward showing off, which can be a great hindrance on the path of integration. The Sufis use the metaphor of comparing the goblet of wine to a seeker's capacity for meditative experiences. The smaller the goblet, the less wine it can hold. The Sufi's ability to expand the inner self for experiencing the wine of meditation without outward uncontrolled manifestations is related to the potential for further growth and integration.

Recently there have been a number of reports in the literature concerning the side effects of meditation—particularly Transcendental Meditation, and the experience of acute regression and psychosis. Walsh and Roche (1979) reported on three patients who had experienced psychotic episodes after involvement in intensive meditation. These patients had a history of schizophrenia. After intensive involvement in meditation, they discontinued antipsychotic medication and also began practicing fasting and sleep deprivation, resulting in pathological regression and the recurrence of psychosis.

Nystul and Garde (1979) compared regular Transcendental Meditators with dropout meditators and nonmeditators. The researchers administered the Tennessee Self-Concept Scale twice over a period of 6 months to all three of these groups. They found that regular meditators and nonmeditators, as compared with the dropout meditators, had significantly fewer characteristics associated with psychosis. Regular meditators, as compared to nonmeditators, had more characteristics associated with personality integration and positive self-esteem.

2. Unstressing

In the initial phase of practicing Transcendental Meditation (TM), the meditators may experience agitation, restlessness, headache, insomnia, anxiety, upset stomach, hyperventilation, or fears. The experience of these phenomena is called "unstressing" by the teachers of TM. They feel that this is a natural occurrence in the initial phase of TM, which, following a short period of time (a few days to a few weeks), will dissipate. Because of the possibility of the occurrence of "unstressing," TM teachers strongly recommend that initiates be "checked" a few times to be sure that they are assuming correct postures and are breathing their *mantra* correctly. If "unstressing" continues, it is felt that a change of *mantra* may be indicated.

Otis compared the adverse effects (unstressing) of TM in the following groups:

a.   *Dropout Group* (N121). After an average of 7.4 months of meditation, this group discontinued the practice of TM.

b.   *Novice meditators* (N156). This group had been practicing TM for 3–6 months with an average of 4.2 months.

c.   *Experienced meditators* (N78). This group had been practicing TM for 18 months or more with an average of 22.7 months.

To the researcher's surprise, the dropouts reported many less complaints and adverse symptoms while meditating, as compared to the meditators. The experienced meditators manifested more symptoms of anxiety, confusion, depression, antisocial behavior, and frustrations, as opposed to the novice meditators or dropouts. These symptoms were not short-lived as suggested by the TM teachers, but continued throughout the meditative experience. To explain this, the author suggested that it could be possible that meditation makes a person more sensitive and aware of problems, and also more open and willing to report them. But, he felt that it was more likely that meditation, itself, in some individuals, has adverse effects.

At the same time, 64 percent of the subjects who continued meditation did not report even a single adverse effect. According to Otis,

> Nevertheless, adverse effects do occur in a sizable percentage of those that take up the practice. Furthermore, the probability of occurrence of adverse effects is higher among psychiatric populations. Accordingly, clinicians that incorporate TM, and possibly other relaxation or meditational techniques into their practice, should be vigilant about the possible occurrence of adverse effects and be prepared to deal with them. Experience indicates that frequent, if not daily monitoring of psychiatric patients trained to meditate is advisable. (In Press.)

3. Increased Responsiveness to Medication

As you may recall, Glueck and Stroebel (1975) reported on psychiatric patients who had been taught TM. These patients had increased unacceptable side effects with psychotropic medications and requested significant decrease or discontinuation of their medication.

Benson (1978) noticed that patients who practice Relaxation Response may need significantly lower doses of medication to avoid overdosage. Overdosage may particularly occur in the case of diabetic patients who are taking insulin or in hypertensive patients who are taking propranolol.

Wesch (1977) reported on a patient who, following a thyroidectomy was on thyroxine replacement therapy. This patient was being treated for migraine headaches with thermal electromyographic (EMG) feedback. The patient began to show signs of hyperthyroidism and the dose of thyroxine needed to be decreased to alleviate the symptoms.

4. Decreased Tolerance for Alcohol

Some meditators report a decreased tolerance for wine, beer, or alcohol. They also experienced headaches and lack of pleasure when drinking alcohol, as compared to when they did not meditate.

5. Insomnia

In some individuals, meditation just before going to sleep is not advisable because it alleviates fatigue, drowsiness, and induces hyperarousal which contributes to insomnia.

6. Withdrawal

Individuals with a proclivity for passivity and withdrawal may experience further intensification of these behaviors following meditation. For these individuals, walking meditation, work meditation (service to others), group chanting, Sufi dances, and Hatha Yoga may be indicated rather than passive meditation.

7. Intensification of Severe Psychopathological Disorders

In severe cases of schizophrenia, depression, phobia, anxiety, obsessive compulsiveness, and borderline personality disorder, meditation is not indicated. First, the patient needs to recover from the severe emotional disorder. Then, work meditation or other forms of physically active meditation or exercises, such as Hatha Yoga, may be useful as adjunct therapy. If the patient insists on meditating, short periods of quiescence (2–5 minutes) daily, while counting one's breath may be advised. If the patient tolerates these short periods of quiescence, they may be gradually increased under the daily supervision of an experienced meditator-clinician.

8. Anesthesia

Although I have not seen any report on the effect of meditation on anesthesia, one may postulate that because meditators are more responsive to medication, they may need a lesser amount of analgesic or anesthetic agents.

9. Decrease or Increase of Appetite

Many meditators report a decrease in habitual and automatic eating behavior. A few experienced meditators reported that following deep meditation and ecstasy, they develop a "ravenous" appetite.

10. Withdrawal Symptoms

Some meditators, if they do not meditate for a day or two, report experiencing mild withdrawal symptoms, such as increased tension, grouchiness, restlessness, edginess, anxiety, headache, disjointedness, and the feeling that "something is missing." They report that they tire more easily. Some need more coffee, tea, or colas, or they smoke more cigarettes.

Otis reported that a few TM meditators noticed withdrawal symptoms following discontinuation of TM; these symptoms included headache, insomnia, restlessness, anxiety, and gastrointestinal upset. After resuming meditation, their symptoms disappeared.

Sufis have been aware of the possibility of becoming habituated to meditation. Because of this, the time comes when the Sufi *pir* suggests that the Sufi meditator needs to free him or herself from the ritual of sitting meditation. One is encouraged to integrate the practice of meditation in every moment of life, rather than just during a special time of the day (chapter 2). According to the Sufis, habituation to meditation itself can be a hindrance on the path, and may become a source of self-indulgence and self-aggrandizement.

In the following chapter, we will explore the psychoanalytic perception of silence in the West, and then discuss the creative and integrative aspects of silence in meditation from a psychoanalytic and ego psychological perspective.

Chapter 4

CREATIVE AND INTEGRATIVE SILENCE

Psychoanalytic Study of Meditation[1]

Only silence before the Thou—
silence of *all* tongues, silent
patience in the undivided word
that precedes the formed and vocal
response—leaves the *Thou* free . . .

Buber, Jewish philosopher-mystic,
20th century.

Psychoanalysis and dynamic psychotherapies in the West emphasize
verbalization in the therapeutic situation as a means of achieving understanding and insight of the self and its *modus operandi* (chapter 2).
Quiescence and silence are often interpreted as resistance, defensive
inhibition, guardedness, and a block to self-realization and integration.

[1]An earlier version of this chapter was published in *International Journal of
Psychoanalysis*, 1973, *54*, 431–443, under the title *Silence in the service of ego:
Psychoanalytic study of meditation.*

The significance of silence in the meditative situation for the development of internal peace and harmony has yet to be appreciated.

The experience of silence is a mysterious phenomenon. It is surprising to find that very little has been written on this subject in the psychological and psychiatric literature. However, there are a few significant contributions to the understanding of silence in the psychoanalytic literature. In most of the psychoanalytic studies, silence is conceptualized as a form of inhibition, withholding, transference resistance, and severe ego regression. Only a few authors have emphasized the integrative, creative, and adaptive aspects of silence.

I hypothesize that, in meditation, silence and quiescence represent a temporary, controlled, deep regression in the service of the ego for development, adaptation, and integration. This controlled regression helps the individual re-experience union with an earlier love object on a preverbal level of psychosexual development similar to regression in the service of the ego in the creative processes and in the psychoanalytic situation. *The re-experiencing of earlier cumulative trauma in the silence of meditation facilitates the individual's ability to deal with earlier traumatic experiences beyond verbalization and cognitive awareness.* This contributes to relative freedom from intrapsychic conflicts, and to the experience of internal peace and harmony. Meditation, in the context of developmental ego psychology, is an integrative and adaptive phenomenon, rather than a pathological experience.

PSYCHOANALYTIC ATTITUDE TOWARD SILENCE

In most psychological schools of thought, very little attention has been given to the examination and significance of silence in human development. Descriptive psychiatry has made phenomenological references to silence in the severe forms of psychopathology such as catatonia, mutism, melancholic depression, and childhood autism. In this context, the patient's silence, or inability to use language as a form of communication, is equated with evidence of psychosis, disturbance of reality testing and/or severe withdrawal from the environment.

Silence and Separation Anxiety

However, we know that children as early as 6 months of age equate silence with the absence of mother and show extreme fear and anxiety when left alone. Bowlby (1960) refers to this phenomenon as "separation anxiety" (chapter 1). Children of this age are reassured by hearing their mother's voice, even if she is in another room. Before going to sleep, the child is often comforted by his mother's voice and, when this reassurance is not given, the child may feel lonely and helpless.

It is a common phenomenon for children during their second year of life to have temporary forms of sleep disturbances. These disturbances are often developmentally phase-appropriate and are attributed to the fears of losing control and abandonment (Fraiberg, 1950, p. 285). Bedtime and going to sleep usually mean separation from mother, quietness, darkness, and silence, so it is understandable how children associate silence and quiescence with the fear of separation from mother and loneliness.

Fear of silence in childhood and adulthood may be related to the fear of separation from mother during the first few years of life. The avoidance of psychological exploration and study of silence may have its roots in our repressed unconscious fear of silence.

Silence as Resistance

Psychoanalysis has contributed to the understanding of the role of silence as a form of communication with multiple-level meanings by emphasizing the active quiescence of the psychoanalyst and the verbalization of the patient. Freud (1912) related the patient's silence to transference and resistance:

> For our experience has shown us—and the fact can be confirmed as often as we please—that if a patient's free associations fail, the stoppage can invariably be removed by an assurance that he is being dominated at the moment by an association which is concerned with the doctor himself or with something connected with him. (p. 101).

In the footnote to this statement, Freud added: "I mean when they really cease, and not when, for instance, the patient keeps them back owing to ordinary feelings of unpleasure." Freud wondered about the patient's silence which disregards ". . . the fundamental rule of psychoanalysis which lays it down that whatever comes into one's head must be reported without criticizing it . . ." (p. 101) In this context, Freud viewed the patient's silence in the psychoanalytic situation as *"the most powerful resistance"* of the transference phenomena (p. 101).

Ferenczi (1916–17), on the role of verbalization as a form of discharge of instinctual desires, conceptualized the silence of an obses-

sional patient as a sign of anal eroticism (pp. 250–252). In his formulation, silence was viewed as anal retentiveness, holding, hoarding,
and keeping all feelings within (chapter 1). In this situation, the patient
was encouraged to overcome silence.

Silence as Communication

The task of understanding the psychological meaning of silence
and the impact of the analyst's silence on the transference situation
was finally undertaken by Reik in 1926, in a lecture to the Vienna
Psychoanalytic Society on *The Psychological Meaning of Silence*. It took
more than 40 years for this paper to be translated into English. Reik,
with the acumen of a clinician and the foresight of a psychoanalytic
theoretician, examined the significance of silence and the role of nonverbal communication in psychoanalysis. He stressed that:

> Speaking is in any case the central point of analysis but . . . it is
> nevertheless not correct to attribute the effect of analysis entirely
> to the word. I believe it would be more correct to say that
> psychoanalysis shows the power of the word and the power of
> silence. So much has been said about the subject of talking in
> analysis, that the emotional effect of silence has been almost com-
> pletely overlooked. (p. 173).

Reik also discussed the patient's reaction to the analyst's silence:

> If we follow the reactions of the person being analysed to the
> analyst's silence from the beginning on, it becomes clearly recog-
> nizable that an abbreviated repetition of an old experience is
> mirrored in the course of treatment. It is as if at this point there
> is a return of feelings, which played an important role in the
> patient's relationship to an old love object—from the original
> tenderness to the embitterment over an imagined or actual denial.
> (p. 181).

Reik emphasized the role of object relationship in the psychogenetic formulation of the ability to tolerate silence: ". . . analytic practice
shows that behind a fear of silence stands the unconscious fear of loss
of love . . . people often speak because they cannot bear silence" (p.
184). Reik concluded his paper by associating silent episodes in the
psychoanalytic hour with compulsion to repeat, which will be discussed
later in this chapter.

Contributions of Kris (1952, 1956), Balint (1958), Greenson (1961,

1966) and Nacht (1964), with their vivid and clear exploration of the synthetic and integrative functions of silence, have enriched the psychoanalytic literature. The most extensive psychoanalytic study of silence was presented in a panel, chaired by Loewenstein (1961), on *The Silent Patient* with major contributions by Arlow, Greenson, Loomie, Van der Heide and Zeligs.

Arlow (1961) stated: "Silence in analysis is different from other silences. It has a unique quality by virtue of a special relationship which exists between patient and therapist" (p. 47). He perceived the patient's silence as a form of conscious concealment of information related to the intense relationship between the patient and the analyst and motivated by feelings of ". . . shame, fear, spite, anger, . . ." (p. 48).

Arlow elaborated further on silence as a sign of regression to the preverbal level of psychosexual development and as a manifestation of a temporary ego disturbance:

> Further in the course of regression the derivatives of preverbal experiences may appear or highly complex emotional states or physical sensations may be experienced, situations which are not only confusing but for which a ready reserve of verbal images is hardly available . . . . Silence during analytic treatment is essentially an ego disturbance of longer or shorter duration. (p. 48).

Greenson (1961) recognized that silence is not always indicative of resistance but ". . . may itself be the content which the patient is trying to convey" (p. 80). He felt that the patient may communicate the traumatic memories of seeing or hearing the parents' sexual relationship in the form of restlessness, agitation, and "wide-eyed silence." Clinically he observed that: "Silence with open eyes is more likely to be derived from hatred and rejection whereas silence with closed eyes is usually derived from love and acceptance" (p. 82).

The patient's reaction to analytic interpretation is often manifested by silence as though the patient requires a "silent time" to feel, examine, and integrate new insight. Prolonged silence following interpretation usually indicates improper timing or incorrectness of interpretation (p. 83).

Loomie (1961) reached the following conclusion: "To some extent the chronically silent patient can be considered delinquent toward the basic rule of analysis" (p. 72). With these patients he suggested a modification of the analytic technique wherein the analyst attempts to offer ". . . himself as a model for a less rigid superego and more flexible ego" (p. 77).

Van der Heide (1961) felt that "... the experience of a shared, mutual silence occasionally outweighs in importance the ideational content ... analysis really does not move until the talkative patient becomes silent" (p. 85). He discussed the phenomenon of "blank silence" which he described as "... a special form of transient, often recurrent cessation of speech. It is perhaps best defined as a temporary, functional ego regression, defensive in nature and indicative of a considerable alteration of the dominant object relation" (p. 85). He related this silence to orality and noted that it is most common in the analysis of regressed patients (chapter 1). Blank silence is that which occurs when the patient becomes silent for quite a few minutes or for the rest of an analytic session. The patient at this time is relaxed on the couch and there is no evidence of motor activity. Often after the termination of this silence the analyst is told "... that thoughts were absent and there is no evidence of conscious withholding of thoughts or fantasy" (p. 86). Van der Heide formulated that "... blank silence represents fusion with the object and blissful narcissistic sleep without manifest interference" (p. 87). Silence is seen as a defensive regression in a very disturbed patient.

Zeligs (1961), in a comprehensive study of the psychology of silence, evaluated the meaning of silence in a twenty-seven-year-old unmarried woman patient. From the beginning of her analysis, she fell into long silent periods which persisted on and off for 3 years. He conceptualized multiple-level meanings of silence in this patient at various times. Silence represented revenge against mother, teasing men, fear of aggression, fear of being attacked, death, and death wishes toward her brother, oral and anal respiratory fantasies, re-repression of thoughts, defense against exhibitionism, autohypnotic evasion, feelings of unreality, struggle with identity, and struggle for power (pp. 31–40).

In summary, throughout the preceding studies, silence was conceptualized in the following ways: transference resistance, withholding, severe regressive fusion or as a struggle with the analyst for power and control. The analysts' purpose was to understand the patients' silence and to help them overcome their silent posture in order to verbalize thoughts and fantasies. Silence was not perceived or explored as an adaptive, integrative, and creative experience.

PSYCHOANALYTIC STUDY OF MEDITATION

In early psychoanalytic writings, personal religious experiences, mysticism, and meditation were conceptualized as infantile, regressive, and maladaptive phenomena described as oceanic fusion, oneness with mother, and the wish for re-experiencing intrauterine life (Freud, 1930, pp. 65–67).

In the past, psychoanalysts have not attempted to examine the healing and growth-producing potential of the psycho-religious practices of the East such as meditation in Yoga, Zen Buddhism, and Sufism. However, Fromm (Suzuki et al., 1960) and Fingarette (1963) have compared the similarities and differences of Zen Buddhism and other mystical practices with psychoanalysis (chapters 2 and 5).

Bakan (1958) proposed that the development of psychoanalysis had its origin in the Hassadic milieu and in the mystical tradition of Cabala (p. 25). Striking, significant similarities exist in the meditative, chanting, and dancing practices of Jewish Mysticism, Sufism, Yoga, and Zen Buddhism.

Similarities Between Meditation and the Psychoanalytic Situation

In examining human behavior closely, one notices that we are constantly *doing something*, such as walking, talking, thinking or fantasizing. Most of these behaviors are habitual and repetitive. Frequently internal drives and conflicts gain *partial* discharge and expression through these repetitive activities.

In the psychoanalytic situation, lying down on a couch brings body movement to a minimum and encourages verbalization of free-associated thoughts and fantasies. De-emphasized are repetitive daily behaviors such as body movement, secondary-process thinking, and reality-oriented problem-solving. Through psychoanalytic interpretation, the analysand is encouraged to examine old defensive and repetitive behavior and to free the self from repetitive patterns which are maladaptive, pathological, and uneconomical.

In meditation, a similar situation is created by sitting quietly and letting thoughts and fantasies come to mind without censoring them. Also, in the meditative situation, because body movement, secondary-process thinking, and reality-oriented problem-solving are minimized, a new dimension opens in experiencing and understanding oneself beyond words and thoughts. The major difference is the use of silence in meditation and the use of language in psychoanalysis. In psychoanalysis, emphasis is on understanding through verbalization the previous *modus operandi*, whereas in the meditative experience emphasis is on the silent experience of one's internal feelings beyond words or cognitive understanding (chapters 2 and 3).

Compulsion to Repeat

Freud (1920) observed that because of earlier psychic trauma, the child feels overwhelmed by anxiety due to passivity and helplessness. The child tries to deal with passivity and helplessness in a traumatic situation through repetition of the experience. By repetition the child plays an active role in re-enacting the trauma, thereby partially mastering it. To illustrate this, Freud (1920) gave a brief history of a little boy, one and one-half years old, who was very attached to his mother. When his mother went away, he took, ". . . any small objects he could get hold of and . . . [threw] them away from him into a corner, under the bed, and so on, so that hunting for his toys and picking them up was often quite a business" (p. 14). Later on, he changed his play so that the object would disappear and return. He performed this game over and over again. Freud's interpretation was as follows: "He compensated himself for this [disappearance of mother], as it were, by himself staging the disappearance and return of the objects within his reach" (p. 15). Freud drew the following conclusion:

> At the onset he was in a *passive* situation—he was overpowered by the experience; but, by repeating it, unpleasurable though it was, as a game, he took on an *active* part. These efforts might be put down to an instinct for mastery . . . (p. 16).

This tendency to repeat the traumatic experience has a basic driven quality which overrides the pleasure principle, the reality principle, and the economic aspects of psychic functioning. Freud (1920) called this phenomenon the "compulsion to repeat" and mentioned: ". . . compulsion to repeat . . . seems more primitive, more elementary, more instinctual than the pleasure principle which it overrides" (p. 23). Freud wrote: "The pleasure principle, then, is a tendency operating in the service of a function whose business it is to free the mental apparatus entirely from excitation or to keep the amount of excitation in it constant or to keep it as low as possible" (p. 62).

In all of us exists a basic tendency toward compulsion to repeat. This tendency acquired in childhood, and which at one time appeared to be helpful for the development of mastery, if overemphasized throughout life, may become a major block on the path of growth, maturity, health, and enlightenment.

In the second year of life, two major ego functions develop: motility in the form of walking, and speech in the form of talking. At the same time, the child is very vulnerable due to the development of stranger and separation anxiety and the separation and individuation process (Shafii & Shafii, 1982, pp. 10–43). Along with these developments, the child has more awareness of mother and of the need to separate from her, while, at the same time, has the need to be very close to and dependent upon her (A. Freud, 1965, p. 65).

It is natural that the newly acquired skills of language and motility are used in the form of compulsion to repeat to cope with the anxiety of separation from mother and the fear of losing her. Could it be that our preoccupation with action and speech in adult life has its roots in this phase of life? We use language and movement in adulthood in the same repetitive and habitual manner to cope with internal tension or external pressure as children do in dealing with the absence of their mother. Speech and action, if used judiciously, are essential for the growth of personality and adaptation to the environment, but often they are used in the form of compulsion to repeat for immediate but partial discharge.

We frequently and unknowingly abuse speech and movement in a repetitive compulsive way. Abuse brings only partial discharge and gratification as with an alcoholic who uses alcohol to reduce tension but who only succeeds temporarily. Later, the alcoholic will use alcohol again until depletion of financial and psychophysiological resources.

In meditation by practicing quiescence and silence the individual directly confronts the self to gain freedom from repetitive and compulsive use of body movement, language, and thought processes. The ability to sit quietly without doing anything else such as reading, eating, talking, or thinking, is a major accomplishment which helps the individual tolerate physical pain, master body tension, and develop patience.

In the past, the Sufi *pirs*, the Yoga *gurus*, and the Zen masters did not have the psychological or psychoanalytic sophistication of the present time. Freud and Pavlov were at least 1,000 years in the future. However, from careful observation, these masters of the mind realized that daily conditioned behavior and defensive tendencies limit our ability to understand ourselves. They intuitively realized that voluntarily limiting body movement and transcending dualities of thought processes through meditation bring about an internal integration and synthesis of all the forces within. This integration brings new understanding and insight beyond the limits of words and language. Enlightenment and maturity, which is called *kamāl* in Sufism, *satori* in Zen Buddhism, and *samadhi* in Yoga, is the integration of all contrasting forces within (chapters 5 and 7).

Through meditation and internal repetition of *zikr*, the seeker replaces the neurotic style of compulsion to repeat with a repetitive behavior which is less destructive and uses less psychic energy. Eventually there is a change in the personality in the form of modification of driven and compulsive character traits and a freedom from inhibition and guilt. On a higher level of the meditative experience, the individual transcends the *zikr* and also frees the self from this repetitive behavior.

CREATIVE AND INTEGRATIVE FUNCTION OF SILENCE

In Sufism, Yoga, and Zen, verbalization is discouraged and the practice of silence in meditation is encouraged. Frequently in the East, methods of self-realization, self-integration, and enlightenment are called the paths of silence. The Sufi guide, for instance, is often referred to as a "silent physician." Psychoanalysis and dynamic psychotherapy are means for the development of insight, self-integration, and maturity, through verbalization and free association of thoughts, feelings, and fantasies.

Why do we see these two extreme positions in the East and West? Are verbalization and verbal understanding the only means to insight and freedom from neurotic inhibitions and repetitive behavior? Can learning about the self and self-integration also occur without the use of words? How much that occurs in the psychoanalytic situation is nonverbal and cannot be captured in the structural limitation of words and language?

The role of silence in the development of enlightenment is expressed vividly in the following Japanese story about a Zen master:

> After a long and arduous journey a young Japanese man arrived deep in a forest where the teacher of his choice was living in a small house he had made. When the student arrived, the teacher was sweeping up fallen leaves. Greeting his master, the young man received no greeting in return. And to all his questions, there were no replies. Realizing there was nothing he could do to get the teacher's attention, the student went to another part of the same forest and built himself a house. Years later, when he was sweeping up fallen leaves, he was enlightened. He then dropped everything, ran through the forest to his teacher, and said, "Thank you." (Cage, 1961, p. 85).

Silence, Preconscious Perception, and Insight

Fisher's work on dreams documented the role of the preconscious in visual perception and verified its significance in the formation of dreams and their content. These preconscious perceptions ". . . appear not to be available to free association . . ." (1954, p. 443).

If we can perceive without conscious awareness, and if this perception plays a major role in the development of our unconscious fantasies and dream formation beyond verbal learning, secondary thought-processes, and cognition, can insight also develop without the aid of verbalization or free association and secondary thought-processes?

Kris, in a well-known paper, responded to this question. He stated: ". . . some and perhaps all significant intellectual achievements are products or at least derivatives of preconscious mentation" (1956, p. 447). Kris associated the experience of *insight* with the patient's ability to "tune-in" and with the merging of cognition with assurance. The patient experiences insight as ". . . 'real', 'concrete', [and] 'three-dimensional' . . ." rather than as ". . . 'intellectual', 'flat', [or] 'two-dimensional' . . ." (Ibid., p. 448).

Kris emphasized the preverbal nature of the experience of insight which recreates the nursing experience of the child.

> These experiences I here suggest considering as the id aspect of insight, or as its infantile prototype. They may be of varied kind, oral in nature and reproduce the experience of the nursing situation . . . . But whatever the infantile prototype, all who have surveyed current analytic views on the meaning of insight seem to agree on the point that we are faced with an effect of integrative ego tendencies. (p. 448).

The criteria for the development of insight are closely related to the three functions of the ego:

> I should like to refer to three functions of the ego, which are intimately involved in the gaining of analytic insight by integrative comprehension. I refer to the control of temporary and partial regression, to the ability of the ego to view the self and to observe its own functions with some measure of objectivity, and to the ego's control over the discharge of affects. (p. 450).

Kris posed this important question: Is awareness necessary for the development of insight?

Only gradually is the patient—and every patient in a different way—enabled to view various parts of his unconscious self and the connexions between them. But there is another, perhaps less obvious, but not less significant difference. It concerns the degree to which insight reaches awareness. Interpretation naturally need not lead to insight; much or most of analytic therapy is carried out in darkness, with here and there a flash of insight to lighten the path. A connexion has been established, but before insight has reached awareness (or, if it does, only for flickering moments), new areas of anxiety and conflict emerge, new material comes, and the process drives on: thus far-reaching changes may and must be achieved, without the pathway by which they have come about becoming part of the patient's awareness. (p. 452).

This statement helps us to understand the psychogenetic determinants of the development of insight in the context of ego psychology. Insight and integration need not be verbal, need not reach awareness, and need not have cognitive manifestations. Insight is often experienced on a preverbal level, which helps the development of the feelings of security, wholeness, oneness, and integration.

Three Areas of the Mind

Michael Balint (1958) proposed a new theoretical approach to the understanding of the mind. He suggested three areas of the mind which are operant concomitantly; usually one of these areas is more prevalent in the individual's style of relationship to himself, to the environment, to problem solving, and in the analytic situation. These three areas or levels are as follows.

1. Oedipal level. (a) At this level, all of the relationships are triangular, whether based on genital, anal, or oral experiences (chapter 6). (b) Relationships are inseparable from conflict. The conflict is based on ambivalence and leads to fixation. (c) At this level, adult language is used as a basic form of communication.

2. Basic fault level. This level is basic and more primitive than the oedipal level. (a) The events at this level are exclusively on a two-person relationship. (b) This relationship is very special and different from the oedipal level. (c) The dynamic forces which are functioning at this level are not based on conflict, but are based on faults or weaknesses in the structure. (d) Adult language is not useful for communication at this level and words do not have their conventional object.

3. *Creation level.*   (a) There is no external object. (b) The subject is on his own and ". . . his main concern is to produce something out of himself" (p. 337). Creative processes, scientific discoveries, mathematical and philosophical explorations, development of insight, early stages of mental and physical illness, and the spontaneous recovery from them belong to this level (pp. 333–334, 337).

Balint felt that our knowledge of the creative level is limited because it is a one-person situation. He suggested that the silent patient also belongs to this level and stated:

> What I have in mind is the silent patient, a puzzling problem to our technique. The pedestrian analytic attitude is to consider the silence merely as a symptom of resistance to some unconscious material stemming either from the patient's past or from the actual transference situation. One must add that this interpretation is nearly always correct; the patient is *running away* from something, but it is equally correct that he is *running towards* something, i.e., a state in which he feels relatively safe and can do something about the problem bothering or tormenting him. The something that he will eventually produce and then present to us is a kind of "creation." . . . True, we cannot be with him during the actual work of creation, but we can be with him in the moments just before and immediately after, and, in addition, we can watch him from the outside during his actual work. Perhaps if we can change our own approach—from considering the silence as a symptom of resistance to studying it as a possible source of information—we may learn something about this area of the mind. (p. 338).

Balint's fresh approach to the psychoanalytic study of the mind places passivity, quiescence, introspection, creativity, and, I may add, meditation in a new focus for clinical and psychoanalytic investigation. In conceptualizing the origin of these levels in the context of chronological development, Balint felt that it is simple to say that the level of creation comes first, then the level of basic fault, and, finally, the level of the oedipal conflicts. However, he wondered whether this simplistic formulation could be misleading. Perhaps, the creation level is a solution resulting from development and secondary to the basic fault level rather than primary to it.

> As we know from embryology, it often happens during develop-
> ment that an early complex structure is gradually simplified or
> even completely lost at a later stage. Thus it is thinkable that the
> earliest level might be that of primary love and with it the level
> of the Oedipus conflict develops by differentiation, and on the
> other hand, the level of creation by simplification. (p. 339).

On the creative level, language and words cannot express the
nonverbal experience of silence. In the psychoanalytic situation, all
levels of human development cannot be repeated. By the nature of
verbalization there is considerable distortion in the understanding of
the creative and meditative process. We need a new conceptual
framework and new approaches to understand, evaluate, and validate
the role of silence in learning and its significance in integrative aspects
of ego function.

Silence, Communion, and Integration

Nacht (1964) related his own clinical experience in the analytic
situation and underlined the significance of silence in the development
of the therapeutic alliance and its role in enhancing the patient's
integration and maturity. He spoke of the uniqueness of the analytic
relationship and explained the special aspects of this uniqueness:

> . . . in the course of my personal clinical experience, I have often
> had the impression that an element in this relationship eluded all
> expression, since often the exchanges between patient and analyst
> were on a level where speech no longer took place . . . . Are some
> affects born from speech, while others can flourish only in silence?
> (p. 299).

He also wondered whether some forms of communication are
expressed and fostered by words, whereas others are prevented by
words. The progress of analytic therapy is related to the effect of
"deep inner attitudes of the analyst" and these attitudes are more
significant than interventions or verbal interpretations.

> For some time I have been insisting on the primary importance
> of the role played by the actual unconscious attitude underlying
> the conscious attitude of the therapist, because of the exchanges
> which develop beyond words between the unconscious of the
> physician and that of the patient, and vice versa. This exchange,
> this communication from unconscious to unconscious, seems to

me to find its level at the pre-object phase of the development of
the person (p. 300).

Nacht regarded the development of speech in children as a new
method of communication which isolated the subject from the object.
Language increases and enhances this separation. Language is also
used to recapture the loved object (mother)—for instance, the infant's
babbling or calling mother's name. The need of reunion with mother
persists for most people, ". . . at their deepest core without touching
the conscious" (p. 300).

Nacht postulated that this need

> . . . is the basis for the non-verbal relationship in the analytic
> situation. True transference is first born in the verbal relationship
> and could not exist without it—but I believe it is the non-verbal
> relationship which gives it substance and significance during the
> course of treatment. (p. 300).

The strength of the unconscious need for total union is experienced in the psychoanalytic situation by silence. This experience, if
the analyst is aware of it and allows its temporary blossoming, will
enhance and deepen the therapeutic bond and will help the patient
to explore the depth of his or her unconscious for further growth
and liberation; ". . . the patient will find, in this brief fulfillment of a
profound need, a new peace and strength which will prove invaluable
for achieving normal relationships" (p. 301).

At this stage the analyst should be totally accepting of the patient's
experience of silence, and should be sensitive and silently receptive
to the "unconscious wish for union-communion."

Nacht stated:

> . . . this need expresses itself by a certain quality of silence which
> fosters non-verbal relationship between the patient and his physi-
> cian. In the same way it can occur when the subject, having elimi-
> nated fear and aggression, can tolerate a certain enduring silence
> of authentic peace in the deepest regions of himself, where he
> *feels* finally not only in agreement but even in communion with
> the object. In this state, experienced as a kind of oneness, all
> opposition and all ambivalence lose their sense and their *raison
> d'être*. (p. 301).

These fleeting moments are essential to the resolution of transference
neurosis and to the patient's freedom from neurotic binds. Integration,

freedom of choice, and liberation from repetitive-compulsive behavior and driven attitudes are the outcome of these peak moments of psychoanalytic experience. To help the patient achieve this state, the analyst ". . . must first be capable of it (silence) himself . . ." Nacht concluded:

> Thus, the unconscious need for union fleetingly realized during analysis will guide the subject towards the acceptance of the inevitable separation which constitutes good object relation, separation until then felt unconsciously as painful, if not intolerable . . . human life needs at moments to steep itself in silence, from which it draws essential nourishment and in which it develops its deepest roots. (p. 303).

METAPSYCHOLOGY OF SILENCE IN MEDITATION

Meditation is a temporary suspension of motility and speech. By voluntary limitation of body movement and language, psychic energy and attention cathexis (investment) are directed internally toward fantasies, daydreams, preconscious mental processes, and body perception. At the beginning of any meditative experience there is an upsurge of free-floating thoughts, fantasies, and memories of the past and present. Primary process emerges in the form of fantasy. The individual who meditates with the help of an experienced guide becomes more aware of instinctual tendencies and animalistic desires such as anger and passion (chapter 2). The meditator is encouraged to observe these fantasies but not act upon them. The meditator verbalizes fantasies to the guide on a regular basis, but the emphasis is not on verbalization as it is in the psychoanalytic situation (Chapters 2 and 3). The meditator is encouraged to continue to meditate and to use the internal breathing of *zikr* to gradually transcend the world of fantasy within and reach a state of *no thought*. The state of no thought, or void (*fanā, nirvana, satori*), is not easily achieved (chapter 5). Many meditators never reach this state, and those who do are often not able to express their experience in words. If they can, they may relate their experiences as follows:

> I felt for a few moments a complete silence within myself. There was no thought, no desire, no wish and no fantasy. It was not a blackout because I was aware of my heart beat, my breathing, and even the most quiet noise around me. But at the same time

> I felt one with all parts of myself and with all the things around. The only thing I could feel was the deepest experience of peace and contentment. I felt totally secure and full of trust. I know I am not doing justice in explaining this experience in words because it is so deep that words cannot describe it. If you have experienced it you know what I am talking about and if you have not it is hard for you to feel it through my spoken words.

This is similar to the statements of great mystics when they speak of their mystical experiences, but at the same time it has a resemblance to Nacht's union-communion in the psychoanalytic situation.

Through meditation and active use of silence a profound but temporary and controlled regression occurs. This deep experience helps the individual regress to the preverbal level of the ego state or to somotosymbiotic phase of the mother-child relationship. The re-experience of this preverbal phase of union with mother and the environment rekindles temporarily the phase of "basic trust."

Erikson (1950) defined this stage of basic trust as follows:

> What we here call trust coincides with what Therese Benedek has called confidence. If I prefer the word "trust", it is because there is more naïveté and more mutuality in it: an infant can be said to be trusting where it would go too far to say that he had confidence. The general state of trust, furthermore, implies not only that one has learned to rely on the sameness and continuity of the outer providers, but also that one may trust oneself and the capacity of one's own organs to cope with urges; . . . (pp. 247–248).

This basic trust is modified as the child grows and language and motility develop concomitant with the separation and individuation phase. Daily frustrations and frequent, subtle traumatic experiences in the child's relationship with mother and the environment have a cumulative and troublesome effect.

Khan (1963), in introducing the concept of "cumulative trauma," referred to these frequent and minute traumatic experiences. He stated:

> My argument is that cumulative trauma is the result of the breaches in the mother's role as a protective shield over the whole course of the child's development, from infancy to adolescence— that is to say, in all those areas of experience where the child continues to need the mother as an auxiliary ego to support his immature and unstable ego functions . . . Cumulative trauma thus

derives from the strains and stresses that an infant-child experiences in the context of his ego dependence on the mother as his protective shield and auxiliary ego. (pp. 290–291).

Kahn emphasized that these strains and stresses occur continuously and that they are not similar to a major traumatic experience in the child's life; he stated: "In this context it would be more accurate to say that these breaches over the course of time and through the development process cumulate silently and invisibly" (p. 291).

The breaches in protective shielding ". . . set up a compulsion in the relatively mature child and the grown adult to correct the imbalances and dissociations in ego integration" (p. 296). I hypothesize that cumulative trauma is the basis of compulsion to repeat and the precursor of maladaptive defense mechanisms.

In meditation, the controlled but deep regression returns the individual to the earliest fixation points and to the re-experience of minute and silent traumas of the separation and individuation phase on a *silent and nonverbal level*. This re-experience frees the psychic energies which are bound and overcathected in these numerous, minute silent traumas and makes it available as a form of neutralized and free psychic energy in the service of the ego. Thus cumulative trauma which is experienced in silence is re-experienced and mastered again in silence.

The internal peace and harmony experienced by the Sufis, Yogis, and Zen masters may be related to this phenomenon of *creative silence in meditation* and to their ability to use temporary, but regulated, deep regression in mastering their internal cumulative traumas. Compulsive, repetitive, and driven behaviors and fantasies give way to the feeling of peace, freedom, and enlightenment. According to the *Bhagavad Gita,* "He who cannot meditate must not expect peace, and without peace, how can anyone expect happiness?"

Chapter 5

EXISTENTIAL COMMUNION

Freedom from the Self

*The flower sheds all its petals
and finds the fruit.*

Tagore, Indian poet, twentieth century

According to the Sufis, Universal Reality (Truth, God, Beloved, Thou, *haqq*) is perceived when the seeker becomes one with the Reality. As long as there is separation between "I" and "Thou", one cannot experience the "Thou." The only way that Universal Reality can be experienced is by giving up the "I," the "me," the "mine"—in other words, the conditioned self—to become one with the "Thou." In Sufism this process is called *fanā*, freedom from the self.

MEANING OF FREEDOM FROM THE SELF (FANĀ)

"Fanā" is an Arabic word meaning passing away, vanishing, annihilation, and nothingness. Abu Yazid-e Bestami, a Sufi of the ninth century A.D., is credited with introducing the experience of *fanā* in Sufism, where it refers specifically to freedom from the conditioned self and loss of self in Reality. In English, there is no word which exactly describes the totality and psychospiritual meaning of *fanā*. In this book, *fanā* is translated as "freedom from the self" or "loss of self."

Many Sufis such as Rabe'a have experienced the loss of the self in the Beloved. It was Abu Yazid, however, who advocated loss of self and daringly shared his experiences of *fanā* on the path of Reality. Abu Yazid meditated:

> . . . Lord God, let me not be deluded . . . Let me not become self-satisfied with my own being, not to yearn for Thee. Better it is that Thou shouldst be mine without me, than that I should be my own without Thee. Better it is that I should speak to Thee through Thee, than that I should speak to myself without Thee. (Attār, Arberry's translation, 1966, pp. 106–107).

Abu Yazid exemplified the loss of self:

> A man came to the door of Abu Yazid and called out.
> "Whom are you seeking?" asked Abu Yazid.
> "Abu Yazid," replied the man.
> "Poor wretch!" said Abu Yazid. "I have been seeking Abu Yazid for thirty years, and cannot find any trace or token of him."
> (p. 121).

Freedom from the self is gradual quiescence of one's wishes and desires. Wishes and desires are the signs of preoccupation with the self and a reflection of duality. Sufis, in the highest level of *fanā*, free the self from all desires.

> "Almighty God," said Abu Yazid, "admitted me to His presence in two thousand stations, and in every station He offered me a Kingdom, but I declined it. God said to me, 'Abu Yazid, what do you desire?' I replied, 'I desire not to desire.' " (p. 122).

Loss of self is essential for further integration and development. Jonaid of Baghdad stated:

"For thirty years I sat watching my heart," he said. "Then for ten years my heart watched over me. Now it is twenty years that I know nothing of my heart and my heart knows nothing of me."

"For thirty years," he said again, "God has spoken with Jonaid by the tongue of Jonaid, Jonaid not being there at all, and men were not aware." (p. 203).

Reaching the stage of poverty, the fourth stage of human integration on the Sufi path, is associated with the experience of freedom from the self (Figure 1, chapter 6). The Sufi's freedom from wants is the essence of the stage of poverty and the beginning of *fanā:*

A man brought five hundred dinars and offered them to Jonaid.

"Do you possess anything besides this?" Jonaid asked him.

"Yes, a lot," the man replied.

"Do you need more?"

"Yes, I do."

"Then take it away," Jonaid said, "You have a better right to it. I possess nothing, and I need nothing." (p. 206).

The Sufis emphasize total absorption in the task at hand. Holding back is a sign of self-conceit and insincerity. The lover gives up everything for the Beloved. The moth is totally attracted to the light of the candle and willingly burns in the flame. Sincere involvement *(ikhlās)* and total absorption *(jazb)* are the essence of union-communion. Freedom from the self can only be achieved by total absorption.

A thief had been hanged in Baghdad. Jonaid went and kissed his feet.

"Why did you do that?" he was asked.

"A thousand compassions be upon him!" he replied. "He proved himself a true man of his trade. He did his work so perfectly, that he gave his life for it." (pp. 207–208).

MANIFESTATIONS OF FREEDOM FROM THE SELF

In studying classical Sufi literature and examining the Sufis' personal lives, the following manifestations, it would seem to me, are some of the aspects of freedom from the self *(fanā)*: internal silence, progressive stages of loss of self, loss of self-awareness, experience of light, absorption, joy, ecstasy, vision of Reality, intuition, and certainty.

Internal Silence

In deep meditative states, the Sufi experiences a profound internal silence. Thoughts, fantasies, wishes, dreams, and daydreams vanish momentarily (chapter 4). The mind becomes clear of dualistic thinking. The Sufi is alert and conscious. Through internal silence, the Sufi becomes aware of invisible rhythms within the body and within nature. Some Sufis become so receptive during meditation that they can "hear an ant walking on a blade of grass," or "feel a plant breathing."

Progressive Levels of Loss of Self

A few Sufis in the past perceived loss of self literally as physical and psychological destruction of the self. Most Sufis, however, feel that loss of self is annihilation of self-centered personality characteristics (attributes). Hujwiri, more than 900 years ago, wrote that freedom from the self " . . . is the annihilation of one attribute through the subsistence of another attribute" (p. 245). It is clear that by freedom from the self the Sufis mean a change of one's attitudes, attributes, or, in our present terminology, personality characteristics.

There are several levels of freedom from the self *(fanā)*.

1. *fanā-fi-al-shaykh* is literally translated as passing away or dying in the guide, *shaykh,* or *pir.* But, in actuality, it means losing the attributes of the self and gaining the attributes of the *pir* (chapter 2). In other words, the Sufi gradually sheds the skin of self-consciousness, old habits, and old values.

The *pir,* as a person with a concrete physical and psychological reality, becomes a vehicle for transformation. Changes of attributes can be accomplished only by the Sufi's total commitment, sincerity, and willingness to tolerate frustrations in order to overcome obstacles on the Path. Intense love is the dynamic and moving force which helps the Sufi in this transformation. The *pir* becomes concretely and symbolically the personification of all the ideal attributes of humanity and Reality.

Through the process of loss of self in the *pir,* the Sufi gives up troublesome attitudes and attributes, such as self-conceit, pride, greed, preoccupation with the forces of passion and anger, and intellectual and rationalistic tendencies. Loss of self in the *pir* occurs out of love and will, rather than from blind obedience. Through the intense relationship between the Sufi and the *pir*, which often occurs on a silent and nonverbal level, a gradual communion develops, a oneness, which enhances the humanness and spirituality of both the *pir* and the Sufi.

Giving up attributes and traits is not an easy task. It can be frightening and disorganizing. The Sufi must have total trust in the *pir*, like a passenger on a sea voyage who trusts life and belongings to the ship's Captain. Sometimes doubt and mistrust will haunt the Sufi. At other times, self-conceit and illusionary experiences will become obstacles on the Path. At these times, intense love and total trust will melt doubts and chip away at self-conceit or illusions (chapter 6).

Rumi, in the fifth book of the *Mathnawi*, described a story of a lover boasting about sacrifices for his beloved, and asking if there were anything else he could do. The beloved answered that the lover had done all but the most important:

> Said the lover, what is the most important thing?
> Said the beloved, It is dying [loss of self] and nothingness.
> All that you have done is the sign of your being, rather than your non-being.
> Die, if you are willing to sacrifice your life.
> If you die, you will find complete existence.
> Your good name will remain until eternity. (1933, p. 80).

Loss of self in the *pir*, then, means freedom from the divided self and oneness with the mature and integrated being of the *pir*.

2. *Fanā-fi-al-rasūl* means passing away in the prophet. The word "*rasūl*" symbolizes all of God's prophets, saints, and previous Sufi guides. At the same time, it specifically refers to the universal attributes of Prophet Mohammed, who is, according to the Sufis, *insān-i-kāmil*, an integrated human being (chapter 7).

Depending on commitment, ability, and psychospiritual endowment, a time comes when the Sufi is ready to be free of the attributes of the *pir*. The *pir* senses the Sufi's readiness for further integration, and realizes personal limitations in guiding the Sufi further. Without hesitation, the *pir* encourages the Sufi to continue on the Path independently. The Sufi continues along on the Path with some trepidation and concern. The need for the concrete presence of the *pir* decreases. Eventually, the Sufi loses the self in the self of all integrated beings, whether of the past or present, and receives their attributes.

The communion which begins with two souls results in the communion of all souls. The Sufi is in the temporal self with a physical reality, but has gained an extra dimension by transcending temporal reality and losing the self in the reality of all humanity. In this stage, the differences between Islam, Christianity, Judaism, Buddhism, and other religions and beliefs vanishes.

3. *Fanā-fi-Allah* means passing away or dying in God. This is the ultimate phase of freedom from the self. At this stage, the Sufi loses all attributes and becomes one with the attributes of Reality *(haqq)*. This phase is also referred to as *fanā-al-fanā* (Ghani, 1951, p. 377). The Sufi loses awareness of and preoccupation with *fanā*, and is freed from *fanā*. The Sufi's temporal being disappears in the visionary experience of God *(haqq)*. *Fanā-al-Fanā* is a negation of negation. It is reaching the stage of *baqā* (permanence), or existential communion. Duality, being and nonbeing, and "I" and "Thou" disappear. There is complete illumination (chapter 7).

Attār, the Sufi of the twelfth century, in his mystical book of poetry, *The Conference of Birds,* wrote:

As long as you are preoccupied with
existing and non-existing,
How can you take a step on this Path?
Be nothing until you receive your being
from Him.
As long as you are preoccupied with self,
how can the True Being reach you?
Unless you become annihilated in humbleness and
non-being *(fanā)*,
How can ultimate knowing be received
from the Great Being? (Ghani, 1951, p. 374).

4. *Permanence* or *Baqā* is the final stage of freedom from the self. It is reaching the ultimate state of existence. "*Baqā* is an Arabic word meaning permanency, living, life, and eternity. In Sufism, it refers to the union and oneness with all beings and God. It is existential communion. Being is achieved by non-being (Figure 1, chapter 6; chapter 7).

In this stage, the Sufi frees the self from all conditioned and dualistic attributes, and reaches the state of Universality—at harmony with the self, others, and God. Creature and Creator become One.

Jāmi, a Sufi of the fifteenth century, wrote:

. . . and see the self and the Beloved in the mirror of each other.
In the mirror of the Beloved, the Sufi sees the self, and in the
mirror of the self, sees the qualities and the attributes of the
Beloved. (Ghani, p. 383).

In Sufi poetry, the mirror is symbolic of the purification of the soul and of loss of self. Shabistari, a Sufi sage of the thirteenth century, in *The Secret Rose Garden*, portrayed this metaphor:

> Not being is the mirror of Absolute Being.
> From the mirror shines the picture of God . . .
> Not-being is the mirror, the Universe is the picture,
> And man as the eye of the picture is hidden in it.
> Thou art the eye of the picture, and He is the light
>   of the eye.
> Who has seen his eyes without the light and the mirror?
> The Universe became man and the man the Universe.
> There is no clearer expression than this.
> When you see well into the origin of this act—
> He is the see-er, the eye and the seen. (Ghani, pp. 61–62).

Loss of Self-Awareness

The experience of freedom from the self is manifested in the Sufi with an intense feeling of love and emotion. The Sufi cannot contain these fervent emotions and is carried away like a branch of a tree in a torrential river. The Sufi loses self-awareness and is shaken to the root of existence. He appears confused, bewildered, and disorganized. He does not attend to outward appearance, daily tasks, or responsibilities. He may wander aimlessly. Usually the Sufi keeps silence. If he does talk, his speech appears irrational and illogical. The Sufi is like a drunkard—free of pain and sorrows one moment, and drowning in tears and despair another. The Sufi, at these times, is called *"diwāna"* or *"majnūn,"* meaning "insane" or "deranged." The Sufi is truly in love, and like a deranged lover gives up reasoning, rationality, and the self for the sake of union and oneness with the Beloved. The experience of loss of self-awareness is frequently short-lived, but may last for days, months, or years. It may occur a number of times.

One of the examples of this irrational fervor of love is the story of Hallaj. Hallaj was born in the year 858 A.D., in the Province of Fars, Persia. Hallaj, while intoxicated on the Sufi path, lost all control and did not keep the vow of silence. He uttered aloud, *"An al-haqq,"* which means, "I am God, I am the Truth!" The orthodox theologians were furious by Hallaj's "heretical" pronouncements. Hallaj was imprisoned for a year, but the people still came to seek his advice and spiritual guidance.

It is said on the first night of his imprisonment the gaolers came to his cell but could not find him in the prison. They searched through all the prison, but could not discover a soul. On the second night they found neither him nor the prison, for all their hunting. On the third night they discovered him in prison.

"Where were you on the first night, and where were you and the prison on the second night?" they demanded. "Now you have both reappeared. What phenomenon is this?"

"On the first night," he replied, "I was in the Presence, therefore I was not here. On the second night the Presence was here, so that both of us were absent. On the third night I was sent back, that the Law might be preserved. Come and do your work!" (Attār, Arberry's translation, p. 267).

Hallaj was finally crucified (913 A.D.) and dismembered by the Caliph. It is said that until the last moment he and all the parts of his body uttered, "I am the Truth."

After Hallaj's martyrdom, the Sufis became more discreet in the open expression of their ecstasy and their loss of self to God. They cloaked these mystical and spiritual experiences in symbolic metaphors. The Sufis claimed Hallaj's death was the result of his inability to keep the "secret of love" and his tendency to verbalize the mysteries of existential communion.

Another example of loss of self-awareness is the life of Rumi. Rumi was a well-known and respected theologian and scholar in the city of Konya, Anatolia (present-day Turkey). At the age of thirty-eight, Rumi met a wandering Sufi, Shams-i-Tabrizi. This encounter was so intense that Rumi totally lost his rationality. He gave up his Chair of Theology and forsook his 10,000 disciples to devote himself totally to his *pir*, Shams. The community of Konya and Rumi's followers were distraught and revolted to no avail.

After a year, Shams disappeared. Rumi experienced this loss intensely. While meditating, he would lose himself and would utter spiritually exhilarating mystical love poems about Shams. Before that time, Rumi had never written poetry and in fact did not even care for it. A few of Rumi's close disciples wrote down his poems. When Rumi returned from periods of ecstasy and loss of self, he was astonished to learn that he had uttered poetry. Some of Rumi's mystical poems were collected in a book entitled *Divan-i-Shams-i Tabriz*. In this book Rumi had obviously lost all of his identity to Shams (*fanā-fi-al-shaykh*). In fact, on the surface, one would think that Shams had written the poems (Schimmel, 1978).

Experience of Light

Experiencing Divine Light, Spiritual Light, or the Light of Reality is the ultimate goal of most mystics, particularly the Sufis. Reverence for light emanates from the Koran, especially in the *Sūra* of Light (24:35):

> God is the Light of the Heavens and of the Earth. His Light is like a niche in which is a lamp . . . the lamp within a glass . . . the glass like unto a brightly-shining star. It is lit from a blessed olive-tree belonging neither to the East nor to the West, the oil whereof would almost give light even though fire toucheth it not! It is light upon light. God guideth to His light whom He will and God setteth forth parables to men, for God knoweth all things.

Prophet Mohammed referred to God as "Light of light," and believed that God is veiled ". . . in seventy veils of light." The following prayer is attributed to Mohammed:

> O Light of light, Thou art veiled to Thy creature and they do not attain to Thy light. O Light of light, Thy light illuminates the people of heaven and enlightens the people of earth. O Light of all light, Thy light is praised by all light.

The Sufi in deep meditative states may experience light in the form of a flash of light, a halo, a shining star, a spark, flames of fire, a lighted candle, sun's rays, or sunlight. Sufis differentiate between these internal experiences of light, or "inner light," and actual physical light. They feel that physical light is just one manifestation of "Real Light." The Real Light, or the Light of Reality, is all around us, but we are blind to it. By losing the temporal self in the ocean of *fanā*, one may experience the Light. The only way one can see the Light is by giving up illusions, self-conceit, and the conditioned self. The Light of Reality is eternal and everlasting.

Some of the Sufis, like Najmoddīn Kobrā (d. 1220 A.D.), and, before him, Sohravardī (martyred in 1191 A.D.), extensively used the metaphor of light to describe the Sufis' mystical journey on the Path of Enlightenment. Sohravardī integrated the works of Plato, Zarathustra, and Islam. He referred to the Light, the heavenly I, or alter ego, as "Perfect Nature." Najmoddīn Kobrā guided the Sufis of Central Asia " . . . toward the practice of meditation with particular attention to the phenomena of light . . ." (Corbin, 1971, p. 8). Some time later, Shabistarī (d. 1317 A.D.) exalted the experience of "black light," or the "midnight sun." According to Corbin, "black light," or the "midnight sun," metaphorically represents the North Star, which shines luminously at midnight in the Middle Eastern heavens. The North Star is the guide of all travelers in the desert and on the sea. "The black light is the light of the pure Essence . . . the ability to perceive it depends upon a spiritual state described as 'reabsorption in God' . . ." Reabsorption in God refers to loss of self in God, which is the highest level of *fanā* (Corbin, p. 111).

Nasafi, Sufi of the thirteenth century, wrote: "God is a light unlimited, infinite and is an ocean endless and without shores . . ." (p. 283) Nasafi described the necessity of the Sufi experiencing Light:

> Oh, Dervish, one has to reach out to this unbounded sea, this Infinite Light. One must experience it. Through this light one can see the universe and be freed from duality and polytheism . . . Doubt and protest will disappear and peace with all creatures in the universe will prevail. When you reach this light and see it you will know with certainty *(yaqin)* that the substance of the universe and the essence of living things is light.
>
> God is the essence of all atoms in existence. All living things in relationship to His grandeur are like a drop to the sea, even less than a drop, because all beings are finite but His essence is infinite: one cannot compare finite with infinite. All things in existence are manifestations of His qualities and attributes and because of Him they have come into being. Anything that one worships in actuality is Him although the worshiper may not know. (p. 286).

Nasafi recounted his dialogue with his Shaykh *(pir)* concerning the experience of Light.

> The shaykh of Nasafi began, "I reached to this Light and I saw it. It was a Light infinite and without limits. It was an ocean without shores and without end. It did not have left or right, up or down, or front and back. I was astonished and bewildered by it. I could not sleep, eat, or work. I shared this experience with a dear one [another Sufi guide]. He said, 'Go and take a handful of straw from the harvest of someone without his permission.' I went and did so. Then I no longer saw the Light."
>
> Nasafi asked, "Oh Shaykh, I thought that one could not see this Light with one's eyes. It could only be seen with the 'internal eye.'"
>
> The Shaykh replied, "O Aziz, I believe that one can see this Light both with the outward and inward eye."

Nasafi responded, "Oh Shaykh, anyone who has reached this
Sea of Light will be drowned in it and after that never see himself
again. All he will see is the Sea of Light."
The Shaykh said, "This vision is not permanent."
Nasafi asked, "Oh Shaykh, what is it that is permanent then?
Is it the vision or beholding the vision?"
The shaykh answered, "The vision is not permanent but be-
holding it is." (pp. 286–287).

Qushayri, another Sufi of the eleventh century A.D., described
the experience of Light:

It begins with flashes of light, then rays of light, then the light
shining forth in its full splendour; for the flashes are like lightning
which appears only to vanish again, and the rays appear from the
flashes and do not cease so speedily, but the light in its full splendour remains for a longer time, and is greater in its power and
more enduring in its stay. (Smith, 1931, p. 214).

Absorption (Jazb)

Jazb means pulling, attraction, and absorption. In Sufism, it refers
to total absorption in the Beloved. Total absorption is one of the
manifestations of freedom from the self.

In a deep state of meditation, the Sufis are absolutely quiet, im-
mobile, and silent. All energies and attentions are focused on meditation. At times, they are so deeply absorbed that they are not aware
of their surroundings, the passage of time, pain, discomfort, hunger,
or thirst. They are not in sleep, but, at the same time, they do not
need sleep. They may remain in this deep state of quiescence and
absorption for days.

Shibli, Sufi of the ninth century, said:

I went to see Nuri [another Sufi]. I saw him sitting in meditation
so motionless that not even one hair moved.
I asked, "From whom did you learn such deep meditation?"
"I learned it from a cat waiting by a mouse hole. The cat was
much stiller than I." (Ghani, 1951, p. 320)

The following story demonstrates Abu Yazid's absorption in his
pir. Abu Yazid, while sitting at the feet of his *pir*, was suddenly asked:

"Abu Yazid, fetch me that book from the window."

"The window? Which window?" asked Abu Yazid.

"Why," said the master, "you have been coming here all this time, and you have not seen the window?"

"No," replied Abu Yazid. "What have I to do with the window? When I am before you, I close my eyes to everything else. I have not come to stare about."

"Since that is so," said the teacher, "go back to Bestam. Your work is completed." (Attār, Arberry's translation, p. 103.)

A remarkable example of absorption during meditation and prayer follows:

> Abul Khair Aqta had a diseased hand. The doctors decided the hand would have to be amputated. As he would not consent to this, his disciples advised them to wait until the Sheikh entered into prayer, when he became quite insensible. They followed this advice and it was only when he came out of prayer that he found that his hand had been amputated. (Rice, 1964, p. 81.)

The Sufis perceive absorption as a gift from God and not something for which one strives. Meditation, one-pointed attention, total involvement with the task at hand, and the experience of internal silence facilitate the experience of absorption.

Joy (Shauq) and Ecstasy (Wajd)

Shauq means filling with desire, yearning, and love. In Sufism, it describes the Sufi's complete joy and enthusiasm in seeing the Beloved. The experience of this utter joy could be compared to the intense joy and enthusiasm a young child exhibits when seeing his mother after separation. The Sufi loses the self in joy. Elation and excitement, like rays of the sun, radiate from him or her. Silence and quiescence give way to the frenzy of excitement and enthusiasm. Intense love (*ishq*) is the essence of joy. In joy, the Sufi loses the self in the "ocean of Love," and returns full of hope, enthusiasm, and contentment. One shares these experiences openly and generously with others through oral traditions, music, and poetry, or by one's mere presence.

Wajd means finding, discovery, and recovering. In Sufism, it refers specifically to ecstasy. The word "*wujūd*," "existence," is also derived from *wajd*. It is interesting to notice that "ecstasy" and "existence" originate from the same word. In moments of supreme joy and ecstasy, the Sufi experiences the unitary essence of existence—existential communion (*wahdat al-wujūd*).

Ecstasy is an overpowering experience of emotion, exaltation, rapturous delight, and frenzy of inspiration. Joyful loss of the self is ecstasy. The experience of ecstasy, like total joy, cannot be generated by the whim of the will. Ecstasy may engulf the Sufi after sincere involvement in meditation.

The use of artificial means, such as alcohol, opium, or hashish, to create momentary feelings of rapture is frowned upon. The Sufis feel that using artificial means for experiencing joy and ecstasy is self-indulgence in animal wishes and desires. The use of artificial means are a block on the Path toward freedom from the self. There are no short cuts. One cannot bypass the rigors of discipline and sacrifice to achieve communion, integration, and enlightenment.

In addition to silent meditation, the practice of *samā'*, through chanting, dancing, singing, and listening to music and poetry, is a vehicle for experiencing ecstasy.

Samā'

Samā', in Arabic, means listening to and hearing. In Sufism, it refers to the experience of ecstasy resulting from singing and hearing songs or music while performing a whirling dance. Most of the Sufi orders, particularly the Sufis of the Mevlevi Order, known in the West as the Whirling Dervishes, have used *samā'* extensively throughout the ages. Ghazzali, in the *Alchemy of Happiness*, devoted a chapter to ecstasy and *samā'*:

> Almighty God has placed a secret in the heart of human beings. This secret is hidden like fire in iron. When a stone hits the iron the hidden fire will become evident . . . *Samā'* and listening to beautiful and pleasant music moves the hidden jewel within. It creates a spontaneous situation which connects the heart of human beings with the Universal and spiritual world. The Universal world is the world of beauty and harmony. Any rhythm, beauty and harmony is the manifestation of that world . . . a beautiful voice and a delightful song are reflections of the wonder of that world. *Samā'* creates awareness in the heart and brings total joy *(shauq)*. If a person's heart is filled with the intense love and total joy of the Beloved, *samā'* will fan the fire within.
>
> *Samā'* throws a flame of fire in the heart and burns away all the impurities. Many strive to become pure but they are not able to do so except with the help of *samā'*. In *samā'* one at times becomes unaware, loses physical strength, falls down and becomes unconscious. If this condition prevails and it was the result of real *samā'*, it is the highest form of *samā'*. Other people present will also benefit.

There are times when a seeker without the help of a *pir* may try to experience *samā'*. This is a mistake because often one becomes prey of one's own illusions.

A seeker asked his *pir*, "When will I be ready to experience *samā'*?" The *pir* said, "Don't eat anything for some time. Then cook something very delicious. If you then choose *samā'* over eating, you are ready." (Summary, pp. 370–388).

Vision of Reality (Mushāhada)

Mushāhada means witnessing, seeing, contemplating, sight, vision, and observation. It also refers to ". . . the highest degree of perfection in contemplating the divine essence" (Steingass, 1892, p. 1243).

In Sufism, *mushāhada*—meaning the actual vision of Reality (God)—is the ultimate goal of the Sufi's journey on the Path. The Sufi bears frustrations and suffering in order to polish the heart so that it can reflect Reality. A vision of reality usually occurs suddenly when least expected. The more the Sufi strives to experience a vision of Reality, the more difficult it is to do so.

Sari-al-Saqati stated, "The vision of Reality gives the soul so much joy that one is not aware of the suffering of the body and the torment of the mind. In paradise no pleasure is more perfect than the vision of Reality" (Ghani, 1951, p. 368).

They asked Abu Yazid, "How old are you?" He answered, "Four years." They asked, "How is that?" He said, "Seventy years I was veiled in the world. It is now four years that I see Him. I do not count the years when I was veiled" (Ghani, p. 369).

There comes a time when the Sufi transcends visionary experiences and the see-er and the Seen become one. The see-er disappears and is totally lost in the Seen.

> "The first time I entered the Holy House," stated Abu Yazid, "I saw the Holy House. The second time I entered it, I saw the Lord of the House. The third time I saw neither the House nor the Lord of the House."
>
> By this Abu Yazid meant, "I became lost in God, so that I knew nothing. Had I seen at all, I would have seen God." (Attār, Arberry's translation, p. 121).

Ghazzali reported the following saying from the Prophet Mohammed: "Worship God in such a way that you see Him, if you cannot do so be aware that he sees you" (p. 766). Sayings such as these make the Sufi hopeful that, through meditation, purity of heart, and grace, it may be possible to see Reality, who is everywhere.

> A *pir* had a disciple which he preferred over the others. The other disciples were unhappy about this. One day he gave every disciple a bird, and he told them to go and kill this bird in a place where no one could see them. All of the disciples went and killed their bird. Only the favored disciple brought back the bird alive. The *pir* asked, "Why didn't you kill it?" The disciple answered, "I couldn't find a place where no one could see. He sees everywhere." The spiritual level of this disciple then became obvious to the others. (Attār, Arberry's translation, p. 767).

Abdullah Ibn Dinar reported:

> I was with Omar Ibn Khattab [the second Caliph of Islam] on the road to Mecca. We stopped along the road. A slave shepherd was bringing the sheep down from the mountain. Omar said to the shepherd, "Sell me one lamb." The shepherd answered, "I am a slave and this is not my property." Omar said, "Tell your master that a wolf took the lamb. He would not know." The shepherd answered, "God knows if the master doesn't." Omar wept. Omar sought out the slave's master. He bought the slave and freed him. Omar said, "These words made you free in this world and [I hope] if God is willing will make me free in the next world." (Attār, Arberry's translation, pp. 766–767).

Intuition and Certainty (Yaqin)

Sufis, through the process of freedom from the self, cleanse their hearts of dualities and develop an intuitive perception which transcends temporal reality and the boundaries of time and place. This may be similar to what we now refer to as extrasensory perception, clairvoyance, and telepathy. Most Sufis are silent about these abilities, feeling that discussing them is a sign of self-conceit.

Attār, in writing the life story of Sahl-i-Tostari (d. 896 A.D.), wrote:

> One day Sahl was sitting in the Mosque. A pigeon fell to the ground from heat and exhaustion. Sahl said, "Shah-i-Kirmani [another Sufi] just died." When they looked into it, such was the case. (Ghani, 1951, p. 366).

The Sufis feel that intuition and certainty *(yaqin)* is seeing the Truth and the Essence of all things. There are different levels of certainty (Hujwari, p. 381):

1. *Certainty of knowledge and understanding (ilm-i-yaqin)*— this level of assurance is reached by intellectual endeavors;

2. *Certainty of vision (ayn-i yaqin)*—this level of certainty is achieved through visionary experiences or experimental and internal endeavors of the heart and the mind on the Path;

3. *Certainty of Reality (haqq-i yaqin)*—total and complete certainty of Reality is achieved following freedom from duality.

PSYCHOBIOLOGICAL PRECURSORS OF FANA

Is it possible that the Sufis and other mystics tapped a natural, innate, psychobiological phenomenon in human beings? Are the moments of "no thought" in meditation, which the Sufis, Yogis, and Zen masters experience, precursors of *fanā?*

Some individuals have experienced during wakefulness "fleeting moments of total quiescence and silence of the mind." These moments may manifest themselves in the form of thought stoppage, no thought, facial blankness, not being there, or staring spells.

In medicine, for instance, some of these moments, such as staring spells, are perceived as pathological symptoms which may manifest underlying disorders of the central nervous system, such as seizure disorders, in the form of *petit mal* seizures *(absence)*, psychomotor epilepsy, and *grand mal* seizures. Staring spells are also seen in severe forms of psychopathology such as childhood autism, childhood schizophrenia, adult schizophrenia, hysteria, and severe depressive, dissociative, and depersonalization disorders.

However, as far as I know, no one has described or examined the possibility that, in some instances, these "fleeting moments of total quiescence and silence of the mind" could be integrative and growth-producing rather than pathological. I hypothesize that some of these fleeting moments of internal silence or no thought may be psychobiological precursors of *fanā.*

Description of the Moments of Fanā

In moments of *fanā*, a person is generally sitting quietly relaxed. Attention may or may not be focused. The mind becomes empty of all thoughts, ideas, and feelings. The individual may appear to be "staring" or "not there." In actuality, the person is fully there, and acutely receptive to all signals from within and without. After a short time, the individual returns to the self, feeling refreshed and alert. It is as if the mind has been cleared from distracting thoughts and disturbing noises. The person is now more receptive and responsive.

In talking with an individual who has experienced moments of *fanā*, one might hear the following descriptions:

1. A feeling of being light as though all burdens of the world had been lifted;
2. Absence of thoughts—quiescence of the mind;
3. Quiet elation and profound joy;
4. Increased sensitivity;
5. Receptivity to internal and external clues;
6. Increased perceptiveness;
7. Awareness of invisible rhythms within and around;
8. Perception of future events;
9. Awareness of the whole as well as the parts;
10. Decreased internal conflicts;
11. Increased feelings of security, certainty, integration, and oneness with all.

These moments of no thought, self-transcendence, or *fanā*, need to be examined in depth to see whether they are epiphenomena, aberrant behavior, or in actuality important functions of the brain for deprogramming overloaded circuits.

I hypothesize that the more human beings are bombarded by stimulation and information, the more moments of *fanā* are needed to continue functioning effectively. Perhaps through momentary *fanā* nature has programmed an effective adaptive psychobiological mechanism for responding to overwhelming input.

Western medicine, psychology, psychiatry, and psychoanalysis have yet to explore the therapeutic or integrative significance of these moments. "Loss of self" has usually been perceived as a form of depersonalization, personality disintegration, narcissistic fusion or psychotic behavior.

I hypothesize that moments of *fanā* are essential components of human adaptation:

1. Moments of *fanā* have biological and physiological roots;

2. Every human being has the potential for experiencing these moments;

3. Some may experience moments of *fanā* frequently without being aware of them;

4. Some may experience moments of *fanā* during creative activities or during intense human relationships;

5. Some are very frightened by these moments and consciously or unconsciously defend against them;

6. The moments of *fanā* may contribute to enhanced learning, well-being, and personality integration;

7. Some, through meditation, become aware of the moments of *fanā* and are gradually able to recreate these moments for a longer period of time in order to experience existential communion.

PSYCHOLOGICAL SIGNIFICANCE OF FREEDOM FROM THE SELF

Freedom from the self *(fanā)* is not unique to the Sufis. It is a universal experience transcending the boundaries of culture and occurring throughout the ages in all parts of the world.

According to Fromm:

> What is common to Jewish-Christian and Zen Buddhist thinking is the awareness that I must give up my 'will' (in the sense of my desire to force, direct, strangle the world outside of me and within me) in order to be completely open, responsive, awake, alive. In Zen terminology this is often called 'to make oneself empty'—which does not mean something negative, but means the openness to receive. (Suzuki et al., 1960, pp. 94–95).

In Judaism, Christianity, and particularly Yoga and Buddhism, there are frequent references to the "loss of self." The writings of

Plotinus and St. John of the Cross are two examples of many which vividly portray the significance of loss of self.

Plotinus (d. 274 A.D.) felt that the only way "perfect knowledge" could be obtained was by the union of the subject with the object. He made the following observations:

> Knowledge has three degrees—opinion, science, illumination. The means or instrument of the first is sense; of the second dialectic; of the third intuition. To the last I subordinate reason. It is absolute knowledge founded on the identity of the mind knowing with the object known. (Bucke, 1901, p. 102).

> You ask, how can we know the Infinite? I answer, not by reason. It is the office of reason to distinguish and define. The Infinite, therefore, cannot be ranked among its objects. You can only apprehend the Infinite by a faculty superior to reason, by entering into a state in which you are your finite self no longer—in which the divine essence is communicated to you. This is ecstasy . . . . It is the liberation of your mind from its finite consciousness. (p. 102).

> The last stage is reached when, in the highest tension and concentration [meditation], beholding in silence and utter forgetfulness of all things, it is able as it were to lose itself. Then it may see God, the fountain of life, the source of being, the origin of all good, the root of the soul. In that moment it enjoys the highest, indescribable bliss; it is as it were swallowed up of divinity, bathed in the light of eternity. (p. 103).

St. John of the Cross (d. 1591) frightened Church authorities because of his intense religious experiences and his devotion to the truth in all religions. He was imprisoned for a number of months. While in prison, he had intensive religious experiences and saw the "heavenly light . . . which lasted the night through, and it filled his soul with joy and made the night pass away as if were but a moment." (p. 120)

St. John stated:

> It is clearly necessary for the soul, aiming at its own supernatural transformation, to be in darkness and far removed from all that relates to its natural condition, the sensual and rational parts. The supernatural is that which transcends nature, and, therefore, that which is natural remains below. Inasmuch as this union and transformation are not cognizable by sense or any

human power, the soul must be completely and voluntarily empty
of all that can enter into it, of every affection and inclination, so
far as it concerns itself. (p. 121)

LOSS OF SELF AND WESTERN PSYCHOLOGIES

Western psychologies, particularly psychoanalysis and dynamic
psychotherapies, have ignored the study of the psychological significance of the "loss of self." Fingarette (1963), on mystic selflessness,
wrote:

> To psychoanalysts, the mystic's stress on loss of self and "unity
> of all with all" is likely to suggest that there is a psychotic-like
> confusion of "inner" and "outer," a loss of the self-object distinc-
> tion as in hallucination and paranoid delusions. The decisive evi-
> dence for the inadequacy of this view arises from observation of
> the behavior of great mystics . . . For, far from showing a confu-
> sion between self and environment, they act with unusual effec-
> tiveness and with a clear sense of the social realities. They often
> show great practical organizing ability and a particularly keen
> sensitivity to the real relationships between their own attitudes
> and desires and those of the persons they deal with. (pp. 306–307).

In another place, Fingarette stressed the progressive quality of
mystic selflessness:

> . . . the experience of loss of self and of the loss of the sense of
> subject-object relations is in fact loss of a certain kind of anxiety-
> generated self-consciousness; it is, as such, creative rather than
> regressive movement. Specifically, it results from ego-syntonic
> conflict resolution, drive neutralization (sublimation), and con-
> sequent absence of anxiety and defense. (p. 332).

Richard M. Bucke, William James, Carl G. Jung, and Erich Fromm
have, like voices in the wilderness, tried to bring to the attention of
the healing professions and the community the significance of "loss
of self."
Erich Fromm (1956), in *The Art of Loving*, wrote:

> . . . man . . . has emerged from the animal kingdom, from instinc-
> tive adaptation, . . . he has transcended nature—although he
> never leaves it; he is a part of it—and yet once torn away from

nature, he cannot return to it; once thrown out of paradise—the state of original oneness with nature— . . . Man can only go forward by developing his reason, by finding a new harmony, a human one, instead of the prehuman harmony which is irretrievably lost. (p. 6).

According to Fromm, the development of reason brings with it a sense of awareness: awareness of the moment, the past, the future, the self and others. Awareness contributes to seeing the self "as a separate entity." Separateness brings with it the possibility of choice and freedom. But, at the same time, separateness makes one aware of being alone. This aloneness generates the feeling of

. . . helplessness before the forces of nature and of society, all this makes his separate, disunited existence an unbearable prison. He would become insane could he not liberate himself from this prison and reach out, unite himself in some form or other with man, with the world outside. (p. 7).

It is fascinating to see how Erich Fromm's formulation concerning human beings' separateness from nature is similar to the Sufis' ideas of separation which were discussed earlier (chapter 2). As you recall, Sufis perceived separation as sickness and the anxieties of separation as the origin of fragmentation of personality and the cause of disturbances of the mind and spirit.

Cosmic Consciousness

A physician and well-known Canadian psychiatrist, Richard M. Bucke (d. 1901), was also concerned about the evolution of the human mind or "consciousness." Bucke, at age thirty-six, had a profound ". . . illuminating metaphysical experience that lightened his life thereafter and led . . ." to the writing of *Cosmic Consciousness, A Study in the Evolution of the Human Mind,* in 1901. Bucke, in his position as a physician and psychiatrist, had associations with a number of creative poets and thinkers of the last century, and was a close friend of Walt Whitman.

Bucke proposed that the human mind had progressed through the following levels of evolution.

1.   *Simple Consciousness*—ability for sensory stimulation and perception (p. 9).

2. *Self-Consciousness*—the development of the ability to conceptualize, use language, and be conscious of the self (p. 11). According to Bucke, this development occurred several hundred thousand years ago in human evolution. Now, by age three, children begin to manifest self-consciousness.

3. *Cosmic Consciousness*—humanity's cumulative experiences bring ever-increasing information and knowledge. According to Bucke, there comes a time when in the human mind there is a limit to the "growth of concepts in number and complexity." Nature attempts "in a fit of evolution" to elevate the brain and the mind to a higher level of consciousness which transcends forms and concepts. Bucke referred to this phenomenon as Cosmic Consciousness or "intuitive intellect" which transcends temporal reality and the intellectual conceptualization of self-conscious man.

> ... the basic fact in cosmic consciousness is implied in its name— that fact is consciousness of the cosmos—this is what is called in the East the "Brahmic Splendor," which is in Dante's phrase capable of transhumanizing a man into a god. Whitman who has an immense deal to say about it, speaks of it in one place as "ineffable light—light rare, untellable, lighting the very light— beyond all signs, descriptions, languages." (p. 14).

Bucke—based on his own personal experience and a careful review of the lives of a number of historic figures such as Moses, Isaiah, Buddha, Socrates, Jesus, Paul, Plotinus, Mohammed, Roger Bacon, Dante, Saint John of the Cross, Pascal, Spinoza, Blake, Balzac, Whitman, and a number of lesser-known—established criteria for recognizing cosmic consciousness.

According to Bucke, Moses' experience of the Burning Bush, Buddha's nirvana, Jesus' experience of the Kingdom of God, Paul's experience of Christ, Mohammed's ascension and seeing Gabriel, and the experiences of the Light by St. John of the Cross, Pascal, and Whitman, are the manifestations of human beings' evolution to a higher level of consciousness, cosmic consciousness. Bucke felt that human beings are just beginning to experience cosmic consciousness and that from this time forward more and more people will do so as a natural evolutionary stage of the human mind.

Bucke used the following criteria to define the experience of cosmic consciousness; sudden experience of "subjective light," immense experience of joy and assurance, intellectual illumination, sense of immortality, absence of the fear of death, and freedom from preoccupation with sin and guilt.

According to Bucke, the individual who experiences cosmic consciousness has experienced the joy, agony, and despair of self-conscious life. Usually the person is in the late thirties, forties, or older. It rarely occurs in the twenties or younger. Generally, individuals who have experienced cosmic consciousness are endowed with a strong character, honesty, conviction, and well-rounded personality. They have religious longings and a sense of awe and curiosity about life beyond conventional limitations. Surprisingly, in a short time, profound personality changes occur in the individual. The person becomes full of joy, energy, and enthusiasm. Serenity, security, and humbleness permeate his being. These changes are usually permanent. (pp. 60–62).

Freedom from the Self (Fanā) and Cosmic Consciousness

There are amazing similarities between the manifestations of freedom from the self in Sufism and Bucke's description of cosmic consciousness. Although Bucke did not discuss meditation and internal silence, it is clear that the manifestations of freedom from the self— loss of self-centered personality characteristics, loss of consciousness, experience of light, absorption, joy and ecstasy, vision of Reality, and intuition and certainty—parallel criteria of cosmic consciousness. The difference is only that Bucke did not delineate how an individual could become receptive to the experience of cosmic consciousness.

The Sufis, on the other hand, have developed practical ways, such as meditation, the internal experience of silence, and the intensive psychospiritual relationship between the *pir* and the seeker, to facilitate freeing the self from the conscious self. Freedom from the self leads to existential communion and total personality integration.

Freedom from the Self and Self-Actualization

Abraham Maslow (1964, 1971), a well-known American psychologist, studied the lives of some of his teachers, such as Ruth Benedict and Max Wertheimer. He found that people such as these show very little psychopathology and exude health, strength, creativity, saintliness, and wisdom. Maslow (1971) believed that these types of people are the epitome of "being human," and he referred to them as self-actualized beings (pp. 45–50). Maslow (1971) described the following aspects of self-actualization:

1. "... experiencing fully, vividly, selflessly, with full concentration and total absorption" (p. 45). By "self-lessly," he means freedom from self-consciousness, self-awareness, and ego-centricity.

2. An ongoing process which reflects individual choices toward growth rather than defensiveness and regression.

3. Letting one's true self emerge rather than being enslaved by parental or societal expectations.

4. Honesty at the time of doubt.

5. Listening to oneself at each moment of life.

6. Constant work toward self-improvement and excellence rather than mediocrity.

7. Transient moments of ecstasy—peak experiences. According to Maslow, "... everyone does have peak experiences but not everyone knows it. Some people wave these small mystical experiences aside" (p. 48).

    Maslow (1964) wrote extensively on peak experiences, which he referred to as the "values of Being." The following are some of the "... attributes of reality when perceived in peak-experiences, ..." (pp. 91–94): Truth (honesty, reality); Goodness; beauty; wholeness (unity, integration); transcending dichotomy; aliveness; uniqueness; perfection (completeness); completion (totality); justice; order (symmetry, rhythm); simplicity; richness; effortlessness; playfulness; and self-sufficiency.

8. Discovering one's strengths, shortcomings, and pathological defense mechanisms, and finding effective ways of freeing the self from defensive postures. Allowing oneself to experience "... the sacred, the eternal, the symbolic" (p. 50).

Maslow, the founder of humanistic psychology, emphasized mystical and personal religious experiences and humanistic values as a major force in human adaptation and integration.

In later life, Maslow gained a deeper appreciation of Eastern mystical traditions which emphasize self-transcendence and freedom from the conditioned self *(fanā)* as the means of becoming an integrated human being (p. 271). Maslow, like the Sufis, came to realize that love is the essence of human development and integration. He wrote:

> Love for a person permits him to unfold, to open up, to drop his defenses, to let himself be naked not only physically but psychologically and spiritually as well. In a word, he lets himself be seen instead of hiding himself. (p. 17).

Maslow specifically referred to Taoism as a way for personality integration and development:

> For me it brings back into serious focus the whole *Taoistic* point of view, not only as expressed in contemporary ecological and ethnological studies, where we have learned not to intrude and to control, but for the human being it also means trusting more the child's own impulses toward growth and self-actualization. (p. 14).

Freedom from the Self (Fanā) and Existentialism

The concept of "nothingness" plays an important role in existential philosophy. Kierkegaard felt that *angst* (dread or anxiety) is an essential aspect of life and is related to dread of "nothingness." Sartre further elaborated on the concept of nothingness by suggesting that life has no meaning and man merely invents a reason for being. According to Sartre, human beings have to come to terms with "nothingness." He believed that the past is gone, the future unknown, and only the moment counts. Nothing exists but the moment. On the other hand, Sartre's ideas of "Authenticity" and emphases on *Becoming* and on "good faith" have mystical connotations.

Some existentialists do not value mystical experiences and the urge for transcendence. They emphasize experience of the moment. They advocate "authentic experiences," meaning total involvement with the moment and freedom from the past or future. Existential therapists usually do not emphasize past experiences in the therapeutic situation.

Existentialism *differs* from Sufism in that the existentialists do not believe in the existence of the unconscious or in Reality (God). However, the writings of some of the religious existentialists such as Teilhard de Chardin, Marcel, Heidegger, Jaspers, Tillich and Merleau-Ponty in addition to Kierkegaard and Buber have contributed to the understanding of the interface between mysticism, religion, and psychology.

There are also similarities between Sufism and Existentialism.

1.   The Sufis, like the existentialists, perceive life as suffering. Existentialists feel that suffering originates from fear of "death" and "nothingness." The Sufis, on the other hand, feel that suffering is related to our anxieties of being separated from nature and Reality.

2.   To alleviate this suffering, existentialists feel that we should forget the past and the future and be involved with the moment. They feel that enjoyment of the moment is the only way to deal with the "prison of life" and the "nauseating" experience of "no exit." However, this should not be confused with hedonism. The existential psychotherapist emphasizes observable and manifest phenomena and minimizes underlying forces.

Sufis are also attentive to manifest phenomena and outward behavior. They, too, emphasize enjoyment of the moment, but they do not deny or ignore the past and contributions of underlying forces of *nafs* in the development of personality. Sufis emphasize the experience of the moment through meditation. The difference being that existentialists emphasize sense pleasure of the moment. They feel that the experience of the moment is the means and the end. The Sufis feel that the experience of the moment is the means for total personality integration and union with all forces of nature and Reality.

3.   Sufis are acutely aware of the inevitability of death, but instead of fearing death or avoiding death they welcome the temporary experience of death through *fanā*. Death and rebirth occur in the psychomystical stages on the Path—Repentance, Abstinence, Renunciation, Poverty, Patience, Trust in God, and Contentment (chapter 6 and 7).

The Existentialist and the Sufi are like two travelers reaching the shore of a vast and torrential river. The Existentialist sits by the shore, paralyzed by fear, and feels that there is no way to go either forward or backward. He feels that the only thing one can do is enjoy the moment and wait for death and "nothingness." The Sufi plunges into the river, with the help of an expert swimmer, the *pir*. By diving into the river, the Sufi overcomes fear of death and nothingness. The Sufi hopes to become one with the river, like a fish. The Sufi does not deny physical death, but at the same time does not fear or avoid it. The Sufi views death as transformation. Inherent in death and dying is reintegration and communion. Freedom from the self is acceptance of the inevitability of death and the recognition that every moment we die and are reborn.

"Will to Meaning"   Viktor Frankl (1959), Professor of Psychiatry and Neurology at the University of Vienna and one of the few *existential therapists*, believed that human beings can transcend the prison of the conditioned self and overcome the dread of death and "nothingness." He felt that every person has to find the meaning of existence. He referred to this as the "will to meaning."

Frankl spent 3 years in Auschwitz and other Nazi concentration camps. Almost his entire family, including his wife, were killed during this time. His book, *Man's Search for Meaning,* is about his life in the concentration camps. He convincingly proved that human beings can transcend the worst possible conditions ever known through internal strength and spiritual belief.

Frankl stated:

> In spite of all the enforced physical and mental primitiveness of the life in a concentration camp, it was possible for spiritual life to deepen. Sensitive people who were used to a rich intellectual life may have suffered much pain (these were often of a delicate constitution), but the damage to their inner selves was less. They were able to retreat from their terrible surroundings to a life of inner riches and spiritual freedom. (p. 56).

Frankl described a visionary experience which he had one early winter morning while marching over miles of ice and snow to forced labor:

> We stumbled on in the darkness, over big stones and through

large puddles, along the one road leading from the camp. The accompanying guards kept shouting at us and driving us with the butts of their rifles. Anyone with very sore feet supported himself on his neighbor's arm. . . .

. . . my mind clung to my wife's image, imagining it with an uncanny acuteness. I heard her answering me, saw her smile, her frank and encouraging look. Real or not, her look was then more luminous than the sun which was beginning to rise.

A thought transfixed me: for the first time in my life I saw the truth as it is set into song by so many poets, proclaimed as the final wisdom by so many thinkers. The truth—that love is the ultimate and the highest goal to which man can aspire. Then I grasped the meaning of the greatest secret that human poetry and human thought and belief have to impart: *The salvation of man is through love and in love.* (pp. 57–59).

Frankl felt that his life changed significantly after this experience. Although he was physically and psychologically suffering, the richness of this experience increased his inner strength. It helped him overcome inner emptiness, ". . . desolation and spiritual poverty."

. . . the real aim of human existence cannot be found in what is called self-actualization. Human existence is essentially self-transcendence rather than self-actualization. Self-actualization is not a possible aim at all, for the simple reason that the more a man would strive for it, the more he would miss it . . . self-actualization cannot be attained if it is made an end in itself, but only as a side effect of self-transcendence. (p. 175).

Frankl, in concluding his moving book, wrote:

Man does not simply exist, but always decides what his existence will be, what he will become in the next moment . . .

Yet one of the main features of human existence is the capacity to rise above such conditions and transcend them. In the same manner, man ultimately transcends himself; a human being is self-transcending being. (pp. 206–207).

A SUFI STORY

Let us conclude this chapter with the following Sufi story from Rumi's *Mathnawi*, Book 1:

A group of Chinese artists claimed that they were the best painters. However, a group of Greek artists insisted that they were better. These two groups argued with each other for some time. At last the Chinese artists said to the King, "Give us a room and we will prove to you our ability." So the King gave the Chinese and the Greeks each a room which opened one to the other.

The Chinese started to paint the wall with beautiful pictures and requested hundreds of paint pigments from the King's treasury. The Greeks said, "We do not need any pigments," and they started to polish the wall of the room. They spent all of their time polishing the wall until no rust was left. Finally the wall shone like a mirror. When the Chinese finished painting their wall, they were jubilant and beat upon drums in joy.

At last, the King came and marvelled at the beauty of the Chinese paintings on the wall. Then he came to the Greek's side of the room. The Greeks removed the veil. The reflection of the paintings from across the room on the mirror-like wall was, without a doubt, the most beautiful.

The Greeks in the story symbolize the Sufis who have polished their hearts and their minds and have freed themselves from greed, possessiveness, and prejudice. The mirror represents their inner self which by its openness and purity reflects the numerous aspects of internal and external Reality. (Shafii, 1973a, p. 380).

Part III

THE INFINITE PATH

HUMAN DEVELOPMENT
IN EAST AND WEST

Initial Three Stages on the Sufi Path and Stages of Human Development in Ego Psychology

Simply trust:
Do not also the petals flutter down,
Just like that?

Issa, Zen Poet, nineteenth century

The Sufis pass through seven stages on the infinite path of human development and integration. In this chapter, the initial three stages of human development in Sufism will be described and compared with the stages of human development in ego psychology. Then, in chapter 7, the final four stages of human development in Sufism will be explored. These final stages go beyond the present psychological constructs of human development in ego psychology (Figure 1, chapter 6).

STAGES OF HUMAN DEVELOPMENT

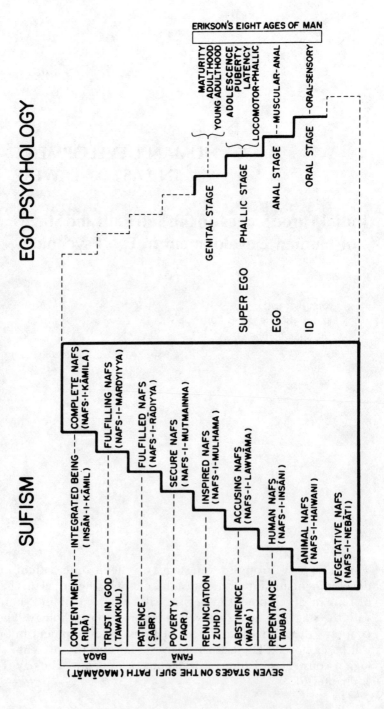

SUFISM

EGO PSYCHOLOGY

ERIKSON'S EIGHT AGES OF MAN

MATURITY
ADULTHOOD
YOUNG ADULTHOOD
ADOLESCENCE
PUBERTY
LATENCY
LOCOMOTOR-PHALLIC
MUSCULAR-ANAL
ORAL-SENSORY

GENITAL STAGE
PHALLIC STAGE
ANAL STAGE
ORAL STAGE

SUPER EGO
EGO
ID

COMPLETE NAFS
(NAFS-I-KÁMILA)
FULFILLING NAFS
(NAFS-I-MARDYIYYA)
FULFILLED NAFS
(NAFS-I-RÁDIYYA)
SECURE NAFS
(NAFS-I-MUTMAINNA)
INSPIRED NAFS
(NAFS-I-MULHAMA)
ACCUSING NAFS
(NAFS-I-LAWWÁMA)
HUMAN NAFS
(NAFS-I-INSÁNI)
ANIMAL NAFS
(NAFS-I-HAIWANI)
VEGETATIVE NAFS
(NAFS-I-NEBÁTI)

INTEGRATED BEING
(INSÁN-I-KÁMIL)

CONTENTMENT
(RIDÁ)
TRUST IN GOD
(TAWAKKUL)
PATIENCE
(SABR)
POVERTY
(FAQR)
RENUNCIATION
(ZUHD)
ABSTINENCE
(WARA')
REPENTANCE
(TAUBA)

BAQÁ
FANÁ

SEVEN STAGES ON THE SUFI PATH (MAQÁMÁT)

SEVEN STAGES OF HUMAN DEVELOPMENT ON THE SUFI PATH

Nothing in the universe is static. Everything, whether inorganic, organic, or living, changes and evolves. During the last century, we have come to realize that evolution is an innate process which helps living organisms modify, change, and develop new ways of adapting for survival. Species which cannot adapt to the environment nor master the challenge of change perish. If matter, organs, and the body modify, change, and evolve, why not also the mind, the psyche, and the spirit?

If mysticism and mystical experiences are perceived as an integral part of furthering human development, then mystical traditions of the East and the West gain new meaning. Human development, in the form of psychological and spiritual evolution, is the essence of Sufism. The Sufis have described seven stages of human development that a traveller on the Path progresses through for further integration and evolution. These stages are referred to as *maqāmāt*.

The word "*maqāmāt*" means places, stations, and musical modes. In olden days, this word was used to indicate the stopping places of caravans. In Sufism, *maqāmāt* refers specifically to the stages of progression on the Path of psychospiritual development (Figure 1, chapter 6). Each stage contributes to the transformation of personality to a more integrated level. The seven stages of human development in Sufism *(maqāmāt)* and the accompanying levels of personality development *(nafses)* are as follows:

MAQĀMĀT	ACCOMPANYING NAFSES
1. Repentance (Tauba)	Human Nafs (Nafs-i-insāni)
2. Abstinence (Wara)	Accusing Nafs (Nafs-i-lawwāmā)
3. Renunciation (Zuhd)	Inspired Nafs (Nafs-i-mulhama)
4. Poverty (Faqr)	Secure Nafs (Nafs-i-mutmainna)
5. Patience (Sabr)	Fulfilled Nafs (Nafs-i-rādiyya)
6. Trust in God (Tawakkul)	Fulfilling Nafs (Nafs-i-mardyiyya)
7. Contentment (Ridā)	Purified, Complete Nafs (Nafs-i-safiyya va Kāmila)

Stage 1: Repentance (Tauba)

The first stage on the Sufi Path of integration is *tauba*, meaning return and repentance. Hujwiri, a Sufi of the eleventh century, in the oldest Persian treatise on Sufism, entitled *Uncovering of the Veils*, wrote: repentance ". . . is the first station of the pilgrims on the way to the Truth, . . ." and it means "return" to Reality (God, Truth) (p. 294).

Al-Tustari, another Sufi of the same period said:

> . . . repentance consists in not forgetting your sins, but always regretting them, so that, although you have many good works to your credit, you will not be pleased with yourself on that account; since remorse for an evil action is superior to good works, and one who never forgets his sins will never be conceited. (p. 296).

Jonaid, the Sufi *pir* of Baghdad, who lived in the ninth century A.D., stated: "There are three meanings of repentance. The first is guilt and remorsefulness, the second freedom from habits, and the third cleansing oneself from injustice and animosities" (Attār, Vol. II, p. 32).

Ghazzali, in *Alchemy of Happiness*, devoted a chapter to repentance. He stated that when human beings were created they were incomplete because they were all passion and impulse. It was not until later that reason and intellect were bestowed to tame the passions (Chapter 1). The Sufis believe that the experience of repentance is essential for controlling passions and impulses. In Sufism, repentance is reawakening and return from ignorance and aimlessness to the Path. The Koran teaches that anyone who hopes for happiness needs to repent. Prophet Mohammed said, "I repent one hundred times everyday" (pp. 647–648).

Repentance: Psychological Reawakening   In Sufi writings, repentance means seeking forgiveness for one's past sins or, what we now refer to as impulsive behaviors and forbidden wishes. Repentance also refers to existential questioning of one's values and reason for being. Generally, a seeker becomes acutely aware of a lack of fulfillment in life. Daily activities and materialistic belongings do not fulfill the inner emptiness nor calm internal agitation. The seeker often feels restless, unhappy, anxious, and despondent. An intense psychological turmoil may occur.

One of the most quoted examples of a Sufi's reawakening is the story of Ebrahim Ibn Adham, the King of Balkh, who lived in the eighth century A.D.:

One night he was asleep on his royal couch. At midnight the roof of the apartment vibrated, as if someone was walking on the roof.

"Who is there?" he shouted.

"A friend," came the reply. "I have lost a camel, and am searching for it on this roof."

"Fool, do you look for the camel on the roof?" cried Ebrahim.

"Heedless one," answered the voice, "do you seek for God in silken clothes, asleep on a golden couch?"

These words filled his heart with terror. A fire blazed within him, and he could not sleep anymore.

(Attār, Arberry's translation, 1966, p. 63).

This was the beginning of Ebrahim's reawakening. Eventually, he gave up his kingdom to follow the Sufi Path of Reality.

Reawakening is one of the functions of the *human nafs* (Figure 1, chapter 1; Figure 1, chapter 6). Reawakening is one of the attributes of the unconscious which manifests itself in affective, emotional, and intellectual experiences. The potential for reawakening exists in all human beings; however, many do not allow themselves to experience it. According to the Sufis, it is essential for a seeker who is psychologically and spiritually ready to have a Sufi guide help with reawakening and further personality development (Chapter 2).

Repentance and Reawakening in Sufism and Anxiety, Guilt and Self-Observation in Psychotherapy   The stage of repentance and reawakening resembles the initial phase of psychoanalysis or dynamic psychotherapy during which the patient becomes aware of the feelings of anxiety, guilt, and lack of fulfillment. The Sufis believe that the first step toward personality integration is becoming aware of the anxieties of separateness from nature and Reality (*haqq*, God, Truth) (Chapter 2). Similarly, the experience of anxiety and guilt is essential for effective and growth-producing psychotherapy. Psychotherapy without suffering is merely an intellectual exercise.

As you recall, Jonaid described multiple levels of the meaning of repentance, and said that the first level of repentance was allowing oneself to feel guilt and remorse. We know that in psychotherapy it is also necessary to experience anxiety and constructive guilt in order to be motivated for change. On the second level, Jonaid stated that repentance was freeing oneself from past habits and repetitive behavior. In psychotherapy, freeing oneself from troublesome habits and pathological character traits is one of the most difficult tasks. Sometimes it may take many years of psychotherapeutic work and self-observation.

Then, on the third level, Jonaid emphasized that repentance was freeing oneself from the tendency toward injustice and animosity. Liberation from the destructive forces of prejudice, injustice, and divisiveness is the final goal of this developmental stage on the Sufi Path. The sensual and rage forces of the animal *nafs*, or, from the ego psychological point of view, the sexual and aggressive drives of the id, need to be watched over and constructively channelized.

Repentance includes the ability and willingness to observe impulses, wishes, and deeds. Awareness is a significant and important part of repentance. As you recall, Prophet Mohammed humbly and sincerely admitted that he repented one hundred times every day, underlining the fallibility of human nature and the strength of urges and impulses. The experience of repentance is a dynamic and continuous phenomenon. Repentance, from a psychodynamic point of view, is a process of self-observation and self-examination which requires constant practice.

Self-observation, examination, and working through impulsive and acting-out behaviors are the significant aspects of effective psychotherapy. Preoccupation with "good" behavior, at the expense of ignoring, denying, or glossing over acting-out tendencies, contributes to narcissistic aggrandizement, self-deception, and, particularly, inability to develop further insight.

Preoccupation with repentance itself can become a source of pride, self-aggrandizement, and a block on the Path of further integration. According to Ruwaym, the Sufi *pir* of the ninth century, the final goal of repentance is the "repenting of repentance," meaning eventually freeing the self from preoccupation with repentance (Sarrāj, p. 43).

Stage 2: Abstinence (Wara')

The second stage on the Sufi Path of integration, according to Sarrāj (d. 988 A.D.), author of the oldest Sufi book written in Arabic, *The Flame of Sufism (Kitāb al-luma' fi' t-tasawwuf)*, is abstinence *(wara')*. *Wara'* literally means being timid, fearful, cautious, pious, temperate, and refraining from anything doubtful (Steingass, p. 1463). In Sufism, *wara'* refers to abstinence, and also to fear of God.

After reawakening, the seeker becomes more aware of wishes, thoughts, and actions, and this awareness often creates inner turmoil regarding ethical, societal, and particularly religious values. The seeker is expected to follow closely religious edicts concerning what is acceptable and approved, what is unacceptable and sinful, and what is in between, or questionable. For instance, in Islam, drinking alcohol, eating pork, adultery, stealing, lying, dishonesty, deception, malicious gossip, unjust behavior, and usury are forbidden and sinful acts. The seeker is not only expected to observe these prohibitions, but also is encouraged to abstain from overindulgence in food and sleep. In most Sufi orders, celibacy was discouraged and marriage encouraged. Abstinence in sexual wishes, except within the context of marriage, was expected and seen as a way of becoming further purified on the Path.

During the stage of abstinence the seeker, on the instruction of the *pir*, is expected to do daily work while at the same time decreasing food intake and nightly sleep. Time is to be spent in meditation and in observation of inner experiences. This period of intensive meditation and observation helps the seeker in the process of dehabituation. Intensive emotional and psychospiritual experiences often occur. Usually, the *pir* is aware of the seeker's inner turmoil, and helps the seeker free the self from disturbing thoughts, fantasies, illusions, and visions (chapter 2).

Consciousness of thoughts and deeds frequently results in an intensive inner experience of fear, shame, and guilt. Fear and guilt at times are projected outwardly as a fear of God. In the early period of Sufism, when the Sufis were more hermetic and ascetic, there was a much greater emphasis on abstinence and "fear of God." But even then, underlying the fear of God was a deep feeling of love and enthusiastic devotion to God (Reality, *haqq*).

The following story illustrates the first two stages on the Sufi Path—reawakening and abstinence. Beshr Hāfi (Beshr the Barefoot), who was born in 767 A.D., was a drunkard.

> . . . one day as he [Beshr] was staggering along the road drunk he found a piece of paper on which was written, "In the Name of God, the Merciful, the Compassionate." He bought some attar of roses and perfumed the paper with it, and deposited it reverently in his house. [It is forbidden to write the name of God on paper and then throw it away.] That night, a certain holy man had a dream in which he was bidden to tell Beshr:
>
> "Thou has perfumed my Name, so I have perfumed thee. Thou has exalted my Name, so I have exalted thee . . ."
>
> "He is a desolate fellow," thought the saint. "Perhaps I am seeing erroneously."
>
> So he made ablution, prayed and returned to sleep. He saw the selfsame dream a second and a third time. In the morning he aroused and went in search of Beshr.
>
> "He is at a wine-party," he was told.

He went to the house where Beshr was.
"Was Beshr here?" he enquired.
"He was," they said. "But he is drunk and incapable."
"Tell him I have a message for him," said the saint.
"A message from whom?" demanded Beshr when he was told.
"A message from God," replied the saint. (Attār, Arberry's translation, p. 81).

This message moved Beshr deeply and prodded his reawakening. Beshr, from that time on, took the path of abstinence and self-denial. Beshr, by being sincerely respectful to the name of God, although he was drunk and staggering, indicated, we might postulate, that he was unconsciously ready entirely to change his life style.

The Sufi saint's dream demonstrates several points:

1.   The significance of dreams in the process of reawakening;

2.   Reliance on outward appearance is misleading;

3.   When one is ready to be reawakened, it is possible that without direct knowledge, someone else—sometimes a Sufi *pir*—will receive spiritual messages and share this information with the seeker;

4.   The essence of Sufism is hope—hope that it is always possible to free the self from troublesome habits and eventually reach total integration and enlightenment;

5.   Reawakening and abstinence continue throughout life.

Beshr, after his reawakening, pursued the path of abstinence. He became constantly observant of his self-indulgent wishes. The following story reflects Beshr's transformation:

Beshr possessed seven book-cases of volumes on Traditions [Islamic laws and codes of ethics and behavior]. He buried them all in the ground, and did not transmit them.
"The reason I do not transmit Traditions," he explained, "is that I perceive in myself a lust to do so. If I perceive in my heart a lust to keep silence, then I will transmit." (p. 83).

This anecdote touches upon an important aspect of the Sufi journey on the path of liberation. The essence of liberation is freedom from lust and impulses. When desiring to do something for self-aggrandizement, it is necessary to deny that desire. Of course, there also comes a time to free oneself from the denying, because the act of denying could itself become an obstacle on the Path. In regard to abstinence, Beshr said, "Abstinence is that which purifies the individual from doubtful deeds and assists in observing *nafs* every moment of life" (Attār, Vol. 1, p. 112).

Types of Abstinence   According to Sarrāj, there are three groups of people who practice abstinence:

1.   Those who abstain from dubious acts which are neither definitely lawful nor unlawful.

2.   Those who listen to the voice of their inner heart [unconscious] and abstain from anything that their heart prohibits.

3.   Those who have reached the final stage of integration and have freed their heart from all thoughts but Reality. (pp. 44–45).

Fear and Hope   The traveller on the Path experiences intense and overwhelming fear and hope during the stage of abstinence.

FEAR (KHAUF). Fear and abstinence are two sides of the same coin. *Khauf* means fearing, fear, phobia, dread, and terror. In Sufism, *khauf* refers to fear of God and fear of one's conscience. Ebrahim Al-Khauwas, a Sufi (d. 904 A.D.), stated: "Abstinence is the sign of the fear of God, fear of God is the sign of knowledge, and knowledge is the sign of nearness to God" (Ghani, p. 273).

According to Ghazzali, fear is one of the stages on the Sufi Path. He quoted the Koran, ". . . knowledgeable people fear God." He also quoted Prophet Mohammed as saying, "The secret of wisdom and knowledge is fear of God." Freedom from passionate impulses and the ability to tolerate frustration can best be achieved by fear. Fear burns passionate impulses (p. 704). Ghazzali categorized fear as mild, moderate, and severe. He suggested that mild fear is not effective and that severe fear can cause hopelessness, phobia, sickness of the mind, unconsciousness, and possibly death. However, moderate fear helps human beings examine shortcomings and overcome fears on the Path of Reality. According to Ghazzali, "Life without fear is ignorance" (pp. 707–708). The result of fear is abstinence and virtue. Fear of God, abstinence, and virtue are the seeds of happiness.

Shebli, a Sufi *pir* (d. 846 A.D.) observed: "Each day that I was overcome with fear, the door of knowledge and insight opened to my heart" (p. 706). This statement clearly demonstrates the dynamic and growth-producing aspects of fear. The Sufis, through inner experiences and by tapping the far reaches of the unconscious, realize that being human is being afraid. The Sufis recognize the psychological and existential inevitability of experiencing fear. They use the experience of fear constructively for psychospiritual development. They do not avoid fear, but face it and experience it. The experience of fear gives emotional and affective momentum—momentum to modify troublesome and unexpected thoughts and behaviors.

For most Sufis the experience of fear and the practice of abstinence strengthened the body and the mind for the arduous journey on the mystical Path. Personality integration and existential communion require sacrifice, physical conditioning, and psychological preparation. Lack of preparation will result in the traveller going astray. Preparation makes one ready to face and experience unexpected situations.

Fear in Sufism is the fear of the unknown and fear of the mysterious core of the unconscious. Affective experience of this fear encourages the traveller to venture to the frontiers of the unknown and to transcend temporal knowledge in order to experience Reality which defies the limits of the rational mind. The traveller's experience of fear and abstinence enhances self-observation, awareness of shortcomings, impulses, hypocrisy, virtuousness, piety, and total immersion on the Path.

HOPE (RAJĀ'). The essence of Sufism is hope. However, during the stage of abstinence, the traveller experiences the feeling of hope more intensely as a counterpart to the experience of fear. Hope gives momentum and energy to action and behavior becoming the dynamic force for the personality integration and existential communion. Lack of hope may lead to hedonism or despair.

Ghazzali, more than 800 years ago, wrote with significant psychological sensitivity on the nature of hope:

> Know that everyone who expects something good in the future is experiencing hope. The ignorant do not differentiate between hope, wish and false hope or self-deception. If one acquires good seed, plants it in plowed grounds, weeds and waters it regularly, relies on God's will to keep away pests and blights, and expects a harvest, this expectation is hope. If one does not search for good seed nor plant in good earth nor weed nor water, and still expects a harvest, this is called false hope or self-deception. If one puts a good seed in the earth and weeds, but does not

water, and waits for rain, particularly in an area of little rainfall,
this is called wish. (p. 697).

A wish is an unrealistic expectation. False hope or self-deception
is total denial of reality.

In psychoanalytic and psychodynamic literature, references to
wishes, guilt, and intrapsychic conflicts related to them abound. However, very little has been written about hope. Hope, as I perceive it,
is one of the major ego functions. Hope motivates the individual to
tolerate frustration, to postpone desires and wishes, to assess carefully
reality, and, above all, to weigh the risks of success or failure. Hope
is anticipating and preparing for the future.

A wish, on the other hand, is the expression of id impulses and
primary process thoughts and fantasies without the test of reality
(Figure 1, chapter 1). It is the manifestation of infantile omnipotence,
egocentricity, and primary narcissism. There is a self-destructive quality in succumbing to a wish. It is like climbing a high mountain without
knowledge or preparation. One may make it to the top by chance,
but the probability of success is minuscule. Indulgence in wishes brings
about the arrest of personality development and serious psychological
disorders.

Sufis recognize the danger of being overwhelmed by wishes. They
feel that by being aware of and containing their wishes, they can
transmute the forces invested in wishes to the energies of hope. Happiness and contentment are the result of transforming the base metals
of animal desires and wishes through abstinence, fear and the elixir
of hope.

Pride, False Hope, and Self-Deception   The Sufis perceive pride
as false hope and self-deception. In Sufi psychology, pride is the
largest block on the Path of Reality. Divisiveness and fragmentation,
the antithesis of integration, are the outcome of pride. Pride brings
animosity, prejudice, and disharmony between people and among
nations. Destructive wars are often the outcome of pride and self-deception.

Nothing is more important for a seeker on the Path than constant
watchfulness over the tendency to be boastful or proud, whether inwardly or outwardly. The biographies of the Sufis are filled with
stories about their struggles to work through prideful tendencies. The
following story is about Abu Yazid of Bestām, the founder of the
ecstatic school of Sufism:

"One day I was seated," Abu Yazid recalled, "when the
thought entered my mind, 'I am the *shāikh* of the time, the saint

of the age.' As soon as this thought occurred to me, I knew that I had been guilty of great error. I rose up and proceeded on the road to Khorasan. I halted in a hospice and swore that I would not leave it until God sent me someone who should reveal me again to myself.

Three days and three nights I remained there. On the fourth day, I saw a one-eyed man approaching on a camel. Observing him closely, I saw in him the marks of divine awareness. I signalled to the camel to halt, and immediately it lowered its two forelegs to the ground. The man gazed upon me."

"You bring me all this way," he said, "to open an eye that was closed, to unlatch a door that was locked, and to drown the people of Bestām along with Abu Yazid?"

"I swooned away. Whence do you come?" I asked. "Since the moment you swore that oath, I have come three thousand leagues." [more than 9,000 miles!] Then my visitor added, "Beware, Abu Yazid! Keep watch over your heart."

"With that he turned his face from me and departed."

(Attār, Arberry's translation, pp. 115–116).

This story graphically demonstrates that pride and self-conceit can plague the Sufi on the Path at any time. Although Abu Yazid was a Sufi *pir* and sage, he was still vulnerable to the thoughts and fantasies of narcissistic self-aggrandizement. The beauty of the story is that Abu Yazid, with honesty and sincerity, shares his struggles with us. At the same time, we became aware that a Sufi sage needs to have further guidance from others or Providence.

One might wonder about the identity of the one-eyed man on the camel. The Sufis, especially when they were further along the Sufi Path, believed in the immortal guide, *Khizr* (Elias). Henry Corbin (1958), the well-known French scholar, extensively discussed *Khizr* and his influence on the Sufi sages. *Khizr* is a prophet, the guide of everyone who is lost, whether physically or spiritually. *Khizr* is timeless and spaceless. He can travel the seven seas in a short time. He has drunk the elixir of life from the spring of immortality. Because of that, he is referred to as *Khizr,* which means green or evergreen. *Khizr* appears from nowhere, frequently in the form of an old man with a grey beard, when a Sufi is in deep distress and helpless on the Path.

In the story of Abu Yazid, the spiritual guide *(Khizr)* appears to him as a one-eyed man. This symbolizes Abu Yazid's momentary self-conceit or narcissistic pride; he became blind on the Path of Reality!

Accusing Nafs   The accompanying *nafs* for the second stage of human development on the Sufi Path, abstinence, is *nafs-i-lawwāmā*, which means accusing or blaming *nafs* (Figure 1, chapter 1; Figure 1, chapter 6). Parental, religious, and societal prohibitions, experience of guilt and shame, fear, self-blame, and self-accusation are manifestations of accusing *nafs*. Humanistic and universal values, ability to delay gratification, sublimation of animal urges, and transformation of these urges to love have their roots in the accusing *nafs*. On a higher level, the ability for self-observation, introspection, and psychospiritual awareness are also the functions of this *nafs*. Abstinence and asceticism are the practical methods for coming in touch with animal urges. According to the Sufis, not only reason and intellect, but also the accusing *nafs* differentiate humans from animals.

ACCUSING NAFS IN SUFISM AND SUPEREGO IN EGO PSYCHOLOGY

The concepts of id and ego in ego psychology were discussed in chapter 1 and compared with animal and human *nafses* in Sufism. Now, accusing *nafs* in Sufism will be compared with the concept of superego in ego psychology (Figure 1, chapter 1; Figure 1, chapter 6).

Accusing *nafs* is similar to the concept of superego proposed by Freud in 1923. The superego is originally derived from the ego. It is that part of the personality which deals with moral and religious values and inhibitions against sexual and aggressive wishes. Most of the superego functions are unconscious. The ego usually mediates between the id and superego to find a healthy or compromised solution for adaptation. According to Freud (1923):

> ... The self-judgement which declares that the ego falls short of its ideal produces the religious sense of humility to which the believer appeals in his longing. As a child grows up, the role of father is carried on by teachers and others in authority; their injunctions and prohibitions remain powerful in the ego ideal and continue, in the form of conscience, to exercise the moral censorship. The tension between the demands of conscience and the actual performances of the ego is experienced as a sense of guilt. (p. 37).

Moore and Fine (1968) define superego as representing

> ... moral attitudes, conscience, and the sense of guilt.... In
> neuroses, symptoms arise as compromises in the conflict between
> *instinctual drives (id* derivatives) and the forces seeking to forbid
> or restrain their expression (the superego). (p. 90).

Parental, societal, and personal prohibitions, along with religious
and moral values are functions of the superego. Some ego psychologists differentiate between ego ideal and superego. They relate the
function of the superego to prohibitions, constrictions, inhibitions,
and severe punishment for transgression of thoughts or deeds. They
believe that the superego is harsh, punitive, and unmerciful. On the
other hand, the ego ideal is perceived as a function of the ego which
relates to one's goals, aspirations, and ideals in life. It is exhilarating
and liberating as opposed to the function of the primitive superego,
which is based on fear of punishment, and is limiting and inhibiting.

In healthy individuals, after adolescence the superego and ego
ideal become fairly well integrated within the function of the ego
through reality testing, discipline, mutual respect for self and others,
and personal political, creative, and spiritual aspirations.

Accusing *nafs* in Sufism and superego and ego ideal in ego psychology are essential for taming animal desires, selfish tendencies,
narcissistic pride, false hope, and self-deception. Over-reliance and preoccupation with abstinence and asceticism in Sufism, or overwhelming preoccupation with a sense of guilt or shame in ego psychology,
limits human development and may contribute to the expression of
psychopathological disorders, such as neurosis, depressive tendencies,
obsessive-compulsive tendencies, severe phobias, or even psychosis.

In early Sufism during the eighth and ninth centuries A.D., some
of the Sufis perceived severe asceticism, abstinence, and preoccupation
with blame and guilt as the only remedies for salvation. Later, however,
in the ninth and tenth centuries most Sufis modified the exaggerated
ascetic and hermetic practices and adopted a more balanced life-style.

*A Comparison Between the Stages of Repentance and Abstinence in Sufism
and the Oral, Anal, and Phallic Stages in Ego Psychology*

We will begin this section with a brief description of the stages
of human development in ego psychology. Then, we will compare
these stages with the stages of repentance and abstinence in Sufism.

Stages of Human Development in Ego Psychology   One of the major contributions of Freud (1905), Abraham (1916), Erikson (1950), and Anna Freud (1965) to the understanding of human development was the construction of the libido theory and its application to all phases of human development from birth onward. Freud concluded that from the moment of birth, different zones of the body are endowed with libido, a pleasure-seeking energy. Before Freud, libido as a sexual energy was attributed only to adolescents and adults. Infants and children were not thought to have any sexual thoughts or desires. They were totally "innocent." Freud (1905), in his famous work, *Three Essays on the Theory of Sexuality*, attacked this myth and associated libidinal energy with the body's anatomical orifices. Abraham (1916) and later Erikson (1950) eloquently described the psychosexual development of infancy and childhood.

In psychoanalysis and ego psychology we are familiar with the following stages of psychosexual development (Figure 1, chapter 6):

1.   Oral Stage (Oral-Sensory)—birth to eighteen months

2.   Anal Stage (Muscular-Anal)—eighteen months to three years

3.   Phallic Stage (Locomotor-Phallic, Latency, Puberty, Adolescence)—three to eighteen years

4.   Genital Stage (Young Adulthood, Adulthood, and Maturity)—eighteen years and onward.

ORAL STAGE. In the oral stage, the infant's mouth and skin are endowed with libidinal energy. Stimulation of the mouth and skin give comfort and pleasure beyond satiating hunger.

Erikson (1950) integrated psychoanalytic, psychosocial, and cultural factors to describe human development. Erikson called this integrated developmental perspective the "Eight Ages of Man."

The oral stage, or according to Erikson the oral-sensory stage, is divided into two phases:

1.   *Oral Receptivity*—this phase spans ages birth to six months. The infant is relaxed and receptive to mother's giving. A "mutuality of relaxation" between the child, mother, and others evolves. The child is totally trusting, and receives great pleasure by ". . . being held, warmed, smiled at, talked to, rocked, . . ." (Erikson, 1963, p. 76). In this phase, there are no ambivalent (love-hate) relationships. When hungry or in pain, the infant cries. Soon the infant learns that, at the

slightest whimper or cry, a loving and caring mother (provider) will attend to all needs. According to Erikson, the development of the sense of "basic trust," which is the foundation of human development, has its roots in the oral-sensory stage, particularly the oral-receptive phase.

2. *Oral Incorporative*—this phase spans ages six to eighteen months. In this phase, the infant usually develops teeth. Biting on hard things and biting through things becomes a pleasurable experience. Also at this time, the infant is able to reach out and grasp objects with both hands. "Taking and holding onto things becomes a social modality" (p. 77).

According to Bowlby (1958, 1960, 1973), by age eight months, the infant is able to differentiate between mother and strangers much more accurately. The infant becomes anxious and panic-stricken and cries in order to become reunited with mother. This reaction is called separation anxiety (chapter 2).

Margaret Mahler (Mahler & Gosliner, 1955; Mahler, 1972; Mahler et al., 1975) contributed significantly to the psychological understanding of the mother-child relationship, especially the development of attachment and love between mother and child during the first three years of life. She calls this process separation-individuation phases. Psychological birth of the self is the outcome of these phases (Shafii & Shafii, 1982, pp. 19–20, 33–35).

It is now recognized that solid attachment behavior develops in these early childhood years. Fractures in human attachments at this time contribute significantly to a number of serious physical and psychopathological syndromes, such as failure to thrive in infancy, mental retardation, developmental disabilities, depressive disorders, behavioral disorders, neurotic disorders, and possible psychotic disorders with resultant ramifications in adolescence and adulthood.

ANAL STAGE. The anal stage, or muscular-anal stage, spans from eighteen months to three years of age. This stage is related to the development of the eliminative organs and body musculature. The libidinal and erotic energy become cathected to the anal zone. The developmental milestones of this stage are toilet training—release and control of bowel function in the form of expelling and withholding, further strengthening of the muscles, and improvement in body coordination. Orderliness, punctuality, thrift, further differentiation between good and bad, the ability for "letting go" and "holding on," and the ability to control oneself are the psychological traits developed during this stage.

Doubt and ambivalence in the form of love-hate are prevalent.

The individual subjects others and the self to harsh and unrelenting punishment at the time of transgression. This reflects the primitive aspects of the superego and the projective identification with parental prohibitions and disciplines.

According to Erikson, healthy development of the individual in the anal stage facilitates the establishment of the sense of autonomy. Pathological development results in an overwhelming sense of shame and doubt which can plague the individual throughout life.

PHALLIC STAGE. The phallic stage usually spans ages three to seven years; however, since the individual from ages seven to eighteen years also manifests many characteristics of the phallic stage, these ages will be included.

Erikson divided human development during ages three to eighteen years in the following way:

Locomotor-Phallic. The locomotor-phallic phase spans ages three to seven years. The developmental milestones of this phase are the attainment of body mastery in the form of walking and running, physical independence, and active involvement in play with other children.

Development of the sense of curiosity about the body with special preoccupation with the genitals occurs. The child becomes acutely aware of the sexual differences between boys and girls. Concern about damage to body parts—particularly the genitals—brings intense fears and anxieties, which are referred to as "castration anxiety."

During this phase, further ethical values and the ability to control sexual and aggressive impulses occur. The superego gradually becomes a consolidated and integrated part of the personality. Initiative and assertiveness evolve during this phase.

The experience of guilt by the ego in the form of the conflict between the wishes of the id and the prohibition of the superego is the major and significant psychosocial development of this phase. At the same time, if one is overwhelmed by the sense of guilt, individual assertiveness and initiative may become inhibited. This could lead to the development of a personality plagued by a multitude of phobias, anxieties, depressions, and neurotic inhibitions.

Latency. The latency phase spans from ages seven to twelve years. During this phase, the child gives up some of the tumultuous wishes and acute fears of the locomotor-phallic phase and moves into a period of relative quiescence. Libidinal and aggressive energies are usually channeled into learning, development of skills, and long-lasting friendships with people of the same sex. According to Erikson, successful expression of the latency phase is industriousness. The child ". . . develops a sense of industry—i.e., he adjusts himself to the inorganic laws of the world. He can become an eager and absorbed unit of a productive situation" (1963, p. 259).

Overwhelming conflicts in this phase contribute to the feelings of inadequacy and inferiority. Mediocrity rather than excellence prevails in the individual's lifestyle.

Puberty and Adolescence.   This phase spans ages twelve to eighteen years. According to psychoanalytic theory, there is an intensive resurgence of the separation-individuation phase and of the phallic stage in puberty and adolescence. A major psychological revolution occurs within the individual. Rapid hormonal increases and body growth contribute to significant personality changes. The maturity of the sexual organs occurs during this period.

Parental, ethical, and societal values, which were internalized in the form of the childhood superego, are re-examined. The adolescent questions, challenges, and doubts everything. With physiological changes, expression of emotions is intensified. The smallest issue may become a point of contention, argument, and debate between adolescents and their parents.

With the physiological and psychological changes, as Erikson put it, an "identity crisis" occurs. The resolution of this crisis gives way to the emerging of a new identity, which transcends childhood identity and in many ways is different from parental identity.

Erikson stated:

> The integration now taking place in the form of ego identity is . . . more than the sum of the childhood identifications. It is the accrued experience of the ego's ability to integrate all identification with the vicissitudes of the libido, with the aptitudes developed out of endowment, and with the opportunities offered in social roles. (p. 261).

One of the tangible promises of this phase is the ability to perceive the possibilities of a future career. The pathological outcome of this phase would be "role confusion." "Where . . . [role confusion] is based on a strong previous doubt as to one's sexual identity, delinquent and outright psychotic episodes are not uncommon" (p. 262).

During late adolescence, the individual becomes ready for the possibility of exploring the uncharted areas in the fields of science, technology, art, literature, politics, aesthetics, philosophy, and particularly religion.

GENITAL STAGE. The genital stage in psychoanalysis and Erikson's phases of young adulthood, adulthood, and maturity are discussed later in this chapter.

Greed in Sufism and Orality-Anality in Ego Psychology

Although the Sufis do not specifically discuss stages of human development in infancy and childhood, they emphasize various human characteristics and traits which resemble the behaviors of the oral, anal, and phallic stages.

The Sufis believe that preoccupation with sensual pleasures, greed, and material possessions contribute further to alienation and separation from nature, the inner self (unconscious), and Reality. They believe that heaven and hell are here with us in this world. Hell is enslavement by one's commanding *nafs*, thereby being at the mercy of animal desires and greed (chapter 1). Heaven is freedom from this enslavement and the mastering of animal desires. Energies liberated from this enslavement bring freedom from preoccupation with the self, allowing further growth, development, and purification. Rumi wrote:

> Oh Son, break your chains and be free.
> How long will you be a slave of silver and gold?
> If you pour the sea into a pitcher,
> It will hold one day's store.
> The eye of the greedy is like the pitcher which
> is never filled.
> The oyster shell does not hold a pearl
> Until it is contented. (*Mathnawi*, Book I, p. 4).

Rumi in another place stated:

> Because you have been able to guide the hellish nature of your *nafses* which are filled with the fire of temptation, they have been transformed to the light of purity and faith; the fire of passion which was flaming within you has turned to the greenness of purity and the light of faith. The fire of anger has been transmuted to patience, the darkness of ignorance to knowledge, the fire of greed to unselfishness and the thorn of envy to roses. (*Mathnawi*, Book II, pp. 388–389).

In Rumi's poem, the metaphor, fire, represents the dynamic and destructive forces and impulses of animal *nafs*. When one becomes aware of the volcano within, it is possible to work through and channelize destructive forces to bring about transformation of the self and enlightenment.

Rumi portrayed the existential dilemma of human beings preoccupied with their animal *nafs*, particularly greed, in the following story of a cow on a green island:

> There is in the world a green island where a sweet-mouthed cow lives alone.
> She feeds on the whole field till nightfall, so that she grows stout and big and choice.
> During the night she becomes thin as a hair from anxiety because she thinks, "What shall I eat tomorrow?"
> At rise of dawn the field becomes green: the green blades and grain have grown up to [a man's] middle.
> The cow falls to ravenously: till night she feeds on that [vegetation and devours it] entirely.
> Again she becomes stout and fat and bulky: Her body is filled with fat and strength.
> Then again at night she [is stricken] by panic [and] falls into a fever [of anxiety] so that from fear of seeking [vainly] for fodder she becomes lean,
> Thinking, "What shall I eat tomorrow at meal time?" This is what the cow does for [many] years.
> She never thinks, "All these years I have been eating from this meadow and this pasture;
> My provender has never failed [even] for a day: what, [then], is this fear and anguish and heart-burning of mind? . . ."
> The cow is the carnal soul, and the field is this world, where she [the carnal soul] is made lean by fear for her daily bread.
> (*Mathnawi*, Book V, Nicholsons' translation, 1925–1940, p. 172)

This story reminds one of the oral stage of psychosexual development. Abraham (1916) described the role of the mouth in psychological development of the first two years of life. During this stage the child expresses intense needs by wishing to devour anything and everything, including mother's breast, mother herself, and the objects around. Abraham refers to this stage as the oral incorporative stage. By wishing to devour everything, the child tries to compensate for feelings of hunger, pain, insecurity, and helplessness. In later life, the conflicts around the oral stage manifest themselves in the form of greediness, feelings of deprivation, demandingness, overindulgence in eating, lack of frustration tolerance, depression, alcoholism, drug addiction, and other severe forms of psychopathological disorders such as psychosis.

Sufis were not aware of the erotogenic aspects of the mouth, but they had a keen understanding of the direct relationship between control and mastery of libidinous and rage forces within and the constant need for eating, greediness, and possession. Selfishness and greed are interrelated in Sufi psychology and are perceived as the manifestations of primitive preoccupation with the self. The Sufis prescribed various methods for enhancing the ability to tolerate frustration, to become more aware of animal *nafs*, and to find a way of handling impulsive and driven desires effectively (chapters 2 and 5). Hujwiri wrote: "Acquiescence in natural habits [impulsive desires and greed] prevents a man from attaining to the exalted degree of . . . spirituality . . ." (p. 149). The hope exists that a human being, through meditation and self-observation on the mystical path, can sublimate sexual and destructive impulses and develop the ability to become tolerant and patient.

Duality in Sufism and Ambivalence in Ego Psychology

According to Erikson (1963), in the oral-incorporative phase, ". . . 'good' and 'evil' enter the baby's world . . . " (p. 78). Until the occurrence of teething, the oral cavity was the source of pleasure; now, teething brings pain and discomfort. Biting of the breast results in mother's anger and the withdrawal of the nipple. The infant then feels frustrated, angry, and helpless.

These developmental events contribute to destroying the child's

> . . . unity with a maternal matrix. This earliest catastrophe in the
> individual's relation to himself and to the world is probably the
> ontogenic contribution to the biblical saga of paradise, where the
> first people on earth forfeited forever the right to pluck without
> effort what had been put at their disposal; they bit into the forbid-
> den apple, and made God angry. (p. 79).

Erikson concluded:

> The oral stages then, form in the infant the springs of the
> *basic sense of trust* and the *basic sense of mistrust* which remain the
> autogenic source of both primal hope and of doom throughout
> life. (p. 80).

It appears that the psychological roots of ambivalence and the tendency for dualistic thinking, such as making divisions into good—bad, heaven—hell, friend—enemy, I—it, and us—them, are related to the oral-incorporative phase of human development. Ambivalent and dualistic tendencies become intensified during the anal phase. Fixation and preoccupation with ambivalent tendencies contribute to the development of rigidity, intolerance, racial and religious prejudice, and, in severe cases, to pathological mistrust, paranoid and destructive behavior, and a multitude of psychopathological disorders.

Sufis did not discuss the concept of oral or anal stages of human development, but they were acutely aware of the human tendency toward divisiveness, fragmentation, and dualistic thinking. The Sufis' search for unity and existential communion consists of transcending the dualistic thought processes and attitudes within, and developing an integrated universal perspective of life.

One wonders why the Sufis attempted to transcend duality and searched with fervor for unity and oneness. Some early psychoanalysts hypothesized that the mystics' desire for oneness and union was a form of pathological regression to the womb.

Fingarette (1963), in *The Self in Transformation,* examined the mystics' search for oneness and communion from an ego-psychological point of view. He perceived communion and oneness as a total psychological integration of various levels of personality, and as freedom from

> Ignorance, pride, lust, and hatred—here is the universally acknowledged "syndrome" associated by mystics with the disease of self-ishness. The psychoanalytic explanation of neurosis is analogous. Unsublimated libido and aggression (lust, hatred and greed) result in distorted, fantasy-colored experiences ("ignorance," "illusion") . . .
>
> "Freedom from striving" and "acceptance," key notions of the mystic, are often misinterpreted to mean systematic refusal to take the initiative, consistent absence of goals of any sort, submissiveness. This the enlightened read into the words in spite of the evidence before their eyes that those who best exemplify mystic enlightenment are people who obviously do take the initiative, who clearly execute well-organized, purposeful behavior, and who have indeed modified the world. (pp. 316–317).

Stage of Abstinence in Sufism and the Phallic Stage in Ego Psychology

As discussed earlier, the stage of abstinence is the second stage on the Sufi Path to Reality. Fear, one of the major psychological attributes of this stage, is related to the accusing *nafs* (Figure 1, chapter 6). The Sufis' practice of abstinence is an attempt to control instinctual desires, confront and experience fears, and channel energies toward further psychospiritual development.

The concept of accusing *nafs* closely resembles the concept of superego in ego psychology. Fear, from a psychodynamic point of view, has its roots in the anxieties of the phallic stage. Although Sufis do not discuss the various phases of psychosexual stages in childhood, they are acutely aware of the psychology of fear—fear originating from religious prohibitions, parental inhibitions, and internal values. In ego psychology, fear is related to the conflict between id impulses and superego prohibitions as experienced by the ego. Sufis are acutely aware of not allowing themselves to become overwhelmed or paralyzed by the intensity of these fears. They feel that intensive fear may result in severe phobia, inhibition, cowardice, inaction, overwhelming doubt, paralysis of the mind and soul, and even unconsciousness and death. This explanation is similar to our present psychodynamic understanding of an individual who becomes extensively traumatized in the phallic stage. Castration anxiety becomes overwhelming and contributes to feelings of helplessness. Severe psychopathology, such as anxiety disorder, phobia, obsessive-compulsive disorders, panic disorders, hysterical paralysis, and inhibitive personality may be the result.

Sufis, by confronting fears directly and by allowing themselves to experience these fears, have found an effective way of mastering them. They use the anxieties and energies generated from fears constructively for further psychomystical evolution. We know that the most effective treatment for unrealistic fears or phobia is being exposed to the phobic-inducing object or situation. Behavioral therapy, psychoanalytic psychotherapy, and other forms of psychotherapy are generally in agreement with this approach. Avoiding the phobic situation reinforces the phobic behavior and contributes further to a panic reaction or severe inhibition.

The Sufis recognize that being human means having fears. They even suggest that life without fear is ignorance. The Sufis openly face their fears, master them, and eventually use the freed energy for continuing on the Path of Reality.

Recently some clinicians using a technique called "flooding" have helped patients overcome phobias. In "flooding" the phobic patient is subjected extensively to the phobic object. The patient may experience panic and anxiety. After the initial panic, the patient gradually adapts and accepts the fear. The patient's psychophysiological reaction becomes milder. Through direct exposure, the patient masters his or her fear. The Sufis' experience of fear during sleepless nights of meditation may be similar to the "flooding" phenomenon.

Stage 3: Renunciation (Zuhd)

The third stage on the Sufi Path of integration is *Zuhd,* which literally means abstaining from or treating with indifference things of this world. In Sufism, *Zuhd* refers to renouncing and giving up longings for things of the world.

There are three types of renunciation:

> *First*—The seeker is materially poor and also his heart is free from greed for worldly things. They asked Jonaid of Baghdad, "What is renunciation?" He said, "Emptiness of the hand from worldly goods and emptiness of the heart from greed."
>
> *Second*—The seeker frees the self from everything in the world. Renunciation itself becomes the source of comfort, internal peace, and harmony. The Sufi, Ruwaym, stated, "Real renunciation is when the heart gives up all pleasures."
>
> *Third*—The seeker renounces renunciation, and frees the self from preoccupation with renunciation. Dwelling on renunciation itself is a form of self conceit and pride. Some of the seekers, because of their own shortcomings and limitations, become fixated at this point. Outwardly, they might have the appearance of abstinence and renunciation but inwardly they are still the slaves of their impulsive wishes and prideful tendencies concerning their act of renunciation. (Ghani, 1951, pp. 273–274).

There are many stories written about the Sufis and their experience of renunciation. The following story is attributed to Abu Yazid of Bestām:

> There was a certain ascetic who was one of the great saints of Bestām. He had his own followers and admirers, and at the same time he was never absent from the circle of Abu Yazid. He listened to all his discourses, and sat with his companions.
>
> One day he remarked to Abu Yazid, "Master, today is thirty years that I have been keeping constant fast. By night too I pray,

so that I never sleep at all. Yet I discover no trace in myself of this knowledge of which you speak . . ."

"If for three hundred years," said Abu Yazid, "you fast by day and pray by night, you will never realize one atom of this discourse."

"Why?" asked the disciple.

"Because you are veiled by your own self," Abu Yazid replied.

"What is the remedy for this?" the man asked.

"You will never accept it," answered Abu Yazid.

"I will so," said the man. "Tell me, so that I may do as you prescribe."

"Very well," said Abu Yazid. "This very hour go and shave your beard and hair. Take off these clothes you are wearing, and tie a loincloth of goat's wool about your waist. Hang a bag of nuts round your neck, then go to the marketplace. Collect all the children you can, and tell them, 'I will give a nut to everyone who slaps me.' Go around all the city in the same way; especially go everywhere people know you. That is your cure."

. . . "This I cannot do," the man protested. "Give me other directions."

"The remedy is what I have said," Abu Yazid declared.

"I cannot do it," the man repeated.

"Did I not say that you would not do it, that you would never obey me?" said Abu Yazid. (Attār, Arberry's translation, pp. 112–113).

This story signifies that although the disciple himself was an ascetic with a number of followers, he had not appreciated the inner meaning of renunciation. Fasting, praying, and deprivation are counterproductive if they become a source of pride and aggrandizement. From a psychodynamic perspective, renunciation became an extension of his narcissism. Abu Yazid was aware of this ascetic's shortcomings and his preoccupation with outward appearance. Abu Yazid suggested a seemingly absurd approach to confront directly the ascetic's pretenses.

Also, the story underlines the significant role of the Sufi guide or spiritual physician in helping the seeker free the self from fixations and prideful preoccupations in various stages of psychomystical development on the Path (chapter 2).

The saying we have earlier quoted from Abu Yazid succinctly summarizes the stage of renunciation:

"Almighty God," said Abu Yazid, "admitted me to His presence in two thousand stations, and in every station He offered me a kingdom, but I declined it. God said to me 'Abu Yazid, what do you desire?' I replied, 'I desire not to desire.' " (p. 122).

The Sufis' final goal is experiencing Reality. Renunciation is a means of overcoming internal obstacles. Fixation on renunciation becomes a veil or obstacle in knowing, seeing, or experiencing Reality.

Another example of renunciation is a story about Ebrahim-Ibn-Adham:

> One day Ebrahim came to a well. He let down the bucket, and it came up full of gold. He emptied it and let it down again, and it came up full of pearls. In merry mood he emptied it once more.
>
> "O God," he cried, "Thou art offering me a treasury. I know that Thou art all-powerful, and Thou knowest that I shall not be deluded by this. Give me water, that I may make my ablution [washing before prayers and meditation]." (p.78).

Renunciation, in the true sense, is giving up old values and longings. It is freeing the mind from indulgent wishes and self-conceit. Renunciation is achieved not by words, but by deeds. It is internal transformation, and giving up of infantile illusions and delusions. It is constantly being aware of one's narcissistic longings and impulsive wishes, and gradually neutralizing these wishes rather than suppressing them. Transformation turns creative energies of these wishes to the spontaneous expression of mystical hopes and feelings, and toward further communion and integration.

Renunciation in Sufism and Genital Stage in Ego Psychology

The highest level of personality development in ego psychology and psychoanalysis is the "genital stage," which corresponds with Erikson's stages of young adulthood, adulthood, and maturity (Figure 1, chapter 6). Freud (1933), regarding the genital stage of psychosexual development, wrote, "We have reserved the name of *genital* phase for definitive sexual organization which is established after puberty . . ." (p. 99). In another place, he stated that the development and organization of sexual function becomes complete with the ". . . genital phase." Freud (1938), in one of his last works, entitled *An Outline of Psychoanalysis* clearly discussed the genital stage:

> . . . In the early phases [oral, anal and phallic] the different component instincts set about their pursuit of pleasure independently of one another; in the phallic phase there are the beginnings of an organization which subordinates the other urges to the primacy of the genitals and signifies the start of a co-ordination of the general urge towards pleasure into the sexual function. (p. 155).

Freud, and most psychoanalysts after him including Erikson, believed that the genital stage is the final stage of psychosexual development. The genital stage is the integration of the oral, anal, and phallic stages. Maturity in psychoanalytic theory is defined as the "primacy of genital organization."

During the last few decades in psychoanalytic circles, there has been discussion concerning the concepts of the genital stage, maturity, health, and personality integration. Erikson (1963) addressed the issue of human development after adolescence. Regarding the concept of the genital stage, he wrote: "A system must have its utopia. For psychoanalysis the utopia is 'genitality' " (p. 92).

In another place regarding adult sexuality, maturity, and integration, Erikson stated:

> Adult sexuality is marked by genitality, by the capacity for a full and mutual consummation of the sexual act. An immense power of verification pervades this meeting of bodies and temperaments after a hazardously long childhood, . . . Freud observed that mature genitality alone guarantees that combination . . . of intellectual clarity, sexual mutuality, and considerate love, which anchors man in the actuality of his responsibilities. (pp. 128–129).

Erikson conceptualized the genital stage as comprising three phases: young adulthood, adulthood, and maturity (Figure 1, chapter 6).

YOUNG ADULTHOOD. Young adulthood follows puberty and adolescence. Consolidating identity and becoming ". . . willing to fuse [one's] identity with that of others" occurs in this phase (p. 263). The individual is ready for "intimacy" and has "the capacity to commit" oneself to a strong affiliation and partnership with others. Intimacy and affiliation contribute to the feeling of close friendship, surging fighting spirit, whether physical or psychological, and orgasm in sexual union. The counterpart of intimacy is the sense of isolation.

ADULTHOOD. An adult person ". . . needs to be needed, and maturity needs guidance as well as encouragement from what has been produced and must be taken care of" (pp. 266–267).

Generativity is the healthy psychological expression of this phase. According to Erikson, "Generativity . . . is primarily the concern in establishing and guiding the next generation, . . ." (p. 267). Generativity includes productivity and creativity. In generativity one gives up something for survival of the next generation and for the transmission of knowledge. "It has taken psychoanalysis some time to realize that the ability to lose oneself in the meeting of bodies and minds leads to a gradual expansion of ego-interests and to a libidinal investment in that which is being generated" (p. 267). If generativity fails it will result in ". . . regression to an obsessive need for pseudo-intimacy . . . often with a pervading sense of stagnation and personal impoverishment" (p. 267).

MATURITY. Maturity is the highest phase of Erikson's epigenetic theory of human development. The developmental task of this phase is "ego integrity versus despair." Erikson defines ego integrity as follows:

> It is the ego's accrued assurance of its proclivity for order and meaning. It is a post-narcissistic love of the human ego—not of the self—as an experience which conveys some world order and spiritual sense, no matter how dearly paid for. (p. 268).

During this phase, the individual experiences failure and victories. Pleasure in giving as well as receiving characterizes relationships. Erikson defined integrity as finding "meaning to human striving." He elaborated further, ". . . the possessor of integrity is ready to defend the dignity of his own life-style against all physical and economic threats" (p. 268). Fear of death "loses its sting."

Developmental failure in this phase is a lack of ego integration which results in fear of death and the experience of "despair." "Despair expresses the feeling that the time is now short, too short for the attempt to start another life to try out alternate roads to integrity. Disgust hides despair . . ." (p. 269).

Erikson concluded his psychological observation of human development by saying, "Ego integrity, therefore, implies an emotional integration which permits participation by followership as well as acceptance of the responsibility of leadership." He added, ". . . healthy children will not fear life if their elders have integrity enough not to fear death" (p. 269).

Renunciation in Sufism and Ego Integrity in Ego Psychology

For some time I puzzled over how to compare Sufi stages of human development with the stages of human development in ego psychology and, particularly, with Erikson's "Eight Ages of Man." This comparison was most difficult at higher developmental levels. For instance, Erikson, in his final phase, talks about maturity and ego integrity. Is ego integrity basically the same as the concept of the integrated human being in Sufism? If they are not the same, what are the differences? Although I had an internal feeling that they were not the same, I had no objective documentation to verify this internal perception. I had read and reread Erikson's "Eight Ages of Man" many times in the last 15 years, but was still perplexed. Recently, by chance, I saw Erikson's footnote in the Second Edition of *Childhood and Society* (1963) concerning a further elaboration on the "Eight Ages of Man." It opened new vistas and, in the essence of Sufism, showed me that truth is often at hand but we are frequently too blind to see it.

In his footnote, Erikson discussed the concept of "basic virtues" or "ego strengths." According to him, ego strength or basic virtue changes in each psychosocial stage. For instance, in the oral-sensory stage, "drive and hope," which are the result of the ratio between "basic trust versus basic mistrust" are the ego strengths. The following chart shows the mode of each psychosocial stage and the optimal virtue of each stage:

Psychosocial Stage	Mode	Ego Strength or Virtue
I — Oral-Sensory	Basic Trust vs. Basic Mistrust	Drive and Hope
II — Muscular-Anal	Autonomy vs. Shame and Doubt	Self-Control and Will Power
III — Locomotor-Phallic	Initiative vs. Guilt	Direction and Purpose
IV — Latency	Industry vs. Inferiority	Method and Competence
V — Puberty-Adolescence	Identity vs. Role Confusion	Devotion and Fidelity
VI — Young Adulthood	Intimacy vs. Isolation	Affiliation and Love
VII — Adulthood	Generativity vs. Stagnation	Production and Care
VIII — Maturity	Ego Integrity vs. Despair	Renunciation and Wisdom

Ibid., p. 274

From these data it is clear that Erikson perceived the final stage of human maturity and development as the optimal ratio between ego integrity versus despair. The ego strength or virture of this final stage is "renunciation and wisdom." By renunciation and wisdom, Erikson (1961) meant:

> Ego-strength in the old takes the form of "wisdom" in all of its connotations from ripened "wits" to matured judgement, which constitute the ability to maintain the *wholeness of experience* even as the body's faculties gradually fall "apart" . . . If vigor of mind combines with the gift of responsible renunciation, some old people can envisage human problems in their entirety (which is what *integrity* means) . . . (p. 161).

Erikson compared virtues to past universal values. He suggested that one can find a similarity ". . . in the idea of the all-healing power of genital union," the ". . . mystics consummation of relationship with God," and ". . . the idea of *perfect Christian love*" (p. 163, footnote).

Regarding wisdom, Erikson (1964) insightfully wrote:

> As we come to the last stage, we become aware of the fact that our civilization really does not harbor the concept of the whole of life, as do the civilizations of the East: "In office a Confucian, in retirement a Taoist." In fact, it is astonishing to behold, how (until quite recently and with a few notable exceptions) Western psychology has avoided looking at the range of the whole cycle. (p. 132).

Erikson defined wisdom as follows: "*Wisdom, then, is detached concern with life itself, in the face of death itself.*" (p. 133). He did not clearly define renunciation, but it appears that he used the concepts of renunciation and wisdom synonomously as a basic virtue or ego strength of the final phase of human development.

Erikson felt that wisdom came with maturity and aging. Wisdom ". . . maintains and conveys the integrity of experience, in spite of the decline of bodily and mental functions. It responds to the need of the oncoming generation for an integrated heritage and yet remains aware of the relativity of all knowledge" (p. 133).

BEYOND MATURITY. Final stages of human development beyond maturity and adulthood have not been explored in Western psychologies. The emphasis in the West has been on learning about symptoms, behaviors, psychopathologies, and human development and adaptation in childhood and adolescence. Emphasis has also been on the development of techniques and approaches to decrease anxiety, alleviate symptoms, and enhance the capacity for adjustment to daily life. Most psychotherapeutic practices in the West, whether they be analytic, behavioral, or any other, emphasize elimination of symptoms and adjustment to daily realities.

Exploration and experience of a reality beyond our temporal and individual reality is frowned upon. A psychotherapist or psychoanalyst may tolerate a short venture in this direction, but if the individual wants to pursue Universal Reality beyond temporal reality, it is often perceived as philosophizing, intellectualization, resistance, narcissistic preoccupation, or psychotic regression!

The stage of renunciation in Sufism approximates the stage of maturity and integration of personality in Western psychotherapies and psychoanalysis. In the most successful psychotherapeutic experiences, the patient renounces symptoms. The patient develops a detached concern towards the self, others, and life, and gives up to some extent the insecurities of possessing and possession. The individual experiences guilt and anxiety, but, through an expanded observing ego, masters these feelings and is not overwhelmed by them. In the most successful analytic and therapeutic experiences, one frees the self from the illusions and delusions of childhood, and becomes aware of one's strengths and limitations in the light of reality.

The following saying is attributed to Karen Horney, the well-known psychoanalyst: "Maturity is a gradual disillusionment." When I once shared this saying with one of my patients who was working toward her Doctoral Degree in Spanish literature, she said that it reminded her of a Spanish word, *desenganche,* which means disengagement and disillusionment, but at the same time also means enlightenment.

Erikson's "detached concern," and the Sufis' "renunciation" mean freeing onself from the habits, behavior, and symptoms which hinder growth and development. It means, specifically, renouncing one's grandiose and infantile fantasies and illusions. Sudden disillusionment may result in severe depression and the feelings of hopelessness and helplessness. Gradual disillusionment brings about feelings of sadness and loss. However, eventually the loss of illusions and distortions brings about freedom from narcissistic, traumatic, neurotic, and conditioned behaviors which burden the body, the mind, and the soul.

Psychoanalysis and Western psychotherapies have contributed to the understanding of the human mind from birth through adulthood. These contributions are significant because they are supported by clinical, naturalistic, and laboratory observations. Mysteries of the mind are being unraveled through clinical, psychological, and psychophysiological studies. The scientific community is becoming receptive to Eastern psychospiritual schools of thought and practices.

In Sufism, after the stage of renunciation, the Sufi may continue on to experience four additional stages: poverty *(faqr)*; patience *(sabr)*; trust in God *(tawakkul)*, and, finally, contentment *(ridā)*. It is in this

206 FREEDOM FROM THE SELF

last stage that the Sufi becomes an integrated or complete human being *(insān-i-kāmil)* (chapter 7).

Psychoanalysis and Western psychotherapies and varieties of Western psychologies do not visualize any further stages of human development beyond maturity. Studies of Sufi psychology may provide a blueprint for discovering the unbounded human potential beyond temporal reality.

Inspired Nafs The accompanying *nafs* in the psychomystical stage of renunciation is called the inspired *nafs* or *nafs-i-mulhama.* (Figure 1, chapter 6). The word *"mulham"* means inspired, and originates from the world *"ilhām,"* meaning inspiration and divine revelation. According to Idries Shah (1964), inspired *nafs* is "The beginning of real mental integration, when the mind is becoming capable of operating on a higher level than was its previous futile custom" (p. 394). Why do the Sufis use the term "inspired" to describe personality development in the stage of renunciation? What do they mean by inspiration or *ilhām?* What is the relationship between renouncing something and then becoming inspired?

The process of renunciation is like digging through the crust of habits, defensive postures, and illusionary fantasies to reach the reservoir of unbounded energies of the unconscious. The experience and expression of unbounded unconscious energies is actualized by the inspired *nafs.* Mystical poetry, books on meditation, stories, and anecdotes are concrete representations of the creative expression of the Sufi's journey on the Path of Reality.

The inspired *nafs* in the stage of renunciation provides the Sufis with a vehicle for transcending the boundaries and limitations of temporal reality, the inhibitions of the internal self, and the oppressions of time, space, and culture for expressing the creative urges and inspiration of the unconscious and Universal Reality.

CONCLUSION

Sufism is a Path toward further personality development and integration. This is also true of ego psychology and psychoanalysis. By comparing Sufism with ego psychology, one becomes aware of amazing similarities and also significant differences.

The following striking parallels exist between Sufism and ego psychology:

1. Both have a theory of human development;
2. Both propose practical methods for further personality integration;
3. Both believe in the concepts of conscious, preconscious, and unconscious;
4. Both tap the unconscious for further integration;
5. Both emphasize experiential rather than intellectual aspects of human development;
6. Both agree in the need for a guide or a therapist;
7. Both propose various stages of human development on the Path of Integration.

The final stage of personality integration in ego psychology is the genital stage which parallels the stage of renunciation in Sufism.

Western psychologies, particularly ego psychology, do not explore the spiritual, universal, and transcendental stages of human development. In Sufism, there are four additional stages beyond the stage of renunciation: poverty, patience, trust in God, and contentment.

We have seen amazing similarities between Sufism and ego psychology. If there are so many similarities in the earlier stages of personality integration, perhaps there are also comparable higher stages not yet identified in Western psychologies. Exploring the Sufi's methods of human integration from a cognitive and experiential perspective may help in deciphering the mysteries within, and may provide a map which will lead to the discovery of uncharted areas of personality integration (chapter 7).

BEYOND EGO PSYCHOLOGY

Final Four Stages of Human Development on the Sufi Path

> *In the depth of your hopes and desires lies your silent knowledge of the beyond;*
> *And like seeds dreaming beneath the snow your heart dreams of spring.*
> *Trust the dreams, for in them is hidden the gate to eternity.*
>
> *Kahlil Gibran, Lebanese and American Poet, twentieth century*

SEVEN STAGES OF HUMAN DEVELOPMENT ON THE SUFI PATH

In chapter 6, repentance, abstinence, and renunciation, the initial three stages of human development in Sufism, were described and compared with the oral, anal, phallic, and genital stages of ego psychology and Erikson's "Eight Ages of Man."

In this chapter, the stages of poverty, patience, trust in God, and contentment on the Sufi Path of Integration will be discussed. These final four stages of human development in Sufism have no counterpart in ego psychology (Figure 1, chapter 6).

Stage 4: Poverty (Faqr)

The fourth stage on the Sufi Path of Reality is called *faqr*. The word *"faqr"* means piercing, perforating, digging, excavating, poverty, want, and need. In Sufism, *faqr* refers to poverty and, specifically, to freedom from wants and desires. Frequently, the Sufi Path is referred to as the Path of Poverty, and the seeker is called *faqir* or dervish. The accompanying *nafs* in this stage is secure *nafs* (*nafs-i-mutmainna*).

The Sufis feel that the lighter one travels, the easier it is to reach the goal. The more one is burdened with worldly goods, the harder it is to move forward. Attention and energies used in protecting and caring for goods hinder progression along the Path of Reality.

The practice of poverty is not unique to Sufism. In Yoga, Buddhism, and Christianity, a vow of poverty may be taken. Many cultures have recognized the liberating aspects of the practice of poverty for enhancing psychospiritual development, and for freeing the human mind and spirit to surge to a higher level of consciousness. Sufism differs from most of the other esoteric traditions in that it recognizes that preoccupation with the outward practice of poverty and becoming fixated on this stage itself may become a hindrance on the Path of Integration.

Origin of the Practice of Poverty in Sufism   In early Islam, during the beginning of the seventh century A.D., the practice of poverty was highly exalted. Several specific references are made in the Koran to poverty:

> God is the needless one and you all are *faqirs* [the needy ones].

* * *

> The *faqirs* receive protection on the path of God.
> (Sūra II, Verse 274).

Prophet Mohammed, himself, owned very little. He said, "Poverty is my grace." Ghazzali quoted Prophet Mohammed in *Alchemy of Happiness:*

"Oh dervishes, from the bottom of your heart be content with
not having, and then you will find the reward of poverty . . . "
The true dervish is totally satisfied, patient and content. Satisfaction with what one receives is the core of poverty. (pp. 719–723).

During the eighth and ninth centuries A.D. the followers of Islam
had conquered the Persian and Byzantine Empires and had created
an Islamic Empire, which spanned from Iberia in the West to the
Indus Valley in the East. Gold and riches from the conquered ter-
ritories poured into Damascus and Baghdad, the capitals of the Ca-
liphates. The ascetic values of Prophet Mohammed and his early suc-
cessors gave way to the aristocratic and materialistic life styles of the
conquered Empires.

The Sufis, however, inspired by the Koran and the Islamic
pioneers, continued to practice renunciation and poverty even though
it was totally opposed to the ethos of that time and threatened the
values of the establishment. Shaqiq, martyred for his Sufi beliefs in
810 A.D., wrote of poverty:

Three things are close to poverty; freedom from worries, detach-
ment from worldly things, and peace of mind. Three things are
characteristic of those who are wealthy; suffering of the body,
constant worries, and enslavement to worldly goods. (Ghani, 1951,
p. 276)

Attributes of Poverty   Books on Sufism are encrusted with gems
about the attributes of Sufis who have experienced the stage of poverty.
In the following pages some of these attributes such as freedom from
having and wanting, freedom from the self, generosity, and being of
the world while free of the world will be explored.

Poverty and Freedom from Having and Wanting   Poverty by choice
is highly valued in Sufism. The first Caliph of Islam, Abu Bakr, who
followed Prophet Mohammad in guiding the Moslems said:

"Oh God, give me plenty of the world and make me desirous of
renouncing it!" This saying has a hidden sense, . . . "First bestow
on me worldly goods that I may give thanks for them, and then
help me to abstain from them for Thy sake, so that I may have
the treble merit of thanksgiving and liberality and abstinence, and
that my poverty may be voluntary, not compulsory." (Hujwiri, pp.
70–71).

212 FREEDOM FROM THE SELF

Immam' Ali, the fourth Caliph of Islam and the son-in-law of
Prophet Mohammed, was the essence of the ideal Sufi. He gave up
all worldly longings on the Path of Truth and Poverty.
One day, Immam' Ali was asked,

> . . . what is the purest thing that can be acquired. He said: "It is
> that which belongs to a heart made rich by God." . . . The heart
> that is so enriched is not made poor by having no worldly goods
> nor glad by having them. (p. 74).

To some Sufis, owning anything, no matter how insignificant,
was a distraction and a sign of belonging to the world rather than
totally pursuing the Path of Reality:

> One night Abu Yazid could find no joy in worship.
> "Look and see if there is anything of value in the house," he
> said.
> His disciples looked and discovered half a bunch of grapes.
> "Fetch them and give them away," Abu Yazid commanded.
> "My house is not a fruiterer's shop."
> And he rediscovered his composure. (Attār, Arberry's trans-
> lation, p. 119).

Sufis believe that being rich has nothing to do with how much
you have, but rather with how little you desire. The more you want,
the poorer you are; the less you want, the richer you are. Hujwiri told
this story:

> . . . A dervish met a King. The King said: "Ask a boon of
> me." The dervish replied: "I will not ask a boon from one of my
> slaves." "How is that?" said the King. The dervish said: "I have
> two slaves who are thy masters: covetousness and expectation."
> (p. 20).

The following story is one of many about Ebrahim Ibn Adham,
who gave up his Kingdom to pursue the Path of Poverty and reflects
the Sufis' internal state of freedom from want.

> A man once brought Ebrahim a thousand dinars.
> "Take," he said.
> "I do not accept anything from beggars," Ebrahim replied.
> "But I am wealthy," the man retorted.
> "Do you want more than you own already?" Ebrahim asked.
> "Indeed," the man exclaimed.

"Then take it back," said Ebrahim. "You are the chief of beggars."
(Attār, Arberry's translation, pp. 71–72).

The Sufis feel that one needs to be worthy of experiencing the essence of poverty. This is a gift from God bestowed on the heart of a sincere seeker. True freedom cannot occur unless one internally detaches the self from the tendencies of possessing and having. The "wish" to have, itself, can imprison the self. As the Sufis say, "The poor man is not he whose hand is empty of provisions, but he whose nature is empty of desires" (Hujwiri, p. 25).

Poverty and Freedom from the Self

The stage of poverty is the beginning of freedom from the self (*fanā*) which was discussed extensively in Chapter 5. Freedom from the self means giving up the conditioned self and becoming one with Reality. One cannot experience freedom from the self unless one has experienced poverty.

> ... Poverty has a form ... and an essence. ... Its form is destitution and indigence, but its essence is fortune and free choice. He who regards the form rests in the form and, failing to attain his object, flees from the essence; but he who has found the essence averts his gaze from all created things, and, in complete annihilation [freedom from the self], seeing only the All-One he hastens towards the fullness of eternal life. ... (p. 20).

Rumi directly related the experience of poverty with freedom from the self.

> When *fanā* [freedom from the self] is adorned by poverty,
> The Sufi becomes like Mohammed full of light.
> Poverty purifies [the self].
> It becomes like the flame of the candle,
> pure light free of shadows. (Ghani, 1951, p. 277).

Poverty and Generosity

One of the attributes of poverty is generosity. When the Sufis receive, whether it be through hard work or offerings, they share selflessly and humbly with others.

Ahmad Ibn Khazruya was a Sufi and a prominent citizen of Balkh:

> A thief broke into Ahmad-i-Khazruya's house. He searched
> everywhere but could not find anything. He was about to leave
> disappointed when Ahmad called out to him.
>
> "Young fellow, take the bucket and draw water from the well
> and purify yourself, then attend to your prayers. When something
> comes I will give it to you, so that you shall not leave my house
> empty-handed."
>
> The youth did as Ahmad bade him. When daylight returned,
> a gentleman brought a hundred dinars and gave them to the
> shaikh.
>
> "Take this as a reward for your night of prayers," he said to
> the thief.
>
> The thief suddenly trembled all over. He burst into tears.
>
> "I had mistaken the road," he cried. "I worked for God just
> one night, and He favoured me so."
>
> Repenting, he returned to God. He refused to take the gold,
> and became one of Ahmad's disciples. (Attār, Arberry's transla-
> tion, p. 176).

This moving story reflects the essence of the Sufi's character and
personality. The Sufi neither rejects material goods nor hoards them.
Two stages of human development in Sufism are evident here:

1.   The stage of poverty—the Sufi does not have any
     possessions and when given 100 gold coins is willing
     to part with them;

2.   The stage of repentance—the thief is reawakened by
     the Sufi's generosity and acceptance, and frees himself
     from past behaviors to begin the search for "wealth"
     through poverty.

Poverty and Being of the World and Free from the World

Most Sufis discourage hermitic life. They feel that it is important
to live among people, toil for daily bread, have a family and raise
children, while also freeing the self from constant want or worry
concerning possessions (chapter 2). The true practice of poverty is
not experienced by retreat from the world and its temptations. The
following story is attributed to the Sufi *pir*, Sari al-Saqati (d. 867 A.D.),
a dealer in secondhand goods in the Baghdad bazaar:

One day a man came from Mount Locam to visit him. . . .
"Shaikh So-and-So from Mount Locam greets you," he said.
"He dwells in the mountains," commented Sari. "So his efforts
amount to nothing. A man ought to be able to live in the midst
of the market and be so preoccupied with God, that not for a
single instant is he absent from God." (Attār, Arberry's translation,
p. 167).

Secure Nafs   The accompanying *nafs* in the stage of poverty is
secure *nafs, nafs-i-mutmainna* (Figure 1, chapter 6). The word *"mut-
mainna"* means quiet, secure, content, acquiescing, and safe. Shah
(1964) referred to *nafs-i-mutmainna* as serene *nafs* that are manifested
by "serene balance," and "equilibrium of the individuality" (p. 395).

At the stage of poverty, the Sufi experiences inner security and
serenity. He or she transcends the constant struggle of having versus
not having and possessing versus not possessing. The Sufi is hard-
working and committed to the task at hand, enjoying work for the
sake of work, with monetary rewards secondary. The Sufi is parsimoni-
ous and avoids waste, but, at the same time, is generous to others.

Secure *nafs* and the experience of poverty provide unbounded
psychological and spiritual riches beyond imagination. This internal
attitude of freedom from want, total devotion to the task at hand,
and enjoyment of the moment generate the feelings of serenity,
strength, effectiveness, and psychospiritual power beyond the ordinary.

The Sufi, by internally experiencing poverty, becomes free—a
freedom which unleashes unbounded sources of energy, love, and
affection. Honesty, openness, and frankness replace timidity, evasive-
ness, and deceptiveness. Attaining the stage of secure *nafs* means
freedom from intrapsychic conflicts, giving up worldly attachments
and possessive tendencies, and becoming closer to the invisible rhythm
of life and Existence.

Psychological Significance of Poverty

From a psychodynamic perspective, constant wanting, greed, and
hoarding are psychopathological traits related to basic internal insecurity and deprivation. They bear no relationship to what one actually
possesses. Many people who are materially wealthy are, in fact, poor
because they lack internal satisfaction and contentment.

Early Sufis perceived poverty in a concrete way. They gave up all of their possessions. If they received something through work or offering, they gave it away before nightfall. The Sufis felt that poverty freed them from all worldly longings and facilitated their total devotion to the Beloved. Rumi, regarding the psychological significance of poverty wrote: "Security is in poverty . . . " (Ghani, 1951, p. 277).

Gradually the Sufis modified their concern about material poverty. They came to realize that preoccupation with "not having" and deprivation from the joys of life could be a sign of conceit, ungratefulness, and a hindrance on the Path. They changed their emphasis to psychological and emotional attitudes toward possessing. The "craving for having," whether in the poor or the wealthy, is perceived as a sign of giving in to the animal *nafs* and as a hindrance on the Path of Integration. Worries and anxieties about daily bread, future savings, and luxuries are signs of duality and lack of faith and trust. The Sufis feel that one needs to be a part of daily life, "a person of the world," and, at the same time, "free of the world."

Psychological attachment to possessions and position, at the expense of "being" and "living," is a block on the Path. The Sufis feel that it is the person's internal perception of material objects which determines true poverty. The Sufi can be outwardly rich or poor as long as not "imprisoned" or "enslaved" by possessions or by the "wish to have more."

The psychological significance of poverty includes:

1. Decrease of "wanting" and "hoarding;"
2. Decrease of "consuming;"
3. Decrease of exploiting others or natural resources;
4. Decrease of waste;
5. Decrease of fantasies and wishes for "having" and "owning;"
6. Increase of sharing with others;
7. Increase of internal security and freedom;
8. Increase of appreciation for the bounties of nature;
9. Development of life style of seeing how little one can use, rather than how much.

The experience of poverty in a psychological sense requires a total change of values. Human nature is constantly driven by the frenzy of greed and the dread of becoming poor. The Sufi masters this pervasive anxiety and insecurity by willingly welcoming poverty, hunger, pain, and the dread of not "having." Fears such as these have plagued humankind throughout the ages. Wars between nations, states, and tribes, and feuds within families frequently occur over possessions and fear of "not having." More than ever, with the energy crisis and recognition of the limitation of resources, conflicts over "having" are becoming more acute. The Sufi practice of poverty might help us to recognize that "using less" is perhaps the essence of civilization rather than "consuming more."

Stage 5: Patience (Ṣabr)

The fifth stage of human development in Sufism is ṣabr. Ṣabr means patience, tolerance, endurance, resignation, and constancy. In Sufism, ṣabr specifically refers to patience. The accompanying *nafs* in this stage is the fulfilled *nafs*, *nafs-i-rādiyya* (Figure 1, chapter 6).

The Koran refers to ṣabr in more than seventy places:

> Those who are patient receive immeasurable rewards. (Sūra 39, Verse 13).
>
> * * *
>
> God is with patient people.
>
> * * *
>
> Patience is so great and dear to God that He did not give it to everyone—only a little to His friends.

The following ancient Islamic saying is heard frequently in daily conversations:

> *As-ṣabru miftāhu' l-fara-j*
> "Patience is the key to happiness."

Prophet Mohammed said, "The most precious gifts are patience and certainty. If you have these, have no fear even if you do not have power or strength . . . " (Ghazzali, p. 666).

Difficulty in Becoming Patient   Hasan of Basra (d. 728 A.D.), the Sufi *pir*, emphasized the difficulty of experiencing patience:

> . . . a Bedouin [tribesman] came to [Hasan] and asked him about patience . . . Hasan replied: "Patience is of two sorts: firstly, patience in misfortune and affliction; and secondly, patience to refrain from the things which God has commanded us to renounce

and has forbidden us to pursue." The Bedouin said: "Thou art an ascetic; I never saw anyone more ascetic than thou art." "O Bedouin!" cried Hasan, "my asceticism is nothing but desire, and my patience is nothing but lack of fortitude." The Bedouin begged him to explain this saying, "for . . . thou hast shaken my belief." Hasan replied, "My patience in misfortune and my submission proclaim my fear of Hell-fire, and this is lack of fortitude . . . ; and my asceticism in this world is desire for the next world, and this is the quintessence of desire. How excellent is he who takes no thought of his own interest! So that his patience is for God's sake, not for the saving of himself from Hell; and his asceticism is for God's sake, not for the purpose of bringing himself into Paradise. This is the mark of true sincerity." (Hujwiri, p. 86).

Attributes of Patience   Some of the attributes of the Sufis who have experienced the stage of patience are maturity, tolerance of suffering, faith, and human qualities. A discussion of these attributes follows.

Patience and Maturity   To the Sufis, patience is not an abstract idea. It is essential for the Sufis during all developmental stages, and especially in the stage of patience, to experience internal patience and practice it in thoughts, words, and deeds. Patience is a sign of maturity. The Sufis believe that by being patient, diversities, animosities, and conflicts—both within and in relation to others—decrease or melt away. They feel that polishing one's soul and mind on the Path of Reality can only occur through patience. Ibrahim Khawwas, the Sufi *pir* of the ninth century, said, "Most people take flight from the heavy burden of patience. The seekers take refuge in patience and rely on it" (Sarrāj, p. 49).

Jonaid of Baghdad was the essence of patience, both in word and deed. When Shebli, as a seeker, first encountered Jonaid, he demanded:

> "You are recommended as an expert on pearls," . . . "Either give me one, or sell one to me."
> "If I sell you one, you will not have the price of it, and if I give you one, having so easily come by it you will not realize its value," Jonaid replied. "Do like me; plunge head first into this Sea, and if you wait patiently you will obtain your pearl." (Attār, Arberry's translation, p. 278).

Acquiring the pearl of wisdom and experiencing internal freedom, enlightenment, and personality integration, are only achieved
through patience. Shebli had to wait many years and perform numerous arduous tasks before Jonaid accepted him as a disciple (chapter 2).

Patience and Suffering Tolerance of pain, whether physical or
psychological, without complaining, is the sign of patience. Sufis
frowned upon praying to God for alleviation of pain and suffering.

> One day Jonaid was suffering from a severe pain in his leg. He
> recited the opening Sura of the Koran and blew it at the painful
> leg [reciting a prayer and blowing it toward the source of discom-
> fort is thought to have a healing effect].
> At once he heard a voice within, "Aren't you ashamed to use
> the word of God for yourself?" (Attār, Part II, p. 13).

The Sufis perceive endurance of pain and the experience of patience as an active psychological process. Nuri observed

> I saw an old man [a Sufi] who was weak and frail. They were
> whipping him severely. He was patient. Then they put him into
> jail. I went to him and said, "You are so weak and frail. How did
> you so patiently endure all these whippings?" He replied, "Oh
> So⌐. one endures suffering through strength of the mind (*himmat*)
> r⌐ ⌐r than through strength of the body." I asked him, "What
> does patience mean to you?" He answered, "Being the same,
> whether suffering or free from suffering." (Attār Part II, p. 286).

Patience and Faith Patience is the essence of faith and belief.
True faith can only be experienced through patience. Rumi stated:
"The Prophet said, God does not give faith to a person who does not
have inner patience" (Ghani, p. 284).

Rumi frequently referred to the significance of patience on the
Path of Reality:

> Patience is from the certainty of Reality (God). Impatience is
> from the detested Satan.
>   * * *
> In humanity, impulsivity and impatience are the signs of
> Satan's work. Patience is the sign of God's mercy.
>   * * *
> God created hundreds of thousands of remedies, but no rem-
> edy is better for human beings than patience. (p. 284).

In Sufism, Satan frequently symbolizes impatience, impulsivity, and giving in to the desires of animal *nafs*. Sufis believe that Satan is actually within each human being, just as is the capacity for freedom from impulsive desires and human integration. They asked Prophet Mohammed, "What is faith?" He answered, "Patience." . . . (Ghazzali, p. 665)

Patience and Human Qualities   Ghazzali, in *Alchemy of Happiness*, perceived patience as a uniquely human quality which helps in taming the forces of rage and passion, in developing insight, and in strengthening faith.

> . . . know that, patience is one of the characteristics of human beings. Animals do not have patience and because of that they do not have the capacity for maturity and integration. Animals are driven by desires and passions. Nothing will quiet them except satisfaction of desires. In the beginning, human beings were created with animal characteristics. They were dressed with the clothes of passion and the need for pleasure.
> Then, at the time of maturity, a light from the lights of angels appeared within human beings so they could gain insight into the outcome of their actions. . . . This ability for insight helps human beings contain and resist passion, and anticipate the harmful outcome of passionate impulses.
> There are two armies within human beings fighting against each other. One is saying, "Be patient, conquer desires through faith." The other encourages giving into desires. This war is called the battle of [animal] *nafs*. Patience strengthens faith for combating immoral desires.
> . . . there are two major desires in human beings. One is passion, and the other rage. Patience is the remedy for conquering these two desires. Conquering these desires is the essence of faith and maturity. (pp. 665–669).

Psychological Significance of Patience   From a psychological and psychodynamic point of view, the stage of patience can be conceptualized in the following way:

1.   Patience, on one level, is an active psychological process. It is experienced on cognitive, affective, and unconscious levels. At the same time, patience transcends psychological processes and becomes spiritual. Patience engulfs the whole being of the Sufi.

2. Conscious control of impulses practiced in the stages of repentance, abstinence, renunciation, and poverty is further internalized and transmuted into patience on the unconscious and transconscious level. By active emphasis on the internal experience of patience, the Sufis underline the significance of harnessing the destructive forces of the sexual and aggressive drives. The transformation of these forces into the integrated energy of love (*ishq*) through patience enhances internal peace and harmony.

3. Silence and quiescence are behavioral manifestations of patience. The internal experience of silence is a powerful psychological force which facilitates further personality integration (chapters 3 and 4).

4. Sublimation and creative expression of impulses are actualized through patience.

5. The stage of poverty prepares the Sufi for the experience of patience. The Sufis realize that the psychomystical experience of patience is more difficult than the practice of poverty.

6. For the Sufi, patience is the essence of faith and belief. Through patience and by gradually and continuously freeing the self from past beliefs, the Sufi discovers faith experientially.

Stage 6: Trust in God (Tawakkul)

Tawakkul is an Arabic word derived from "wakl," meaning entrusting one's affairs to another. In Sufism, *tawakkul* means total trust in God. It is the sixth stage on the Sufi Path. The fulfilling *nafs* (*nafs-i-mardyiyya*) is the accompanying *nafs* in this stage (Figure 1, chapter 6). Few Sufis reach the stage of *tawakkul*.

The Koran refers to "trust in God" in a number of places:

Trust in God is the bond of faith. (Sūra 5, Verse 26).

* * *

The faithful are those who have trust in God. (Sūra 14, Verse 15).

* * *

He who trusts in God and relies on Him frees the self from everything else. (Sūra 65, Verse 3).

The Sufis take these Koranic verses to heart. They incorporate the process of trust in God into their psychomystical and spiritual practices.

Attributes of Trust in God   Some of the attributes of the Sufis who have experienced the stage of trust in God are: knowledge of God, sincerity, unbounded faith and hope, and existential communion.

Trust in God and Knowledge of God   Hujwiri (1967) described the internal experience of knowledge of God:

> Real trust in God proceeds from right knowledge, for those who know Him aright have that confidence that He will give them their daily bread, and they speak and look with right knowledge, so that their food and drink is only love, and their speech is only ecstasy, and their looking is only contemplation. (p. 115).

Trust in God and Sincerity
> I heard an old man relate that one day he went to the place where al-Daqqáq held his meetings, with the intention of asking him about the state of those who trust in God. . . . Al-Daqqáq was wearing a fine turban manufactured in Tabaristán, which the old man coveted. He said to al-Daqqáq: "What is trust in God?" The Shaykh replied: "To refrain from coveting people's turbans." With these words he flung his turban in front of the questioner. (p. 163).

On a superficial level, this story illustrates the necessity of freeing oneself from wanting before even beginning to experience the meaning of trust in God. On a deeper level, the experience of trust in God is not an intellectual exercise, but rather evolves from unconditional confidence in God, profound sincerity, and commitment to the Path of Truth.

Trust in God and Unbounded Faith and Hope   Habib the Persian (d. 714 A.D.) was a wealthy man who loaned money for usury (this is forbidden in Islam). After he was reawakened, he repented and gave away all his belongings.

> Time passed, and he was completely destitute. His wife asked him for housekeeping money constantly. So Habib left his house

and made for the hermitage to resume his devotions. When night came he returned to his wife.

"Where have you been working, not to bring anything home?" his wife demanded.

"The one I have been working for is extremely generous," Habib replied. "He is so generous that I am ashamed to ask him for anything. When the proper time comes, he will give. For he says, 'Every ten days I pay the wages.'"

So Habib repaired daily to the hermitage to worship, till ten days were up. On the tenth day at the time of the midday prayer a thought entered his mind.

"What can I take home tonight, and what am I to tell my wife?"

And he pondered this deeply. Straightway, Almighty God sent a porter to the door of his house with an ass-load of flour, another with a skinned sheep, and another with oil, honey, herbs, and seasonings. The porters loaded up all this. A handsome young man accompanied them with a purse of three hundred silver dirhams. Coming to Habib's house, he knocked on the door.

"What do you want?" asked Habib's wife, opening the door. "The Master has sent all this," the handsome youth replied. "Tell Habib, 'You increase your output, and we will increase your wages.'"

So saying, he departed. At nightfall Habib proceeded homeward, ashamed and sorrowful. As he approached his house, the aroma of bread and cooking assailed his nostrils. His wife ran to greet him and wiped his face and was gentle with him as she had never been before.

"Husband," she cried, "the man you are working for is a very fine gentleman, generous and full of loving kindness. See what he sent by the hand of a handsome young man? And the young man said, 'When Habib comes home, tell him, You increase your output, and we will increase your wages.'"

Habib was amazed.

"Wonderful!" he exclaimed. "I work for ten days, and he did me all this kindness. If I work harder, who knows what he will do?"

And he turned his face wholly away from worldly things and gave himself up to God's service. (Attār, Arberry's translation, pp. 34–35).

Trust in God is total. This unbounded faith and hope expresses itself in daily life by freedom from worries and anxieties over daily sustenance. When the Sufis receive through work or through offerings they share freely with others.

Two notables of the Faith came to visit Rabe'a and both were hungry.

"It may be that she will give us food," they said to each other. "Her food is bound to come from a lawful source."

When they sat down there was a napkin with two loaves laid before them. They were well content. A beggar arrived just then, and Rabe'a gave him the two loaves. The two men of religions were much upset, but said nothing. After a while a maidservant entered with a handful of warm bread.

"My mistress sent these," she explained. Rabe'a counted the loaves. There were eighteen. "Perhaps it was not this that she sent me," Rabe'a remarked.

For all that the maidservant assured her, it profited nothing. So she took back the loaves and carried them away. Now it so happened that she had taken two of the loaves for herself. She asked her mistress, and she added the two to the pile and returned with them. Rabe'a counted again, and found there were twenty loaves. She now accepted them.

"This is what your mistress sent me," she said.

She set the loaves before the two men and they ate, marveling. (pp. 43–44).

Rabe'a explained that she believed wholeheartedly that God repays tenfold. So when she gave her two loaves of bread to the beggar, she was certain that she would receive twenty loaves in return. When the maidservant brought eighteen loaves, she knew that either there was "some misappropriation," or that they were not "meant" for her. This faith and total trust in God is all-encompassing in the lives of the Sufi *pirs*.

Shah-e Shoja' (d. 884 A.D.) of Kerman was a Sufi *pir* of a princely family. He gave up all of his worldly attachment and pursued the Path of Poverty. The following story reflects not only his, but also his daughter's practice of poverty, trust in God, and unbounded faith and hope:

Shah-e Shoja' . . . had a daughter. The king of Kerman asked for her hand in marriage. He requested three days' grace, and during those three days he went from Mosque to Mosque, till at last he caught sight of a dervish praying earnestly. Shah-e Shoja' waited patiently until he had finished his prayers, then he addressed him.

"Dervish, do you have any family?"

"No," the dervish replied.

"Do you want a wife who can recite the Koran?"

"Who is there who will give such a wife to me?" said the dervish. "All I possess is three dirhams."

BEYOND EGO PSYCHOLOGY   225

"I will give you my daughter," said Shah-e Shoja'. "Of these three dirhams you possess, spend one on bread and one on attar of roses, then tie the marriage-knot."

They agreed accordingly. That same night, Shah-e Shoja' dispatched his daughter to his house. Entering the dervish's house, the girl saw some dry bread beside a jug of water.

"What is this bread?" she demanded.

"It remained over from yesterday. I kept it for tonight," the dervish told her.

Thereupon the girl made to leave the house.

"I knew," the dervish observed, "that the daughter of Shah-e Shoja' would never be able to live with me and put up with my poverty."

"Sir, it is not on account of your lack of means that I am leaving you," the girl replied. "I am leaving because of your lack of faith and trust, in that you set aside bread from yesterday, not relying on God's provision for the morrow. At the same time, I am surprised at my father. For twenty years he has kept me at home, always saying, 'I will give you to a god-fearing man.' Now he has given me to a fellow who does not rely on God for his daily bread."

"Is there any atonement for this sin?" the dervish asked.

"Yes," said the girl. "The atonement is that only one of the two remains in this house—myself, or the dry bread." (p. 184).

Trust in God and Existential Communion (Tauhid)   The word *tauhid* derives from *wahd,* meaning one, being single, alone, or incomparable. *Tauhid* means making one, declaring God to be one, a belief in the unity of God, and unitarianism. In Sufism, it also refers to the process of integration, perfection, and existential communion. The Sufis pursue the idea and experience of existential communion to the farthest frontiers of imagination. Existential communion means the unity of all forms of existence, manifest or hidden, organic or inorganic, human or spiritual. The flame of existential communion is the source of the integrative energy of love. Everything the Sufi does and every suffering he or she goes through is for the sake of existential communion (chapter 5).

Sufis, with all atoms of their being, believe in *La Ilaha Ill-al-Allah,* which means There is no God but God. The Sufi feels that the essence of this proclamation of faith and *tauhid* is that nothing exists in the universe but God. Everything in the world of existence is the manifestation of His Light and His Essence. *La* is an Arabic word indicating "no" and negation. The Sufis feel that it is at first necessary to negate all forms of beliefs and attachments to past values in order deeply to experience the oneness of all. Sufis chant and meditate upon *La Ilaha Ill-al-Allah* continuously to help them shed selfish attitudes and dualistic tendencies with the hope of experiencing trust in God and existential communion.

Tagore, the well-known Indian poet and philosopher, echoes this conviction:

> I believe in God because
>   He allowed me to deny Him.

The Sufi would say:

> I love God because
>   He allowed me to deny Him.

Ghazzali, in *Alchemy of Happiness,* wrote:

> Know that trust in God is a stage of those closest to God. It is of the highest degree. Attaining this stage and practicing it is most difficult because the process of recognition itself is the sign of separation and lack of existential communion. . . .
> Know that trust in God is a state of the heart. It is the fruit of sincere faith and belief. There are many forms of faith, but trust in God is built on two pillars of faith. One is faith in existential communion or unity of all and the other is faith in the complete affection and mercy of God. (pp. 798–799).

Ghazzali described four kinds of faith in God:

> In the first kind is the person who says: "There is no God but God," but does not really believe it. This is the belief of hypocrites.
> In the second kind, the person believes in the meaning of the oneness of God. This includes most people [who are brought up in the culture] and those who by discussion and discourse accept it [such as scientists, philosophers, and theologians].
> In the third kind are those who experience the vision of God. They have the insight that everything is based on a unitary principle, and that there is only one Creator and Mover. . . . This realization is a light which appears in the heart, and is the foundation of a firm belief. It is the belief of gnostics. In this level of belief in God the person perceives the creation and the Creator

separately. There is still multiplicity and to some extent duality.

In the fourth kind, or ultimate or complete belief, existential communion, the Sufi does not see, hear or know anything but the One. Duality does not exist. The Sufis call this *"fanā* in *tauhid"* or loss of the self in existential communion. (pp. 799–800).

Degrees of Trust in God   Ghazzali, concerning the degrees of trust in God, stated:

> Know that there are three degrees:
> 1.   In the first degree, the state of trust in God is like a person who is in an adversarial situation and hires and puts his trust in an eloquent, honest, brave, kind, and brilliant lawyer.
> 2.   The second degree is like the relationship of a child to his mother. The child knows no one except mother. If the child is hungry he calls only mother. This total trust in the mother is instinctual, spontaneous, and automatic. The child is not aware of his total trust.
> 3.   The third degree is like a dead corpse in the hands of a mortician. The mortician moves the body. Everything is in the hands of the mortician. A dead person does not have any expectation, does not pray, nor wish.
>
>   This is not like a child who calls upon the mother, but like a child who knows deeply that even if he does not call for the mother, the mother will be totally aware of his condition and will look after him. This is the ultimate degree of trust in God. (p. 809).

The time comes when the Sufi needs to free the self from preoccupation with trust in God:

> Ibrahim Khawwas [a Sufi *pir*] . . . came to Kufa, and having heard of Al-Hallaj, went to see him. Al-Hallaj said: "O Ibrahim, during these forty years of your connexion with Sufiism, what have you gained from it?" Ibrahim answered: "I have made . . . trust in God . . . peculiarly my own." Al-Hallaj said: "You have wasted your life in cultivating your spiritual nature: what has become of annihilation in Unification . . . [loss of self in existential communion]?" (Hujwiri, p. 205).

Ibráhím Khawwás was the first to suggest the experience of "trust in God" as a developmental stage in Sufism. Here, Al-Halláj pointed out to Khawwás his narcissistic preoccupation with this stage and reminded him that the essence of Sufism is freedom from the self (fanā) in existential communion (tauhid).

Psychological Significance of Trust in God   Ghazzali, with the psychological acumen of an astute clinician and synthetic ability of a universal scholar, conceptualized the meanings of trust in God in Sufism. From a psychological and psychodynamic perspective, trust in God is the rekindling and re-emergence of the basic trust of early infancy. What is the difference between the Sufi's experience of trust in God and Erikson's concept of basic trust (chapter 6)? The differences are none, and many! None, in that they both originate from the love and affection of a devoted and sensitive mother—a love which is a reflection of the integrative energy of life.

The differences are many, in that:

1.   The child does not have a choice—survival depends upon the early mother-child bond and the development of basic trust;

2.   The child does not have any cognitive awareness of this process, although on a sensory-motor and perceptual level, responds automatically;

3.   Usually, this basic trust is "given" and easily available to the child;

4.   The Sufi's development of total trust is a hard-won battle; the Sufi must go through a multitude of trials and tribulations, work through numerous defenses, fantasies, and illusions, and melt away self-conceit and narcissistic tendencies to reach communion with Reality. Many begin this arduous journey with high hopes and sincere effort, but only a few reach the goal.

Understanding existential communion is beyond human cognition which is based on differentiation. Existential communion is experiencing loss of the self in *fanā* (chapter 5). It is freeing the self from the constant avalanche of passionate impulses and destructive drives. Trust in God is experiencing regression and disintegration for further reintegration.

A person does not need to be a Sufi to experience total trust in

God. A few are blessed with the experience of this psychospiritual process without being aware of it. An individual who has experienced trust in God may manifest the following attributes:

1. Total involvement in the task at hand, as if all life depended upon it;
2. Initiative and hard work;
3. Deep internal security;
4. Childlike joy and enthusiasm which is contagious and a source of unbounded energy;
5. Profound faith and trust;
6. Experiences "failure" as a source of rejuvenated energy and does not give up;
7. Persistency;
8. Acute sense of awareness and a sharpened sense of observation;
9. Perceives the common principle of unity and oneness underlying manifest diversities;
10. Lives with ease among people of all classes, creeds, and races; the poor and the rich, the oppressed and the oppressor, the known and unknown are all the manifestations of the One;
11. Freedom from animosities;
12. Deep appreciation and gratitude for everything in life;
13. Attainment of an extra dimension beyond time, space, and place—this is not sought, dwelled upon, or discussed;
14. Disappearance of the fear of death and the unknown.

Stage 7: Contentment (Riḍā)

The seventh and final stage of human development on the Path of Reality is *riḍā. Riḍā* in Arabic, or *rizā* in Persian, means satisfaction, consent, agreement, acquiescence, and contentment. In Sufism, *riḍā* means a deeper inner satisfaction and total contentment. The accompanying *nafs* in this stage is purified and complete nafs, *nafs-i-kāmila.*

A Sufi who reaches this stage of final integration is called *insān-i-kāmil,* an integrated human being (figure 1, chapter 6).

The Sufis are inspired by the following Koranic sayings concerning contentment:

> God is content with those who are content with Him. (Sūra 5, Verse 119).
>
> * * *
>
> . . . contentment is the greatest road to God and the experience of it is heaven on earth. . . . (Sūra 9, Verse 73).

Attributes of Contentment   Some of the attributes of the Sufis who have reached the stage of contentment are: poverty, freedom from duality, integrity, acceptance of God's will, joy of union, and freedom from expectation.

Contentment and Poverty   Hujwiri, regarding contentment and poverty, wrote:

> The . . . [sufi] has nothing and can suffer no loss. He does not become rich by having anything, nor indigent by having nothing: both these conditions are alike to him in respect of his poverty. It is permitted that he should be more joyful when he has nothing, for the shaykhs have said: "The more straitened one is in circumstances, the more expansive (cheerful and happy) is one's (spiritual) state," because it is unlucky for a dervish to have property: if he "imprisons" anything . . . for his own use, he himself is "imprisoned" in the same proportion. The friends of God live by means of His secret bounties. Wordly wealth holds them back from the path of quietism (riḍā). (p. 20).

Contentment and Freedom from Duality   They asked the Sufi *pir,* Ḥabíb Al-'Ajamí,

> "With what thing is God pleased?" He answered: "With a heart which is not sullied by hypocrisy [duality]," because hypocrisy . . . is the opposite of concord . . . , and the state of being well pleased (*riḍā*) [contentment] is the essence of concord. There is no connexion between hypocrisy and love, and love subsists in the state of being well pleased (with whatever is decreed by God). Therefore acquiescence (*ridā*) is a characteristic of God's friends, while hypocrisy is a characteristic of His enemies. (p. 89).

Contentment and Integrity   Fuḍayl Ibn' Iyáḍ was a Sufi sage who lived at the time of Harun, the Caliph of Baghdad, in the eighth century A.D. One day, Harun was despondent. He went with one of his companions to visit a few wise men to receive help for his sorrows. Harun went to visit Fuḍayl and knocked at his door, but Fuḍayl was reluctant to see the Caliph because he did not want to associate with people in power. However, after the Caliph's insistence, Fuḍayl opened his door. He

> . . . extinguished the lamp and stood in a corner. Hárún went in and tried to find him. Their hands met. Fuḍayl exclaimed, 'Alas! Never have I felt a softer hand: 't will be very wonderful if it escape from Divine torment.' Hárún began to weep, and wept so violently that he swooned. When he came to himself, he said, 'O Fuḍayl, give me a word of counsel.' Fuḍayl said: "O Commander of the Faithful, thy ancestor ('Abbás) was the uncle of Mustafá [Prophet Mohammed]. He asked the Prophet to give him dominion over men. The Prophet answered, "O my uncle, I will give thee dominion for one moment over thyself," i.e., one moment of thy obedience to God is better than a thousand years of men's obedience to thee, since dominion brings repentance on the Day of Resurrection' . . . (p. 99).

When Harun was leaving, he asked Fuḍayl whether he had any debts that he could pay. Fuḍayl answered:

> 'Yes, the debt which I owe to God, namely, obedience to Him; woe is me, if He call me to account for it!' Harun said, 'O Fuḍayl, I am speaking of debts to men.' He replied, 'God be praised! His bounty towards me is great, and I have no reason to complain of Him to His servants.' Harun offered him a purse of a thousand dinars, saying, 'Use the money for some purpose of thine own.' Fuḍayl said, 'O Commander of the Faithful, my counsels have done thee no good. Here again thou art behaving wrongly and unjustly.' Harun exclaimed, 'How is that?' Fuḍayl said, 'I wish thee to be saved, but thou wouldst cast me into perdition: is not this unjust?' We took leave of him with tears in our eyes, and Harun said . . . 'Fuḍayl is a king indeed.' (pp. 99–100).

This story exemplifies the total contentment of Fuḍayl. He had freed himself from material longings and worldly expectation, and this freedom gave him unbounded human strength and integrity.

Contentment and Acceptance of God's Will (Qazā)   Rumi wrote in *Mathnawi* (*Book 3*) regarding Sufi *pirs* who are totally content with God's will.

> Now listen to the story of those travelers who have freed themselves from complaints about this universe. . . . I know a group of *pirs* who have even closed their mouths to prayers. The happiness of these benevolent *pirs* comes from contentment. They do not avoid God's will (*qazā*) for in God's will they see the enthusiasm of love. It would be hypocrisy and duality to seek relief from God's will. Their hearts are open to benevolence and deep trust. They do not wear the dark clothes of despondency. They are content with anything that comes to them whether it be the elixir of life or a tormenting fire. Poison in their mouth is sweet sugar. Stones in their paths are jewels and diamonds. Because of their inner benevolence and deep trust, good and bad are the same to them (Ghani, pp. 313–314).

Dhu' L-Nun the Egyptian who had reached the stage of contentment said, "Contentment is the joy of the heart in the bitterness of His Will." They asked Dho' L-Nun, "Who is most insightful about his own self?" He replied, "The one who is content with his lot in life" (Ghani, 1951, p. 317).

Harith Muhasibi, Sufi *pir* of the ninth century, discussed the significance of contentment. Contentment " . . . is the quiescence . . . of the heart under the events which flow from the Divine decrees" (p. 180). Sufi al-Ghulam, in his meditation, frequently said, "If Thou chastise me I love Thee, and if Thou have mercy on me I love Thee" (p. 180). Hiri, a Sufi *pir*, wrote:

> During the last forty years God has never put me in any state that I disliked, or transferred me to another state that I resented. (p. 180).

Ghazzali, regarding the acceptance of God's will, related the following story:

> A religiously devoted man of the Jewish faith spent many years in worship and prayer. One night while dreaming he was told who his woman companion would be in Paradise. He asked to see her so that he might gain insight into the nature of her devotion. After finding out that she did not spend sleepless nights in prayer or fast frequently he asked her, "What have you done to deserve Paradise?" She replied, "Nothing but what you see." He insisted

and insisted and at last she said, "I have this little attitude. If I am sick or in affliction, I do not desire health. If I am in the sun, I do not desire to be in the shade, and if I am in the shade, I do not desire to be in the sun. I am content with anything He does."

The devoted man raised his hands in awe and said, "This is not a little attitude, it is a great virtue." (p. 858).

Ghazzali summarized: ". . . contentment with God's will is the highest stage. No stage is above it because love is the highest of all. Contentment with God's will is the fruit of love" (p. 857).

Contentment and Joy of Union   For the Sufis, contentment is the essence of happiness and joy. This joy is permanent and everlasting. It has evolved from satisfaction and acceptance. This is the joy of union between the lover and the Beloved. "Happiness is happiness only when it leads to the Giver of happiness . . . " (Hujwiri, p. 178).

Those who are

> . . . chosen by God are His lovers . . . whose hearts dwell in the presence of Purity and in the garden of Intimacy; who have no thought of created things and have escaped from the bonds of "stations" and "states" and have devoted themselves to the love of God. Their satisfaction involves no loss, for satisfaction with God is a manifest kingdom. (p. 179).

Contentment and Freedom from Expectations   The experience of contentment transcends the boundaries of temporal knowledge and understanding. Jonaid stated that the Sufi *pir* has

> . . . no fear, because fear is the expectation either of some future calamity or of the eventual loss of some objects of desire, whereas the *pir* is the son of his time . . . : he has no future that he should fear anything; and he hath no fear so he hath no hope, since hope is the expectation either of gaining an object of desire or of being relieved from a misfortune, and this belongs to the future; nor does he grieve, because grief arises from the rigour of time, and how should he feel grief who is in the radiance of satisfaction, contentment . . . and garden of concord? (Hujwiri, p. 216).

The Sufis are totally content and free from any form of expectation, even the hope of becoming a saint.

Ibrahim Adham asked a Sufi:

... whether he desired to be one of God's saints, and on his replying "Yes," said: "Do not covet anything in this world or the next, and devote thyself entirely to God, and turn to God with all thy heart." (p. 217).

Types of Contentment   According to Hujwiri, four groups of people experience contentment (p. 178):

1. Those who are content with God's gift—that is to say content with all bounties of Nature; they are called gnostics;

2. Those who are content with happiness in this world;

3. Those who are content with afflictions;

4. Those who are content with having been chosen; that is to say those who are blessed to be the lovers of Reality.

Psychological Significance of Contentment   Contentment is the total acceptance of Universal Wisdom and God's will and judgement. It is the recognition that individual will and wisdom is the reflection of Universal Wisdom. This recognition and insight is cognitive, emotional, and spiritual; it permeates the Sufi's whole being.

Contentment is the highest form of *fanā*, freedom from the self (chapter 5). The Sufi, through the states of repentance, abstinence, renunciation, poverty, patience, and trust in God, gradually loses the layers of individuality, and becomes one with the One.

Deep internal satisfaction, compassionate love, empathy toward others, sincerity in devotion, and constant service to mankind—humbly and silently—are the manifestations of contentment. Trust and security are the internal expressions of contentment. All forms of striving, whether worldly or spiritual, disappear in quiescence and contentment. Contentment is appreciation and acceptance of life as *it is*. Erich Fromm wrote: "A Sufi transcends the union with God to achieve union with life" (Arasteh, 1965b, p. IX).

Contentment is an active process of total integration. It is the existential communion of the Sufi with the rhythm of life, similar to the oneness of a drop of water with the ocean. The basic instinct for existential communion reaches fulfillment in the contentment of union. The Sufi in the stage of contentment frees the self from the habits and memories of the past, and the wishes, fantasies, and concerns of the future.

The Sufi lives in the moment and is one with the moment. Rumi states, "Oh friend, the Sufi is the child of the moment. Talking about tomorrow is not a condition of the Path." Communion with the moment means the loss of subject and object duality, the loss of I-Thou, the loss of past or future, and the loss of concern about the present. The idea of "communion with the moment" shatters the rational mind. It defies all rationalities and all manifest physical and psychological laws. It can be awesome and frightening. At the same time, communion "with the moment" has liberating possibilities.

Existential communion has been the hope of humanity throughout the ages—hope for freeing the self from the prison of the past, the bondage of time, and the mirage of the future. Transcending the temporal self and becoming one with all aspects of existence results in the experience of contentment. The Sufi who reaches the stage of contentment is called *insān-i-kāmil*, an integrated human being (figure 1, chapter 6).

Integrated Human Being (Insān-i-kāmil)   A Sufi who reaches the stage of contentment, or final integration, is called *insān-i-kāmil*. *Insān* means man, mankind, human being, and mortal. *Kāmil* means perfect, complete, full, entire.

Insān-i-kāmil is frequently translated into English as the "perfect man." This translation, although literally correct, does not fully describe *insān-i-kāmil*. Actually, the word *"insān"* refers to a human being in a general sense, encompassing both male and female. *"Kāmil"* in this context refers to maturity and integration. Throughout this book, *insān-i-kāmil* is translated as "integrated human being," or "integrated being."

Ibn Abrabi, Sufi sage of Andalusia, who lived in the thirteenth century, wrote extensively about *insān-i-kāmil*. He used more than 22 terms synonymously with *insān-i-kāmil*, including "the Reality of Realities, the Reality of Mohammad, the Spirit of Mohammad, the First Intellect, the Most Mighty Spirit, the Most Exalted Pen, the Vicegerent, God's representative, the Perfect Man, The Real Adam, The Pole, The Servant of the All-embracing One, etc" (Affifi, 1936, p. 66).

According to the Sufis, Universal Wisdom, or the Wisdom of Reality, manifests itself in the form of an integrated human being. The potential for becoming an integrated being is endowed in every human. Only a few realize this potential.

Some Sufis believe that only one person at each given period of time may become an integrated human being, the Logos, *qutb* (pole), or God's representative to humanity. They feel that this person, although among us, is often not recognized. But most Sufis feel that the potential for becoming an integrated human being and the "pole" of one's existence is in every human being.

According to Ibn Arabi, an integrated human being

> . . . is not perfect . . . unless he realizes his essential oneness with God. This is what distinguishes any man from a Perfect Man. Every man is a microcosm in this sense, but only *potentially* so. The Perfect Man is an actual microcosm, because he does *actually manifest* all of God's attributes and perfections, and such manifestations are incomplete without the full realisation of his essential unity with God. (p. 81).

ATTRIBUTES OF AN INTEGRATED HUMAN BEING. Nasafi, the Sufi author who lived in the thirteenth century A.D., wrote a book in Persian entitled *The Book of an Integrated Human Being (Kitāb al-Insān al-Kāmil)*. In this book, Nasafi discussed the qualities of an integrated human being. I have translated the following material from Nasafi's book in order to give the reader a feeling of the attributes and qualities of an integrated human being as perceived by the Sufis.

1.   *Complete Realization and Insight*
       . . . an *insān-i-kāmil* is the one who has completely realized religion, the Path and the Reality. If you do not understand this statement, I can say it differently. An *insān-i-kāmil* is the one who has reached the ultimate of these four attributes; good words, good deeds, good manners, and true insight.
       Oh dervish! All seekers are working for the attainment of these four attributes. Anyone who reaches the ultimate of these four attributes has reached the total integration of the self. Many come to this Path and go in this direction but do not reach the goal.
       Now that you know the meaning of *insān-i-kāmil*, know also that it has many other names. Oh dervish! An *insān-i-kāmil* is called Shaykh, guide, leader, wise man, mature, integrated, *Imam*, vicegerent, *qutb*, universal cup, mirror of the universe and great elixir of

life. An *insān-i-kāmil* is like Jesus who brought the dead to life. He is like *Khizr* who drank the elixir of life. He is like Solomon who knew the language of birds. An *insān-i-kāmil* is always present in the world and is not more than one because all existence is one. The heart of existence is *insān-i-kāmil.* . . . (pp. 4–5).

Nasafi elaborated further:

> *Insān-i-kāmil* is the manifestation of the first intellect. . . . all knowledge emerges from *insān-i-kāmil.* (p. 162).

2. *Mirror of Reality*

   Oh dervish! You frequently hear that in the Ocean of Being there is a reflecting mirror. Everything which occurs in the universe reflects in this mirror. . . . this Ocean is the Ocean of the universe unknown and the mirror is the heart of an *insān-i-kāmil.* The secret of the universe manifests itself in the world of existence and reflects it in the heart of an *insān-i-kāmil.* The *insān-i-kāmil* then becomes aware of it. The heart of an *insān-i-kāmil* also reflects everything which is in the heart of those who are close to him.

   There are other human beings who because of their simplicity and purity of heart can reflect the internal condition of human beings and animals. There are also animals that because of the purity of their heart can reflect natural events and the internal conditions of human beings. Some people understand these things and some do not. (pp. 237–238).

3. *Oneness of Existence*

   Oh dervish! Existence is nothing but One. This Oneness has an outward and inward existence. The inward existence is Light. This Light is the essence of the universe. The universe is infused with the Light. It is a Light without limit and infinite. It is a Sea without end and without shores. Life, science, devotion and power of all beings are from this Light. Vision, hearing, speech, and the understanding . . . of all beings is from this Light. Nature, character, and action of beings is also from this Light. Outward phenomena of this existence is the reflection of this Light and the mirror of this Light. (p. 249).

4.   *Evolution, Integration, and Existential Communion*
Oh dervish! All creatures are part of human existence. All aspects of the universe were busy developing and evolving until finally human beings emerged. . . . Humanity is the completion and maturity of this evolution . . . (p. 251).

An integrated human being, *insān-i-kāmil*, is the one who is in communion with all aspects of nature. Because of this, according to the Sufis, an integrated human being becomes aware of the hidden laws of nature and can communicate with animals, birds, plants, and other aspects of existence beyond words.

Oh dervish! The goal is for a human being to reach integration of the self and return to his Creator enriched. In the proximity of His Presence . . . a human being becomes secure and full of joy. The human spirit is in constant search for integration and completion. The integration and completion of a human being is through knowledge, insight, purity of heart, and closeness to God. . . . One cannot turn to anyone but God. Face the Creator and know the self and the Creator. Be totally in love with the Creator and be at His disposal. Then be able to transcend insight, knowledge, purity, joy, spiritual and higher levels of understanding in order to reach the First Essence. Then the circle will be complete. The circle is not completed until it reaches its beginning. (pp. 360–361).

5.   *Death before Dying*
Death, an inevitable occurrence for all human beings, has frightened, puzzled, and fascinated them throughout the ages. Erikson considered one of the major criterion of personality integration to be the acceptance of the inevitability of death.
The Sufis not only accept the inevitability of death, but also welcome the death of the conventional self, or *fanā*, as an important step in becoming an integrated human being (chapter 5).

Nasafi wrote:

.... the prophets and the Sufi *pirs* experience death of the
conventional self (*fanā*) before dying a natural death. They die
voluntarily before dying naturally. They see and experience before dying what other people experience after natural
death. . . . They transcend the stage of "knowledge of certainty"
to the stage of "vision of certainty . . . " (p. 107).

6. *Reflecting Heart*
    According to the Sufis, the heart of an integrated
    human being is so purified that it reflects like a shining
    mirror the rhythm of nature, the laws of the universe,
    and future events.

Nasafi wrote:

. . . any affliction or blessing which becomes apparent in this
manifest world from the unknown and hidden universe at first
appears in the heart of an *isān-i-kāmil*. What others see in dreams,
he will see in wakefulness . . . (p. 237).

7. *Beyond Time and Place*
    According to the Sufis, an integrated human
    being is able to transcend time, space, and place.

(Their) abilities . . . are such that earth, water, air, fire, desert, and mountain will not interfere with their visions. If
they are in the East they can see the people of the West and
hear their communications. If they are in the West they can
see the people of the East and hear their communications.
If they want to go from East to West, they can go in a
moment. Earth, sea, mountain, and desert are the same to
them. Fire and water are equal to them . . .
(They) live in such a way that people do not notice them.
They do not claim virtue, renunciation, or Sainthood. On
a conscious level they are like others, and they do not appear
outwardly different. Their unconscious is more sublime
than others. (pp. 318–319).

The following stories about Rabe'a succinctly summarize the qualities of an integrated human being.

> Rabe'a was asked, "Do you love God?"
> She answered, "Yes."
> "Do you hate the devil?"
> She answered, "No, my love of God leaves me no time to hate the devil."
>
> * * *
>
> Rabe'a saw Prophet Mohammed in a dream. He asked her, "Oh Rabe'a, do you love me?"
> She said, "Oh Prophet of God, who does not love you, but love of God has absorbed me that neither love nor hate of any other being remains in my heart."
>
> * * *

PSYCHOLOGICAL QUALITIES OF AN INTEGRATED HUMAN BEING

1. Freedom from fears, greed, and sexual and aggressive impulses

2. Freedom from duality

3. Freedom from the temporal or the conditioned self

4. Total integration of all *nafses* within—vegetative, animal, human, accusing, inspired, secure, fulfilled, fulfilling, and complete

5. Experience of all seven stages of human development—repentance, abstinence, renunciation, poverty, patience, trust in God, and contentment

6. Experience of affective and psychomystical states (*hālāt*)—hope, fear, despondency, vision, ecstasy, joy, doubt, trust, security, and certainty

7. Total involvement with life and total integration with the moment

8. Freedom from the past and future

9. Realization of one's relationship to the ecological order of nature and the invisible rhythm of life

10. Experience of transcendental and trans-temporal reality

11. Existential communion (*fanā* and *baqā*).

The Sufis who have reached the stage of contentment and have become integrated human beings are silent. They do not have the need nor the urge to describe their psychomystical state. Even if they would want to, they cannot, because words usually cannot express universal, holistic, and primarily nonverbal experiences. The descriptions of an integrated human being are, at most, only a part of the perceivable and communicable truth.

In the *insān-i-kāmil*, the tumultuous ecstatic and peak experiences of the earlier phases of *fanā* have given way to calmness, serenity, and oneness with all aspects of life. The Sufi toils for a crust of bread like any other person in the community, is a part of life and does not separate from any aspect of it. The Sufi performs any task with total love and devotion, particularly service to others. The Sufi becomes one with the moment. Sereneness and tranquility exude from one's deeds and actions. One's face has a glow and emanates a special light. One began the journey with all the anxieties, despair, and drudgeries of daily life. Now one has completed the circle and returns to the beginning. Daily life and outward circumstances may be the same, better, or worse than before. Inwardly, the Sufi exudes openness, trust, and the enthusiasm of a child.

The *insān-i-kāmil* has experienced all of the states of human development, and has spiritually passed through all of the stages of psychomystical experiences in realizing fulfillment and maturity.

PSYCHOLOGICAL PERSPECTIVE OF AN INTEGRATED HUMAN BEING. The complexity and elusiveness of Sufi ideas are most evident when attempting to describe the final stages of human development, and particularly, the concept of *insān-i-kāmil*, an integrated human being. *Insān-i-kāmil* is a hope-inspiring ideal which encourages the best in humanity. It is a guiding light which can help human beings transcend the fragmentations of the past, dualities of the present, limitations of culture, and preoccupations with the self. Awareness of the potential for becoming an integrated human being and genuine endeavor on the Path of Reality, itself, stimulates psychological and spiritual integration. Although one may not reach the ideal, ust being a traveler on the Path and having the goal in mind can be a source of continuous encouragement, development, and hope.

REFERENCES

Abraham, K. The first pregenital stage of the libido. In *Selected papers of Karl Abraham*. London: Hogarth, 1948.

Affifi, A.E. *The mystical philosophy of Muhyid Din-Ibnul Arabi*. Lahore: S. Ashraf, 1964.

Akishige, Y. A historical survey of the psychological studies in Zen. *Kyushu Psychological Studies, V, Bulletin of the Faculty of Literature of the Kyushu University*, 1968, *11*, 1–56.

Anand, B.K., Chhina, G.S., & Singh, B. Some aspects of electroencephalographic studies in yogis. *Electroencephalographic Clinical Neurophysiology*, 1961, *13*, 452–456.

Arasteh, A.R. *Final Integration in the Adult Personality. A Measure for Health, Social Change, and Leadership*. Leiden: E.J. Brill, 1965a.

Arasteh, A.R. *Rumi the Persian: Rebirth in creativity and love*. Lahore: S. Ashraf, 1965b.

Arlow, J.A. Silence and the theory of technique. *Journal American Psychoanalytic Association*, 1961, *9*, 44–55.

Assagioli, R. *Psychosynthesis*. New York: Penguin Books, 1981.

Attār, F. (d. 1220). *Muslim saints and mystics: Episodes from the Tadhkirat al-Auliya (memorial of the saints)*. The Persian Heritage Series. (A.J. Arberry, trans.) Chicago: University of Chicago Press, 1966.

Attar, F. (d. 1220). *The Tadhkiratul-Auliya*, (R.A. Nicholson, ed.) (Vol. 1 and 2). London: Luzac, 1907. In Persian.

Attar, F. (d. 1220). *Mantiq ut-Tair; A philosophical religious poem in prose (The conference of the birds)*. London: Routledge & Kegan Paul, 1961.

Avicenna (Ibn-i-Sina, Sh. Huain Ibn Abdullah) (d. 1037). *Tarjuma Ravān Shināsi Shifa. Al-Fann Al-Sādis Men Kutob Alshifa*. Fourth Printing. A. Dānāsarisht, trans. from Arabic into Persian. Tehran: Ibn-i-Sina Publishing Company, 1352, hijri shamsi, 1973.

Azima, H., Vispo, R., & Azima, F.J. (1961). Observations on anaclitic therapy during sensory deprivation. In P. Solomon, (Ed.), *Sensory deprivation*. Cambridge: Harvard University Press, 1961.

Bagchi, B., & Wenger, M. Electrophysiological correlates of some Yogi exercises. *Electroencephalographic Clinical Neurophysiology*, 1957, 7, 132–149.

Bakan, D. *Sigmund Freud and the Jewish mystical tradition*. New York: Schocken Books, 1965.

Balint, M. The three areas of the mind. *International Journal of Psychoanalysis*, 1958, *39*, 328–340.

Banquet, J.P. Spectral analysis of the EEG in meditation. *Electroencephalographic Clinical Neurophysiology*, 1973, *35*, 143–151.

Basmajian, J.V. Conscious control and training of motor units and motor neurons. In *Muscles alive: Their functions revealed by electromyography.* (2nd ed.). Baltimore: Williams & Wilkins, 1967.

Beary, J.F., Benson, H., & Klemchuk, K. A simple psychophysiologic technique which elicits the hypometabolic changes of the relaxation response. *Psychosomatic Medicine,* 1974, *36,* 115–120.

Bennett, J.E., & Trinder, J. Hemispheric laterality and cognitive style associated with transcendental meditation. *Psychophysiology,* 1977, *14,* 293–296.

Benson, H. *The Relaxation response.* New York: Morrow, 1975.

Benson, H. Systematic hypertension and the relaxation response. *Journal of Human Stress,* 1978, *4,* 38–42.

Benson, H., Dryer, T., & Hartley, L.H. Decreased VO-Sub-2 consumption during exercise with elicitation of the relaxation response. *Journal of Human Stress,* 1978, *4,* 38–42.

Benson, H., Herd, J.A., Morse, W.H., & Kelleher, R.T. Behavioral induction of arterial hypertension and its reversal. *American Journal of Physiology,* 1969, *217,* 30–34.

Benson, H., & Wallace, R.L. Decreased blood pressure in hypertensive subjects who practiced meditation. Supplement II to *Circulation 45 and 46,* 1972, 516.

Bibring, E. Psychoanalysis and dynamic psychotherapies. *Journal of American Psychoanalytic Association,* 1954, *2,* 745–770.

Bloomfield, H.H., Cain, M.P., & Jaffe, D.T. *T.M.: Discovering inner energy and overcoming stress.* New York: Delacorte, 1975.

Bloomfield, H.H., & Kory, R.B. *The holistic way to health and happiness: A new approach to complete lifetime wellness.* New York: Simon &Schuster, 1978.

Bowlby, J. The nature of the child's tie to his mother. *International Journal of Psychoanalysis,* 1958, *39,* 350–373.

Bowlby, J. Grief and mourning in infancy and early childhood. *Psychoanalytic Study of the Child,* 1960, *15,* 9–52.

Bowlby, J. *Separation, anxiety, and anger.* New York: Basic Books. 1973.

Bruche, H. *Learning psychotherapy. Rationale and ground rules.* Cambridge: Harvard University Press, 1974.

Buber, M. *I and thou.* New York: Charles Scribner's Sons, 1970.

Bucke, R.M. *Cosmic consciousness: A study in the evolution of the human mind.* New York: Citadel Press, 1970.

Cage, J. *Silence.* Cambridge, Mass.: MIT Press, 1971.

Cannon, W.B., & de la Paz, D. Emotional stimulation of adrenal secretion. *American Journal Physiology,* 1911, *28,* 64.

Carpenter, J.T. Meditation, esoteric traditions—Contributions to psychotherapy. *American Journal of Psychotherapy*, 1977, *31*, 394–404.

Carrington, P. *Freedom in Meditation*. Garden City, N.Y.: Anchor Press/Double-day, 1977.

Cauthen, N.R., & Prymak, C.A. Meditation versus relaxation: An examination of the physiological effects of relaxation training and of different levels of experience with transcendental meditation. *Journal of Consultative Clinical Psychology*, 1977, *45*, 496–497.

Corbin, H. *Creative imagination in the Sufism of Ibn Arabi*. (R. Manheim, trans.) Princeton: Princeton University Press, 1969.

Corby, J.C., Roth, W.T., Zarcone, V.P., & Kopell, B.S. Psychophysiological correlates of the practice of tantric yoga meditation. *Archives of General Psychiatry*, 1978, *35*, 571–577.

Das, N., & Gastaut, H. Variations de l'activité électrique de cerveau, de coeur et des muscles squelettiaues au cour de la méditation et de "l'extase" yoguique. *Electroencephalographic Clinical Neurophysiology*, 1956, *Supplement 5*, 211–219.

Davidson, R.J., & Schwartz, G.E. The psychobiology of relaxation and related states: A multi-process theory. In D.I. Motofsky (Ed.), *Behavior control and modification of physiological activity*. New Jersey: Prentice-Hall, 1976.

Deikman, A. Deautomatization and the mystic experience. *Psychiatry*, 1966, *29*, 324–338.

Deikman, A.J. Sufism and psychiatry. *Journal of Nervous and Mental Diseases*, 1977, *165*, 318–329.

Dwivedi, K.N., Gupta, V.M., & Udupa, K.N. Preliminary report on some physiological changes due to vipashyana meditation. *Indian Journal of Medical Science*, 1977, *31*, 51–54.

Elson, B.D., Hauri, P., & Cunis, D. Physiological changes in Yoga meditation. *Psychophysiology*, 1977, *14*, 52–57.

Engel, B.T., & Hansen, S.P. Operant conditioning of heart rate slowing. *Psychophysiology*, 1966, *3*, 176–187.

Erikson, E.H. *Childhood and society*. (2nd ed.) New York: Norton, 1963.

Erikson, E.H. The roots of virtue. In J. Huxley, (Ed.), *The humanist frame*. New York: Harper & Brothers, 1961.

Erikson, E.H. *Insight and responsibility. Lectures on the ethical implications of psychoanalytic insight*. New York: Norton, 1964.

Erikson, E.H. *The life cycle completed: A review*. New York: W.W. Norton & Co. 1982.

Fee, R.A., & Girdano, D.A. The relative effectiveness of three techniques to induce the trophotropic response. *Biofeedback Self Regulated*, 1978, *3*, 145–157.

Fenwick, P. Computer analysis of the EEG during mantra meditation. Paper presented at conference on the effects of meditation, concentration, and attention on the EEG. University of Marseilles, 1960.

Fenwick, P.B.C., Donaldson, S., Gillis, L., Bushman, J., Fenton, G.W., Perry, I., Tilsey, C., & Serafinowicz, H. Metabolic and EEG changes during transcendental meditation: An explanation. *Biological Psychology*, 1977, *5*, 101–118.

Ferenczi, S. Silence is golden. In *Further contributions to the theory and technique of psychoanalysis*. London: Hogarth Press, 1950.

Fingarette, H. *The self in transformation: Psychoanalysis, philosophy, and the life of the spirit.* New York: Basic Books, 1963.

Fisher, C. Dreams and perception. *Journal of American Psychoanalytic Association*, 1954, *2*, 389–445.

Fraiberg, S. On the sleep disturbances of early childhood. *Psychoanalytic Study of the Child.* 1950, *5*, 285–309.

Frank, J. *Persuasion and healing.* New York: Schocken, 1963.

Frankl, V.E. *Man's search for meaning: An introduction to logotherapy.* (Original title: *From Death-Camp to Existentialism*) New York: Washington Square Press, 1963.

Freud, A. *The ego and the mechanisms of defense.* New York: International Universities Press, 1936.

Freud, A. *Normality and pathology in childhood: Assessments of development.* New York: International Universities Press, 1965.

Freud, S. *The interpretation of dreams. Standard ed. Complete psychological works of Sigmund Freud, 4 & 5,* 1900, London: Hogarth Press, 1968.

Freud, S. Three essays on the theory of sexuality. *Standard ed. Complete psychological works of Sigmund Freud,* 1905, *7*, 123–243.

Freud, S. The dynamics of transference. *Standard ed. Complete psychological works of Sigmund Freud,* 1912, *12*, 99–108.

Freud, S. Beyond the pleasure principle. *Standard ed.,* 1920, *18*, 7–64.

Freud, S. The ego and the id. *Standard ed.,* 1923, *19*, 3–66.

Freud, S. Inhibitions, symptoms, and anxiety. *Standard ed.,* 1926, *20*, 87–156.

Freud, S. Civilization and its discontents. *Standard ed.,* 1930, *21*, 64–145.

Freud, S. Anxiety and instinctual life. *Standard ed.,* 1933, *22*, 81–111.

Freud, S. Analysis terminable and interminable. *Standard Ed.,* 1937, *23*, 216–253.

Freud, S. An outline of psychoanalysis. *Standard ed.,* 1938, *23*, 141–313.

Fromm, E. *The art of loving.* New York: Harper & Row, 1956.

Fromm, E. Psychoanalysis and Zen Buddhism. In D.T. Suzuki, E. Fromm, & R. DeMartino, (Eds.), *Zen Buddhism and psychoanalysis.* New York: Grove Press, 1960.

Galin, D. Implications for psychiatry of left and right cerebral specialization.

Archives of General Psychiatry, 1974, *31,* 572–583.

Galin, D. Lateral specialization and psychiatric issues: Speculation on development and the evolution of consciousness. *Annual of New York Academy of Science,* 1977, *299,* 397–411.

Galin, D., & Ornstein, R. Lateral specialization of cognitive mode: An EEG study. *Psychophysiology,* 1972, *9,* 4.

Gellhorn, E. *Principles of autonomic-somatic integrations: Physiological basis and psychological and clinical implications.* Minneapolis: University of Minnesota Press, 1967.

Gellhorn, E., & Kiely, W.F. Mystical states of consciousness: Neurophysiological and clinical aspects. *Journal of Nervous & Mental Diseases,* 1972, *154,* 399–405.

Ghani, M.Q. *Ta'rikh-i-tasawwuf dar Islam.* Tehran: Ibn-i-Sina, 1330h. hijri shamsi, 1951. (In Persian).

Ghazzali, Abu Hamid Muhammed al- (d. 1111). *Kitab-i-Kimiya-i-Seadat (Alchemy of happiness).* Tehran: Markizi Bookseller, 1352. hijri shamsi, 1973. (In Persian).

Gibran, K. *The Prophet.* New York: Alfred A. Knopf, 1963.

Glueck, B.C., Stroebel, C.F. Biofeedback and meditation in the treatment of psychiatric illness. *Comprehensive Psychiatry,* 1975, *16,* 303–321.

Goethe, J.W. *West-Eastern divan (West-Ostlicher Divan),* 1819.

Goethe, J.W. *Faust: The second part of the tragedy, in five acts.* Garden City, N.Y.: Doubleday, 1961.

Goleman, D. *The Varieties of the Meditative Experience.* New York: E.P. Dutton, 1977.

Goleman, D.J. & Schwartz, G.E. Meditation as an intervention in stress reactivity. *Journal of Consultive Clinical Psychology,* 1976, *44,* 456–466.

Green, E.F., Walters, E.D., Green, A.M. & Murphy, B. Feedback technique for deep relaxation. *Psychophysiology,* 1969, *6,* 371–377.

Greenson, R.R. On the silence and sounds of the analytic hour. *Journal of the American Psychoanalytic Association,* 1961, *9,* 79–84.

Greenson, R.R. That 'impossible' profession. Journal of the American Psychoanalytic Association, 1966, 14, 9–27.

Greenson, R.R. *The technique and practice of psychoanalysis (Vol. 1).* New York: International Universities Press, 1967.

Hafiz, K.S.M. (d. 1389). *Divan-i-Khwajeh Shams uddin Mohammad Hafiz.* (Eds.) M. Ghazvini & G. Ghani, Tehran: Zawwar, 1321 hijri shamsi, 1941. (In Persian).

Hafiz, S.M. (d. 1389). The *Divan-i-Hafiz* (H.W. Clarke, trans). New York: Samuel Weiser, 1970. (Originally published, 1891).

Happich, C. Das bildbewusstsein als ansatzstelle psychischer behandlung. *Zentralblatt für Psychotherapie,* 1932, *5,* 663–677.

Happich, C. Bildbewusstsein und schopferische situation (Symbolic conscious-ness and the creative situation). *Deutsche Medizinische Wochenschrift, 2,* 1939.

Happich, C.. *Anleitung zur Meditation (Introduction to Meditation).* (3rd ed.) Darmstadt: E. Rother, 1948.

Hartmann, H. *Ego psychology and the problem of adaptation.* New York: Interna-tional Universities Press, 1958.

Hartmann, H. *Essays on ego psychology: Selected problems in psychoanalytic theory.* New York: International Universities Press, 1964.

Haynes, C.T., Hebert, J.R., Reber, W., & Orme-Johnson, D.W. The psycho-physiology of advanced participants in the transcendental meditation program: Correlations of EEG coherence, creativity, H-reflex recovery, and experience of transcendental consciousness. In D.W. Orme-Johnson & J.T. Farrow, (eds.), *Scientific Research on the Transcendental Meditation Program. Collected Papers. Vol. 1.* New York: Maharishi European Research University Press, 1977.

Hirai, T. *Psychophysiology of Zen.* Tokyo: Igaku Shoin Ltd., 1974.

Hoffman, J.W., Benson, H., Arns, P.A., Stainbrook, G.L., Landsberg, J.L., Young, J.B, & Gill, A. Reduced sympathetic nervous system responsivity associated with the relaxation response. *Science,* 1982, *215,* 190–192.

Hujwiri, A.U.J. (d. 1072). *Kashf al-Mahjub, The oldest Persian treatise on Sufism (The uncovering of the veils).* (R.A. Nicholson, trans). London: Luzac & Co., 1967.

Ibn 'Arabi, M. (d. 1240). *Sufis of Andalusia: The Ruh al-quds and al-Durrat al-fakhira.* (R.W.J. Austin, trans). London: George Allen & Unwin Ltd., 1971.

Issa. (19th century). In R.H. Blythe, *Haiku, Vol. 2, Spring.* Tokyo: Hokuseido Press, 1950, p. 363.

Jami, A.R. (d. 1492). In R. Beny, *Persia: Bridge of turquoise.* Boston: New York Graphic Society, 1975.

Jami, A.R. (d. 1492). *Nafahat al-uns.* (Ed.) M. Tauhidipur. Tehran, 1336 hijri shamsi, 1957 (In Persian).

Janby, J. Immediate effects of the transcendental meditation technique: In-creased skin resistance during first meditation after instruction. In D.W. Orme-Johnson & J.T. Farrow, (Eds.), *Scientific research on the transcendental meditation program. Collected papers.* (Vol. 1). New York: Maharishi Euro-pean Research University Press, 1977.

Jevning, R., Wilson, A., VanderLaan, M.A., & Levine, S. Plasma prolactin and cortisol during transcendental meditation. In D.W. Orme-Johnson & J.T. Farrow, (Eds)., *Scientific research on the transcendental meditation program. Collected papers.* (Vol. 1). New York: Maharishi European Re-search University Press, 1977.

Jones, E. *The life and work of Sigmund Freud (3 Vol).* New York: Basic Books, 1953.

Jung, C. *The integration of the personality.* London: Lowe & Brydone, 1940.

Kamiya, J. Operant control of the EEG alpha rhythm and some of its reported effects on consciousness. In C. Tart (Ed.), *Altered states of consciousness. A book of readings.* New York: John Wiley & Sons, 1969.

Kamiya, J., Barber, T.X., DiCara, L.V., Miller, N.E., Shapiro, D., & Stoyva, J. (Eds.), *Biofeedback and self-control.* Chicago: Aldine-Atherton, 1971.

Kasamatsu, A., & Hirai, T. An electroencephalographic study on the Zen meditation (Zazen). *Folio, Psychiatry & Neurology Japonica,* 1966, *20,* 315–336.

Kasamatsu, A., & Hirai, T. An electroencephalographic study on the Zen meditation (Zazen). *Journal of American Institute of Hypnosis,* 1973, *14,* 107–114.

Kelman, H. Communing and relating. *American Journal of Psychotherapy,* 1960, *14,* 70–96.

Kernberg, O. *Borderline conditions and pathological narcissism.* New York: Aronson, 1975.

Khan, H.I. *The Sufi Message of Hazrat Inayat Khan.* (Vol X) London: Barrie & Jenkins, 1964.

Khan, M.M.R. The concept of cumulative trauma. *Psychoanalytic Study of the Child,* 1963, *18,* 286–306.

Kohut, H. *The analysis of self: A systematic approach to the psychoanalytic treatment of narcissistic personality disorders.* New York: International Universities Press, 1971.

Kohut, H. *The restoration of the self.* New York: International Universities Press, 1977.

Kohut, H. *Search for the self: Selected writings of Heinz Kohut, 1950–1978, (Vol 1 & 2).* New York: International Universities Press, 1978.

Kora, T., & Sato, K. Morita therapy—A psychotherapy in the way of Zen. *Psychologia,* 1958, *1,* 219.

Koran (*The Holy Qur-an: Pts. I to XXX, Text, Translation, and Commentary*). Ed. & Trans. A. Yusaf Ali, Lahore: S. Ashraf, 1969.

Kretschmer, W. Meditative techniques in psychotherapy. In C. Tart, (Ed.), *Altered states of consciousness. A book of readings.* New York: John Wiley & Sons, 1969.

Kris, E. *Psychoanalytic explorations in art.* New York: Schocken Books, 1967.

Kris, E. On some vicissitudes of insight in psychoanalysis. *International Journal of Psychoanalysis,* 1956, *37,* 445–455.

Laing, R.D. Transcendental experience in relation to religion and psychosis. *Psychedelic Review,* 1965, *6,* 7–15.

Laurie, G. An investigation into the changes in skin resistance during the transcendental meditation technique. In D.W. Orme-Johnson & J.T. Farrow (Eds.), *Scientific research on the transcendental meditation program.* Col-

lected papers. (Vol. 1). New York: Mahirishi European Research University Press, 1977.

Lings, M. *A Sufi saint of the twentieth century, Shaikh Admad al- Alawi. His spiritual heritage and legacy.* (2nd ed.) Berkeley: University of California Press, 1971.

Loewenstein, R.M. The silent patient. *Journal of the American Psychoanalytic Association,* 1961, *9,* 206.

Loomie, L. S. Some ego considerations in the silent patient. *Journal of the American Psychoanalytic Association,* 1961, *9,* 56–78.

Luthe, W. Autogenic training: Method, research, and application in medicine. In C. Tart (Ed.), *Altered states of consciousness. A book of readings.* New York: John Wiley & Sons, 1969.

Mahler, M.S., & Gosliner, B.J. On symbiotic child psychosis: Genetic dynamic, and restitutive aspects. *Psychoanalytic Study of the Child,* 1955, *10,* 195–212.

Mahler, M.S. On the significance of the normal separation-individuation phase: With reference to research in symbiotic childhood psychosis. In M. Schur (Ed.), *Drives, affects, behavior* (Vol. 2). New York: International Universities Press, 1965.

Mahler, M. On the first three subphases of the separation-individuation process. *International Journal of Psychoanalysis,* 1972, *53,* 333–338.

Mahler, M.S., Pine, F., & Bergman, A. *The psychological birth of the human infant: Symbiosis and individuation.* New York: Basic Books, 1975.

Maslow, A.H. Cognition of being in the peak experiences. *Journal of Genetic Psychology,* 1959, *94,* 43–66.

Maslow, A.H. *Religions, values, and peak-experiences.* New York: Penguin Books, 1977.

Maslow, A.H. *The farther reaches of human nature.* New York: Viking Press, 1973.

Maupin, E.W. Individual differences in response to a Zen meditation exercise. In C. Tart (Ed.), *Altered states of consciousness. A book of readings.* New York: John Wiley & Sons, 1969.

Meissner, W.W., Mack, J.E., & Semrad, E.V. Theories of personality and psychopathology: I. Freudian school. In A.M. Freedman, H.I. Kaplan, & B.J. Sadock, (Eds.), *Comprehensive textbook of psychiatry (II).* (2nd ed.). Baltimore: Williams & Wilkins, 1975.

Michaels, R.R., Parra, J., McCann, D.S., & Vander, A.J. Renin, Cortisol, and aldosterone during transcendental meditation. *Psychosomatic Medicine,* 1979, *41,* 50–54.

Miller, N.E. Learning of visceral and glandular responses. *Science,* 1969, *163,* 434–445.

Moore, B.E., & Fine, B.D. (Eds.) *A glossary of psychoanalytic terms and concepts.* (2nd ed.). New York: American Psychoanalytic Association, 1968.

Morewedge, P. *The metaphysica of Avicenna (ibn Sina). A critical translation-com-*

mentary and analysis of the fundamental arguments in Avicenna's Metaphysica in the Danish Nama-i-ala'i (The Book of Scientific Knowledge). New York: Columbia University Press, 1973.

Morse, D.R., Martin, J.S., Furst, M.L., & Dubin, L.L. A physiological and subjective evaluation of meditation, hypnosis, and relaxation. *Psychosomatic Medicine,* 1977, *39,* 304–324.

Nacht, S. Silence as an integrative factor, *International Journal of Psychoanalysis* 1964, *45,* 299–303.

Naranjo, C., & Ornstein, R.E. *On the Psychology of Meditation.* New York: Viking Press, 1971.

Nasafi, A. (d. 13th century). *Kitab al-Insan al-Kamil (The book of the integrated human being). (Le Livre de l'Homme Parfait).* (Ed). M. Mole, Tehran: Department D'Iranologie, de l'Institute Franco-Iranian, 1962. (In Persian).

Nasr, S.H. *Three Muslim sages: Avicenna, Suhrawardi, Ibn Arabi.* Cambridge, Mass.: Harvard University Press, 1964.

Nasr, S.H. *Studies in comparative religion—The Sufi Master as exemplified in Persian Sufi literature.* Middlesex, England: Tamarrow Press, 1970.

Nasr, S.H. *Sufi Essays.* Albany, N.Y.: State University of New York Press, 1973.

Nasr, S.H. In R. Beny, *Persia: Bridge of turquoise.* Boston: New York Graphic Society, 1975.

Nurbakhsh, D.J. *Mureed Va Murad.* Tehran: Khaneqah-i-N'imutullahi, 1332 hijri shamsi, 1953. (In Persian).

Nurbakhsh, D.J. Sufism and psychoanalysis. Part One: What is sufism? *International Journal of Social Psychiatry,* 1978, *24,* 204–212.

Nurbakhsh, D.J. Sufism and psychoanalysis. Part Two: A comparison between sufism and psychoanalysis. *International Journal of Social Psychiatry,* 1978, *24,* 213–219.

Nystul, M.S., & Garde, M. The self-concepts of regular transcendental meditators, dropout meditators, and non-meditators. *Journal of Psychology,* 1979, *103,* 15–18.

Old Testament. In C.I. Scofield (Ed.), *The Holy Bible containing the Old and New Testaments.* New York: Oxford University Press, 1945.

Orme-Johnson, D.W. Autonomic stability and transcendental meditation. *Psychosomatic Medicine,* 1973, *35,* 341–349.

Otis, L.S. Adverse effects of transcendental meditation. In D. Shapiro & R. Walsh (Eds.), *The science of meditation: Research, theory, and experience.* New York: Aldine, 1982, In Press.

Pagano, R.R., Rose, R.M., Stivers, R.M., & Warrenburg, S. Sleep during transcendental meditation. *Science,* 1976, *191,* 308–310.

Pagano, R.R., & Frumkin, L.R. The effect of transcendental meditation on right hemispheric functioning. *Biofeedback Self Regulating,* 1977, *2,* 407–414.

Reik, T. The psychological meaning of silence. *Psychoanalytic Review,* 1968, 55, 172–186.

Rice, C. *The Persian Sufis.* London: Allen & Unwin, 1964.

Riley, V. Psychoneuroendocrine influences on immunocompetence and neoplasia. *Science,* 1981, *212,* 1100–1109.

Royster, J.E. Sufi as psychotherapist. *Psychologia,* 1979, *22,* 225–235.

Ruesch, J., & Bateson, G. *Communication, the social matrix of psychiatry.* New York: W.W. Norton, 1968.

Rumi, M.J.M. (d. 1273). *The Mathnawi of Jalalu'ddin Rumi (6 Vols).* R.A. Nicholson (Ed.). Leiden: E.J. Brill, 1925–1940. (In Persian and English).

Rumi, M.J.M. (d. 1273). *Selected Odes from the Divan-i-Shams-i Tabriz,* R.A. Nicholson (Ed. & trans.), Cambridge: Cambridge University Press, 1961. (Originally published 1898).

Rumi, M.J.M. (d. 1273). *Fīhi mā Fīhi.* (Trans. A.J. Arberry, as *Discourses of Rumi*). New York: Samuel Weiser, 1972.

Rumi, M.J.M. (d. 1273). *Masnavi-Ī-Ma'navi, The spiritual couplets.* E.H. Whinfield, (Ed. & trans.), Republished under *Teachings of Rumi.* London: Octagon Press, 1973.

Sarrāj, A.N. (d. 988). *Kitāb al-luma'fit't-tasawwuf (The Flame of Sufism).* (R.A. Nicholson, Ed.). Leiden: E.J. Brill, 1914. (In Arabic).

Schalling, D., Cronholm, B., & Asberg, M. Components of state and trait anxiety as related to personality and arousal. In L. Levi, *Emotions: Their parameters and measurement.* New York: Raven Press, 1975.

Schimmel, A. *Mystical dimensions of Islam.* Chapel Hill: University of North Carolina Press, 1975.

Schimmel, A. *The triumphal Sun, A study of the works of Jalaloddin Rumi.* revised ed. London: East-West Publications, 1980.

Scholem, G. *On the Kabbalah and its symbolism.* (R. Manheim, trans.). New York: Schocken Books, 1965.

Schultz, J. *Das Autogene Training.* Stuttgart: Theime Verlag, 1932.

Schultz, J. *Le Training Autogene.* Paris: Presses' Université de France, 1958.

Schwartz, G.E. The facts of transcendental meditation: II. "TM relaxes some people and makes them feel better." *Psychology Today,* 1974, 7, 39–44.

Schwartz, G.E., Davidson, R.J., & Goleman, D.J. Patterning of cognitive and somatic processes in the self-regulation of anxiety: Effects of meditation versus exercise. *Psychosomatic Medicine,* 1978, *40,* 321–328.

Seer, P., Raeburn, J.M. Meditation training and essential hypertension: A methodological study. *Journal of Behavioral Medicine,* 1980, *3,* 59–71.

Selye, H. The general adaptation syndrome and the diseases of adaptation. *Journal of Clinical Endocrinology & Metabolism,* 1946, *6,* 117.

Selye, H. *The physiology and pathology of exposure to stress.* Montreal: Acta, 1950.

Shabistari, S.D.M. (d. 1250). *The secret rose garden.* (F. Lederer, trans.). S.M.

Lahore: S. Ashraf, 1969.

Shafii, M. The pir (sufi guide) and the western psychotherapist. *The R.M. Bucke Memorial Society Newsletter,* 1968, *3,* 9–19.

Shafii, M. Adaptive and therapeutic aspects of meditation. *International Journal of Psychoanalytic Psychotherapy,* 1973a, *2,* 364–382.

Shafii, M. Silence in the service of ego: Psychoanalytic study of meditation. *International Journal of Psychoanalysis,* 1973b, *54,* 431–443.

Shafii, M., Lavely, R., & Jaffe, R. Meditation and marijuana. *American Journal of Psychiatry,* 1974, *131,* 60–63.

Shafii, M., Lavely, R., & Jaffe, R. Meditation and the prevention of drug abuse. *American Journal of Psychiatry,* 1975, *132,* 942–945.

Shafii, M., Shafii, S.L. *Pathways of human development: Normal growth and emotional disorders in infancy, childhood, and adolescence.* New York: Thieme-Stratton, 1982.

Shah, I. *The Sufis.* Garden City, N.Y.: Doubleday, 1964.

Shapiro, D., Turskey, B., Gershon, E., & Stern, M. Effects of feedback and reinforcement on the control of human systolic blood pressure. *Science,* 1969, *163,* 588–590.

Smith, M. *The Way of the Mystics: The Early Christian mystics and the rise of the Sufis.* New York: Oxford University Press, 1978. Originally published as *Studies in early mysticism in the Near and Middle East,* 1931.

Solomon, P., Kubzansky, P.E., Leiderman, P.H., Mendelson, I.H., Brumbull, R., & Wexler, D. (Eds.). *Sensory Deprivation.* Cambridge: Harvard University Press, 1961.

Sperry, R.W. Mental unity following surgical disconnection of the cerebral hemispheres. *Harvey Lectures,* 1967, *62,* 293–323.

Steingass, F. *A comprehensive Persian-English Dictionary.* London: Routledge & Kegan Paul, 1963.

Stigsby, B., Rodenberg, J.C., & Moth, H.B. Electroencephalographic findings during mantra meditation (transcendental meditation). A controlled, quantitative study of experienced meditators. *Electroencephalographic Clinical Neurophysiology,* 1981, *51,* 434–442.

Sugi, Y., & Akutsu, K. On the respiration and respiratory change in Zen practice. *Japanese Journal of Physiology,* 1964, *26,* 72–73.

Surwillo, W.W., Hobson, D.P. Brain electrical activity during prayer. *Psychol. Rep.,* 1978, *43,* 135–143.

Suzuki, D.T., Fromm, E., & DeMartino, R. *Zen Buddhism and psychoanalysis.* New York: Grove Press, 1960.

Tagore, R.R. *Fireflies.* New York: Macmillan, 1928.

Tart, C.T. (Ed.) *Altered states of consciousness: A book of readings.* New York: John Wiley & Sons, 1969.

Tart, C.T. A psychologist's experience with transcendental meditation. *Journal of Transpersonal Psychology*, 1971, *3*, 135–140.

Valiuddin, M. *Love of God*. London: Camelot Press, 1972.

Van Der Heide, C. Blank silence and the dream screen. *Journal of the American Psychoanalytic Association*, 1961, *9*, 85–90.

Wallace, R.K. Physiological effects of transcendental meditation. *Science*, 1970, *167*, 1751–1754.

Wallace, R.K., Benson, H., & Wilson, A.F. A wakeful hypometabolic physiologic states. *American Journal of Physiology*, 1971, *221*, 795–799.

Walsh, R., & Roche, L. Precipitation of acute psychotic episodes by intensive meditation in individuals with a history of schizophrenia. *American Journal of Psychiatry*, 1979, *136*, 1085–1086.

Warrenburg, S., Pagano, R.R., Woods, M., & Hlastala, M. A comparison of somatic relaxation and EEG activity in classical progressive relaxation and transcendental meditation. *Journal of Behavioral Medicine*, 1980, *3*, 73–93.

Watts, A.W. Asian psychology and modern psychiatry. *American Journal of Psychoanalysis*, 1953, *13*, 25–30.

Wenger, M.A., & Bagchi, B.K. Studies of autonomic functions in practitioners of yoga in India. *Behavioral Science*, 1961, *6*, 312–323.

Wenger, M.A., Bagchi, B.K., & Anand, B.K. Experiments in India on "voluntary" control of the heart and pulse. *Circulation*, 1961, *24*, 1319–1325.

Wesch, J.E. Clinical comments section. *Newsletter of the Biofeedback Society*, 1977, *5*.

West, M.A. Changes in skin resistance in subjects resting, reading, listening to music, or practicing the transcendental meditation technique. In D.W. Orme-Johnson & J.T. Farrow (Eds.). *Scientific research on the transcendental meditation program. Collected papers*. (Vol. 1). New York: Maharishi European Research University Press, 1977.

Westcott, M. (1977). Hemispheric symmetry of the EEG during the transcendental meditation technique. In D.W. Orme-Johnson & J.T. Farrow, (Eds.), *Scientific research on the transcendental meditation program. Collected papers*. (Vol. I). New York: Maharishi European Research University Press, 1977.

Whyte, L.L. *The Unconscious before Freud*. Garden City, N.Y.: Doubleday, 1962.

Williams, P., West, M. EEG responses to photic stimulation in persons experienced at meditation. *Electroencephalographic Clinical Neurophysiology*, 1975, *39*, 519–522.

Zeligs, M.A. The psychology of silence. *Journal of American Psychoanalytic Association*, 1961, *9*, 7–43.

AUTHOR INDEX

SUBJECT INDEX